GARDENING
Hints & Tips

GARDENING
Hints & Tips

Pippa Greenwood

LONDON • NEW YORK • SYDNEY • MOSCOW

A DK PUBLISHING BOOK

Senior Editor Linda Martin
Project Art Editor Jayne Carter
US Editors Lynn McGowan, Ray Rogers
Designer Helen Benfield
Managing Editor Stephanie Jackson
Managing Art Editor Nigel Duffield
Senior Managing Editor Krystyna Mayer
Senior Managing Art Editor Lynne Brown
Production Controller Sarah Coltman
DTP Designer Jason Little

First American Edition 1996
2 4 6 8 10 9 7 5 3
Published in the United States by
DK Publishing, Inc., 95 Madison Avenue,
New York, New York 10016

Library of Congress
Cataloging-in-Publication Data

Greenwood, Pippa.
    Gardening hints and tips / by Pippa Greenwood
        p.   cm.
    Includes index.
    ISBN 0-7894-1071-0
    1. Gardening.   I. Title.
SB451. G69 1996   96-13970
635- -dc20   CIP

Color reproduced by Chroma Graphics, Singapore.
Printed and bound in Italy by Lego.

CONTENTS

INTRODUCTION 6

RESTORING LANDSCAPES 10

PLANTS AND PLANTING 38

CONTAINER GARDENING 62

INTRODUCTION

T HE KEY TO CREATING AND MAINTAINING *a beautiful and productive garden is regular, sustained care. Whether starting from scratch, renovating a neglected garden, or keeping a garden in good condition, this book is filled with common-sense solutions, sound advice, and helpful tips that minimize time and effort – giving you more time to relax and enjoy yourself in the garden.*

USING THIS BOOK

ESTABLISHING A GARDEN

Three sections cover the fundamental aspects of gardening – from sowing lawns to clearing overgrown borders or flower beds. *Restoring Gardens* offers advice on successfully renovating a neglected garden without wasting precious time or money. *Plants and Planting* reveals the essential points to consider when selecting plants for a garden and supplies helpful tips on providing the plants with a healthy and promising start. *Lawns* is a comprehensive guide to creating, restoring, and maintaining a green, dense, and healthy lawn.

Planting bulbs
To find out how to plant bulbs so that you avoid unsightly, dying foliage after flowering, see page 56. For advice on planting bulbs in a lawn, see page 126.

MAINTAINING A GARDEN

A garden requires regular care and attention if it is to remain both attractive and fertile. *Plant Care* describes how to look after plants once they are established. *Pests and Diseases* helps you to identify and eliminate unwelcome visitors, while demonstrating that not everything that moves in the garden is harmful. *Propagating Plants* demystifies the satisfying and economical process of producing new plants from existing ones. *General Maintenance* features tips on repairing and brightening up the structural and practical elements of a garden – walls, paths, fences, greenhouses, tools, and furniture.

Dividing clumps
For tips on digging up and dividing clumps of perennials, see page 60. For other methods of propagation, see pages 140-157.

ADDING NEW DIMENSIONS TO A GARDEN

Once a garden is established and thriving, additional features can create further exciting areas of interest. *Container Gardening* outlines the techniques for planting up pots, barrels, hanging baskets, and windowboxes, offers dozens of tips on maintaining containers with the minimum of effort, and gives innovative ideas for displaying pots to their best advantage. *Water Features* highlights the advantages of having water in gardens, with suggestions for introducing water to small gardens with limited space, and hints on attracting wildlife. Finally, the comprehensive index and chapter-by-chapter color coding make it easy to find hints and tips throughout the book.

Saving soil mix
To find out how to stabilize tall containers and save on soil mix when planting up, see page 22.

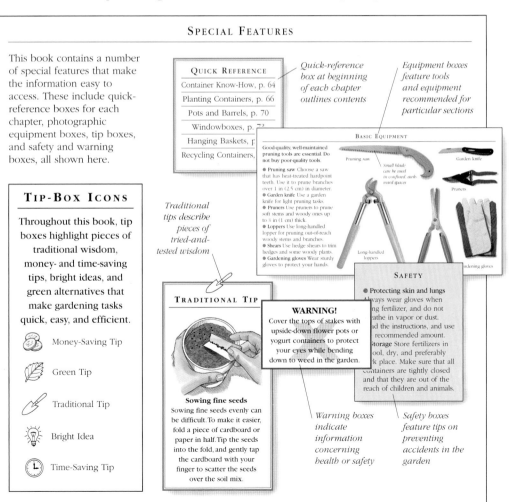

SPECIAL FEATURES

This book contains a number of special features that make the information easy to access. These include quick-reference boxes for each chapter, photographic equipment boxes, tip boxes, and safety and warning boxes, all shown here.

QUICK REFERENCE

Container Know-How, p. 64

Planting Containers, p. 66

Pots and Barrels, p. 70

Windowboxes, p. 72

Hanging Baskets, p.

Recycling Containers,

Quick-reference box at beginning of each chapter outlines contents

Equipment boxes feature tools and equipment recommended for particular sections

TIP-BOX ICONS

Throughout this book, tip boxes highlight pieces of traditional wisdom, money- and time-saving tips, bright ideas, and green alternatives that make gardening tasks quick, easy, and efficient.

Money-Saving Tip

Green Tip

Traditional Tip

Bright Idea

Time-Saving Tip

Traditional tips describe pieces of tried-and-tested wisdom

BASIC EQUIPMENT

Good-quality, well-maintained pruning tools are essential. Do not buy poor-quality tools.

● **Pruning saw** Choose a saw that has heat-treated hardpoint teeth. Use it to prune branches over 1 in (2.5 cm) in diameter.
● **Garden knife** Use a garden knife for light pruning tasks.
● **Pruners** Use pruners to prune soft stems and woody ones up to ⅜ in (1 cm) thick.
● **Loppers** Use long-handled lopper for pruning out-of-reach woody stems and branches.
● **Shears** Use hedge shears to trim hedges and some woody plants.
● **Gardening gloves** Wear sturdy gloves to protect your hands.

Pruning saw

Small blade can be used in confined, awkward spaces

Garden knife

Pruners

Long-handled loppers

Gardening gloves

SAFETY

● **Protecting skin and lungs** Always wear gloves when ...ng fertilizer, and do not ...athe in vapor or dust. ...d the instructions, and use recommended amount. ...torage Store fertilizers in ...ool, dry, and preferably ...k place. Make sure that all containers are tightly closed and that they are out of the reach of children and animals.

TRADITIONAL TIP

Sowing fine seeds
Sowing fine seeds evenly can be difficult. To make it easier, fold a piece of cardboard or paper in half. Tip the seeds into the fold, and gently tap the cardboard with your finger to scatter the seeds over the soil mix.

WARNING!
Cover the tops of stakes with upside-down flower pots or yogurt containers to protect your eyes while bending down to weed in the garden.

Warning boxes indicate information concerning health or safety

Safety boxes feature tips on preventing accidents in the garden

CREATING A MANAGEABLE GARDEN

Gardening can be a time-consuming and labor-intensive job, but it need not be. With careful planning, a low-maintenance plan can be put into effect. After the first year, it will require a minimum of work to keep the garden looking good. Consider paving an area and using plants in containers to create a colorful and manageable display. Cover walls and fences with fast-growing climbers that need little pruning, such as *Pyracantha*. Instead of choosing herbaceous borders, which may need constant care, select plants that need less attention, such as bulbs and shrubs. To deter weeds and conserve moisture in the soil, use groundcover, and apply a thick mulch of compost or bark chips.

Preventing weed growth
Removing weeds from a garden can be a tedious task; it is easier to prevent their growth in the first place. One of the most successful and attractive ways of achieving this is to deprive weed seedlings of light and air by using plants that will cover the soil with foliage.

GROWING FOOD IN YOUR GARDEN

More and more people are discovering the delights of growing their own vegetables, fruit, and herbs. Not only do these plants make attractive additions to borders and containers with the variety of foliage and flowers they offer, they also produce fresh, tasty, and nutritious crops. With the extensive choice now available through seed catalogs and garden centers, it is possible to experiment until you find your own favorite edible plants. Compact, fast-growing, and densely planted crops are ideal for a small garden, while fan-trained fruit trees can make productive and decorative screens for larger areas. For an aromatic, attractive display, consider planting an herb garden. Of use to every cook, herbs add a final, delicate touch to an edible garden.

Choosing crops
When deciding which vegetables to feature in a garden, make sure you choose cultivars that are resistant to disease. If possible, select a range of vegetables that will produce crops in succession and over a sustained period of time.

GARDENING ON A ROOF OR BALCONY

You can create a beautiful garden on a roof or balcony with an array of striking containers overflowing with suitable plants. In a location where weight is an important consideration, use plastic or fiberglass containers, and fill them with styrofoam pieces and lightweight potting mix. Assess the features of the site carefully so that you select plants that thrive in shady or exposed conditions. Train hardy climbers over trellis panels to form attractive screens for privacy or to filter the wind. Avoid tall plants that may be blown over, and choose some fragrant plants so that you can enjoy their scent from indoors as well as outdoors.

Planting containers
Use pots to grow vegetables and fruit, such as lettuce and strawberries.

Protecting your back
Make sure you use a tool of the correct length and weight when digging, and ensure that your back is kept straight.

MAKING THE GARDEN A SAFE PLACE

Although a garden is a place to enjoy and to relax in, some features and tasks require a certain amount of care in order to keep it a safe, accident-free area. When designing a garden from scratch, take into account the needs of those most likely to use it. If this includes young children, consider featuring water in a bubble fountain, rather than a pond. Read plant labels thoroughly before purchase to ensure that you do not choose any potentially hazardous plants. Always use electrical equipment and tools with care. Avoid trailing cords and, where possible, install a circuit breaker. Unplug power tools before repairing them, and never use them while watering, or during or just after rainfall.

WORKING WITH THE SEASONS

One of the pleasures of having a garden is knowing how to work with the seasons to maximum advantage. Differences in climate, soil type, and location will all affect the growth of plants and the timing of various activities. To be successful, a gardener needs to take all these elements into account before deciding when and what to do. However, there are a number of basic tasks that can be carried out at specific times through the year, and helpful suggestions are given on pages 174–181.

Storing apples and pears
Apples and pears may be kept for weeks, even months, if stored in cool, dark conditions. Wrap in tissue paper, taking care not to bruise the fruit.

Restoring Landscapes

RENOVATING OR CHANGING A LANDSCAPE does not need to be hard work. Planning, the right equipment, some basic gardening knowledge, and enthusiasm are all you need to transform your landscape. Begin with improvements that will not take too much time or money. These changes will help make you feel positive about the landscape and will inspire and encourage you to tackle it in more fundamental ways.

Garden Problems and Solutions

Garden Problems	Simple Solutions
Lawn The shape is boring or simply does not appeal to you; the edges are damaged and shabby-looking; the lawn is full of uneven areas, moss, weeds, and brown patches; there is too much of it.	Alter the shape; neaten lawn edges or remake them from scratch; level out humps and hollows; control moss and weeds; reseed bare areas; plant a specimen tree; make an island bed; make a path; create an ornamental divider.
Flower beds and Borders Beds and borders are fine overall, but some plants are overwhelmed by others; some plants are in poor condition; there are gaps in a border.	Divide overcrowded plants, removing some entirely; add climbers to leggy shrubs; use annuals, perennials, and bulbs to fill gaps; grow climbers or groundcovers to cover bare slopes.
Trees Trees are overgrown and out of shape; they are blocking light for shrubs, and other plants, and the house; low branches restrict access around trees.	Create a bed using plants that enjoy woodland conditions; plant spring bulbs and water and feed them to counteract competition; crown-lift or crown-reduce the trees to increase light levels.
Patio The area is untidy and covered with moss, algae, and weeds; the slabs are broken and cracked; you do not like the shape; it is stark and uninviting.	Remove debris; control moss, algae, and weeds; replace or remove broken slabs; add plants; alter the shape; use pots, baskets, and other containers; create a barbecue or water feature.
Paths and Steps They are too angular and harsh, and do not fit in with the garden; they are slippery; they have loose slabs; weeds are growing in the cracks; they are deteriorating; they look untidy.	Plant up with edging to soften harsh lines and to make them look more attractive; remove algae and moss; repair loose or damaged areas; remove weeds and prevent their reappearance; liven them up with plants in containers.
Walls They serve a purpose but are damaged, discolored, and ugly; they do not provide any benefit to the garden; they are uninteresting.	Clean, whitewash, or paint; plant and train fruit trees; plant climbers or thin out existing climbers; clean up the old trellis, or erect a new one; paint a mural; add a mirror; add a seat to make a bower.

A Transformed Landscape

A landscape that has been neglected over a long period of time can be a depressing sight. Restoring it may seem a daunting task, but you will be amazed at the transformation you can make in just one year. Start by clearing away any debris and cutting the grass.

Ideas for Renovating and Restoring a Landscape

Renovation tips

Retain any features that are worth saving, such as a tree or a shrub that provides a focal point. Introduce immediate color with pots of annuals, bedding plants, and fast-growing climbers.

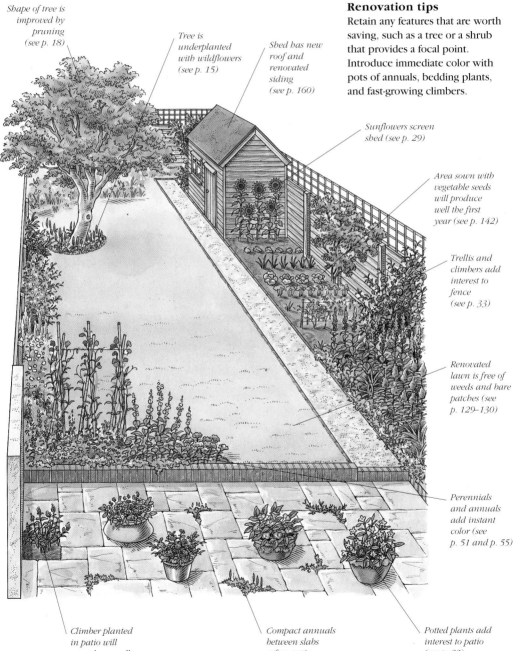

Shape of tree is improved by pruning (see p. 18)

Tree is underplanted with wildflowers (see p. 15)

Shed has new roof and renovated siding (see p. 160)

Sunflowers screen shed (see p. 29)

Area sown with vegetable seeds will produce well the first year (see p. 142)

Trellis and climbers add interest to fence (see p. 33)

Renovated lawn is free of weeds and bare patches (see p. 129–130)

Perennials and annuals add instant color (see p. 51 and p. 55)

Climber planted in patio will cover bare wall (see p. 20)

Compact annuals between slabs soften patio (see p. 143)

Potted plants add interest to patio (see p. 22)

TRANSFORMING LAWNS

A LAWN OFTEN FORMS one of the central parts of a landscape and, in many cases, takes up the largest portion of the area. If the lawn is unkempt or uninspiring, it can make the rest of the landscape look uninviting.

RESHAPING LAWNS

The shape of a lawn is fundamental to the look of a landscape. It may impart a degree of formality, or it may have a casual, relaxed effect. Changing a lawn's shape need not be difficult and does not necessarily involve buying more sod or grass seed.

CURVED LAWNS
● **Marking off** Use string and pegs (see p. 125) to mark regular curves. For complicated curves, use a flexible hose.

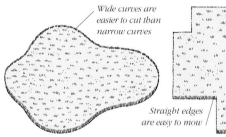

Wide curves are easier to cut than narrow curves

Using curves
Combine a curved lawn with informal plantings to give your landscape a casual look. Keep in mind that curves are harder to mow than straight edges.

STRAIGHT LAWNS
● **Marking off** Pull string tightly between pegs driven into the lawn. Cut along the edge of a board (see p. 128).

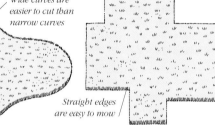

Straight edges are easy to mow

Using straight edges
Use straight edges and right angles to create a formal, elegant look. To retain the effect, keep the lawn edges neat and well maintained (see p. 128).

PLANNING SHAPES
● **Viewing the effect** After marking off the proposed new shape of a lawn, view the design from several different places before starting to make the changes. If possible, check to see what the new shape looks like when viewed from an upstairs window.

PLANTING FOR EFFECT
● **A formal look** Plant neatly clipped shrubs in beds and borders to increase the formal appearance of a straight-edged lawn.
● **An informal look** Allow herbaceous plants with rounded shapes to hang over the edges of a curved lawn.

MAKING AND SHAPING ISLAND BEDS
● **Adapting to conditions** Turn any areas where grass does not grow well – perhaps because the ground is too dry, too wet, or too shaded – into an island bed. Use plants that are suited to the prevailing conditions (see p. 44).
● **Alternative planting** Instead of planting herbaceous and annual flowers or shrubs in an island bed, try filling it with some attractive vegetables and fruits. Rhubarb, chard, runner beans, lettuce, radicchio, and strawberries – or a selection of herbs – will all look good, and will provide fresh produce for several months.

● **Scale** Create an island bed to break up a lawn. Make sure that the scale of the bed is in proportion to the lawn size.

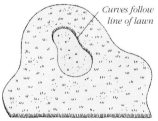

Curves follow line of lawn

Following lawn shapes
To create a coordinated and balanced look in a garden, make a curved island bed in a curved lawn, and make a straight-edged bed in a formal lawn.

TRADITIONAL TIP

Creating a focal point
Transform an expanse of green by planting a specimen tree. Choose one that will grow to a suitable size; a large tree looks confined in a small setting, and a tiny tree is lost in a large area.

BREAKING UP LAWNS

Another way to alter an existing lawn is to divide it up. This can be done, both by altering the structure of the lawn itself and by using plants, paths, or stepping-stones. Dividing a lawn into sections can often make a narrow garden look wider.

DIVIDING LAWNS

● **Different uses** If a lawn is large enough, consider dividing it into two distinct areas – perhaps one for children to play on, and one for adults to relax on.

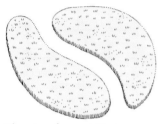

Shaping lawn areas
To create continuity between divided areas of lawn, be sure shapes complement each other. Also make sure the edges are easy to mow, and that any dividing borders are in proportion to the grassy areas.

USING PATHS

● **Ideal width** Make sure that a new path crossing a lawn is unobstructed and that it is wide enough for at least one person to walk along easily.
● **Curved path** If laying a path across a curved lawn, make sure that the path follows the shape of the existing curves.
● **Direction of path** Try to design a path so that it leads either to a particular object, such as a shed or greenhouse, or to a different section of the landscape. A path that obviously leads nowhere can look odd and out of place.
● **Fruit edging** Plant stepover apples, trained to grow to roughly 18–24 in (45–60 cm) above ground level, to create interesting edges on a straight path that crosses a lawn.

USING HEDGES

Creating landscape rooms
Use hedges to divide a large lawn into a series of different "rooms." Each area can have its own distinctive character. Divisions can add interest to a landscape, and also make it seem longer or larger. Screens made up of shrubs planted at intervals, and arranged informally or trained over supports, can be used to create the same effect (see p. 29).

MAKING STEPPING-STONE PATHS

If your planned path is not going to be subjected to heavy use, paving slabs – laid either in a line to make a symmetrical path or informally as a stepping-stone path – can look attractive. If the soil is compacted, the slabs can be laid on sand rather than crushed stone.

LAYING A STEPPING-STONE PATH

1 Mark off the position of the slabs by cutting around them, and remove enough soil to sink each slab just beneath the level of the grass. Allow for at least ½ in (1 cm) of sand or hardcore for bedding in.

2 Note the depth required, and repeat for each slab along the path. Thoroughly compact the soil, add the sand or hardcore, and bed each slab firmly in. Check the level, and adjust the slabs, if necessary.

POSITIONING SLABS

● **Arranging slabs** Experiment with different positions for a series of slabs before cutting and removing turf. Check to be sure the slabs are spaced conveniently for walking.
● **Tools** Use a half-moon edger for cutting turf and a spade or trowel to remove soil.
● **Depth of slabs** Make sure that paving slabs are sunk sufficiently deep into turf that they present no obstruction to a lawnmower.
● **Secondary path** Use stepping stones to provide access from the main pathway to a play area, garden seat, or arbor.

LEVELING LAWNS

I f the look of a landscape is informal, a few small hollows or humps in a lawn may not matter much. If, however, hollows and humps are numerous or obvious, you will need to level them out. Small hollows can be filled with a sandy top-dressing.

LEVELING A HOLLOW OR HUMP IN A LAWN

1 Using a half-moon edger, cut a deep cross through the center of the uneven area. Cut right through the soil and beyond the problem area. Carefully peel back the sections of turf, and fold them back.

2 Turn over the soil lightly with a hand fork. To fill a hollow, add sandy topsoil a little at a time. To remove a hump underneath the turf, remove as much soil as necessary. Firm the soil.

3 Carefully lower the turf back into position. Firm gently, and make sure that the area is completely level. Firm again, and sprinkle top-dressing into any gaps. Water the area thoroughly.

ESTABLISHING CAUSES OF HOLLOWS AND HUMPS

● **Poor drainage** Hollows can be caused by poor drainage, which may be indicated by the presence of moss. Make sure that the soil used to fill the hollow contains plenty of coarse sand. Use a sandy top-dressing mixture.
● **Hidden causes** Check to see if uneven areas are caused by any underlying debris or buried tree roots. If necessary, dig out the cause of the problem, then even out the area using topsoil or a sandy top-dressing mixture.

● **Burrowing moles** Severe hollows in a lawn can be caused by the collapse of mole tunnels, which must be excavated and filled in. To prevent further damage, keep moles from coming back into your yard (see p. 113).

PLANNING REPAIRS

● **Best time** If possible, level out uneven areas in autumn or spring, when turf will re-establish quickly. Water the lawn frequently and thoroughly to encourage rapid rooting.

PROTECTING REPAIRS

● **Regular use** If children use a lawn regularly, consider fencing off repaired areas with stakes and string until the turf is re-established.

BRIGHT IDEA

Making turf resilient
For areas of lawn that develop hollows due to heavy use, add finely chopped car tires to the top-dressing. The rubber will make the turf more resistant to damage from regular pounding.

LEVELING WITH TOP-DRESSING

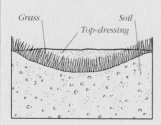
Grass   *Soil*
  Top-dressing

Slight hollows in a lawn can be filled with a sandy top-dressing; the grass will grow through and then root in the top-dressing. Use this method only for shallow hollows, since excessive quantities of top-dressing may smother the grass and prevent growth.

ENHANCING TREES IN LAWNS

A tree planted in a lawn can provide a natural central feature for a landscape, especially if it has an attractive and interesting shape. A tree that offers particular seasonal interest – perhaps spring blossoms or striking color in autumn – can also form a stunning focal point.

PROVIDING SEATING

Adding a seat
Put a large, old tree to good use by placing a bench or seat around or under it. Make sure that there is enough room for the tree trunk to expand without being constricted by the bench.

CARING FOR TREES

● **Trees in lawns** Leave a circle about three or four times the diameter of each tree's root ball free of grass. This makes feeding easy and minimizes competition from the grass.
● **Soil level** If making a flower bed under a tree, do not raise the soil level more than about 2–3 in (5–8 cm). If the bed is any deeper than this, the tree roots may be suffocated.

PLANTING GROUNDCOVER

● **Bulbs under trees** Bulbs form decorative groundcover under trees. Choose bulbs that flower mainly in spring, when the tree will not create much shade.

FEEDING TREES

● **When planting** Give a new tree a good start. Mix plenty of bulky organic matter, with added fertilizer, into as large a planting hole as possible.
● **Stimulating growth** Foliar feed a newly planted tree throughout its first and second growing season. This will help to speed up the tree's establishment by stimulating root growth.
● **Feeding area** When feeding an established tree, lift squares of turf around the outermost spread of the branches, and fork fertilizer into the soil. Replace the turf, and water well.

CREATING WILDFLOWER AREAS

G rass growing directly beneath a tree rarely thrives. Although it is occasionally possible to cultivate a fairly green area if you choose a suitable grass seed mixture or sod, it may be easier to plant flowers instead. Choose plants that are tolerant of shade and dry soil.

PLANTING WILDFLOWERS UNDER TREES

Flowers will attract pollinating insects

Self-seeding foxgloves quickly establish in shade of tree

Small groundcover plants at edges keep weeds down

Choosing appropriate plants
Choose any plants that grow naturally in the conditions found under trees. Because suitable plants all enjoy the same habitat, they will look natural together. Groundcover plants, such as periwinkle, keep the weeds down and are easy to maintain.

SELECTING PLANTS

● **Correct choice** Choose from the following plants, all of which will grow well under a tree: *Anemone* x *hybrida, Anemone nemorosa, Bergenia* spp., *Brunnera macrophylla, Convallaria majalis, Cyclamen, Galanthus nivalis, Geranium macrorrhizum, Hyacinthoides non-scripta, Iris foetidissima, Lamium* spp., *Liriope muscari, Tiarella cordifolia, Viola.*

MAINTAINING PLANTS

● **Watering** Although plants that grow under a tree do not require much water, you will need to water them regularly during dry periods, when little rain penetrates the canopy.

RESTORING BORDERS

A BADLY PLANTED BORDER, or one that has become too crowded, can spoil the look of a landscape. However, if the basic design is good, it may be possible to transform a border with some careful thinning or additional planting.

THINNING OUT BORDERS

It is very easy to overplant a border. Planted at the correct spacing, a border invariably looks sparse until the plants have grown and matured. When they have, you may need to remove a number of entire plants, or simply divide existing plants.

DEALING WITH AN OVERCROWDED BORDER

Rapidly growing, vigorous shrub · *Plant too large for space* · *Perennial clump* · *Small shrub suitable for this border* · *Gap between plants allows for growth* · *Replanted perennial clump*

Border before thinning
Rapidly growing shrubs create competition and shade, and should be removed to allow more space for other plants to grow and develop properly. Herbaceous perennial clumps become crowded and need to be divided every two or three years.

Border after thinning
Divide crowded herbaceous perennial clumps (see p. 60). Keep some sections for the border, and use others to fill gaps elsewhere in the landscape. Move some shrubs (see p. 59) to another site, and prune back others as required.

USING CLEMATIS

Reviving a shrub
Instead of digging up a straggly, leggy shrub, plant a clematis close by, and allow it to scramble through the shrub. This will soon cover any sparseness and will also provide color.

IMPROVING BORDERS
● **Starting again** If a border is beyond repair, move the plants into a spare patch of ground. Redesign the area, and replant.
● **Improving the soil** If you start over, take the opportunity to revitalize the soil. Incorporate compost and well-rotted manure, and use a general fertilizer (see p. 84). If the soil is heavy and sticky, dig in coarse sand to improve the drainage (see p. 42).
● **Digging in winter** Do not do extensive work on a border with heavy soil during during a wet winter; this could damage plants. Wait until spring.
● **Mulching** Cover any bare areas between plants with a 2–3 in (5–7 cm) deep layer of mulch to retain moisture and suppress weeds (see p. 90).

MOVING AND PLANTING
● **Recycling** Move shrubs from a mixed border to other areas of the landscape in late autumn, when the roots are dormant (see p. 58–59).
● **Dividing perennials** Use only the vigorous sections of divided perennials. If you have any spare clumps, you can plant them in containers and in other areas of the garden.
● **Planting distance** When planting, always check a plant's potential height and spread (see p. 51), and group plants together accordingly. This can save a lot of time and effort later.
● **Roots** Always check the roots of any plant you are moving. If they are tangled, soak the root ball for a few hours before loosening them.

FILLING GAPS IN BORDERS

If a mixed or herbaceous border is planted correctly, it will take a few years for it to reach its full potential. The planting will look sparse for the first few years; fill temporary gaps with bulbs, annuals, and potted plants until the border plants are well established.

SPRING COLOR

Planting bulbs
Use bulbs to fill gaps in a newly planted or thinned out border. Spring-flowering bulbs, such as *Narcissi*, are useful because they look their best when shrubs and herbaceous plants are bare.

SUMMER COLOR

Planting perennials
Use herbaceous perennials and a few annuals in spaces between young shrubs in a border to give an immediate, full look. As the shrubs mature, remove the plants as necessary.

SOWING ANNUALS
● **Planting times** Try sowing some traditionally spring-sown annuals in autumn instead. This can often result in a long, sustained flowering period.

USING CONTAINERS
● **Planting pots** Bring temporary color to a border with containerized plants. Bury the pots in the soil up to their rims, or stand them in the border, making sure that the bases are hidden by the foliage of nearby plants.
● **Autumn color** Use pots of autumn crocus and *Colchicum* to brighten up borders in late summer or autumn.

COVERING SLOPES

Sloping areas often help to add interest to a garden, and can provide useful and unusual opportunities for planting. If your landscape varies, use this to your advantage. However, dealing with slopes requires careful planning and planting to avoid soil erosion and slippage.

DEALING WITH SLOPES
● **Terraces** One way of dealing with a steep slope is to terrace it. Build a series of retaining walls to support the soil.

Planting up a slope
If access to plants on a slope is difficult, choose plants that do not need much maintenance. You may need to use groundcover plants initially to help keep the soil in place (see p. 44).

STABILIZING SOIL
● **Retaining walls** Make sure that any wood you use to make retaining walls has been pressure-treated, and that it is sturdy enough to bear the weight of the soil.
● **Netting** Keep soil on a steep slope in place with netting (see p. 44). This is best left in place, although you can cut it away when plants are established, if you prefer.
● **Adding mulch** Use a layer of mulch to disguise netting. The mulch will also help to keep the soil in place.

CHOOSING PLANTS
● **Wet soil** Consider planting moisture-loving plants at the bottom of a slope, where it is usually damp (see p. 44).

TIME-SAVING TIP

Hiding rubble
Instead of disposing of an unwanted pile of rubble, plant a climber to hide it. Many climbers, including roses and clematis, grow well horizontally. If the pile includes concrete, do not use acid-loving plants.

CREATING A WOODLAND GARDEN

Rather than struggling to radically alter a landscape that is planted with trees, it may be more sensible to work with the trees and develop a woodland-style garden. If you have trees growing in a border, underplant them with suitable, dry shade-loving plants.

DEVELOPING A WOODLAND GARDEN

Tree trunk adds to woodland atmosphere

Foxgloves self-seed to produce more plants each year

Thick undergrowth provides shelter for wildlife

Looking natural

For a natural, woodland look, select plants that multiply by self-seeding. Include bulbs in your planting design, too. Choose plants with small, simple flowers and plain leaves.

PLANNING SHADY BEDS

● **Shrubs** Underplant large trees with shade-tolerant shrubs. Take care not to damage the trees' roots as you dig.
● **Groundcovers** Choose herbaceous plants that thrive in shade. Some make useful groundcovers for what would otherwise be bare ground.
● **Gradual shade** Soil at the edge of a tree canopy receives more light than that closer to the trunk, so choose your plants accordingly.

THINNING TREES

A large, mature tree in a landscape is something very special. If a tree causes problems by creating excessive shade, or if its branches are encroaching too far toward a building, it may be possible to remedy the problem without having to spoil the tree.

PRUNING TREES

● **Professional help** Always hire a professional arborist to perform any tree surgery. This type of work can be dangerous and the outcome disastrous, if it is done by somebody who has not been properly trained.
● **Height and spread** If a tree has outgrown its site, and its lower branches are casting shade, it may be possible to have it "crown-reduced," or to have both the height and the spread reduced. If this is done properly, the tree will retain its natural shape after pruning but will be significantly smaller.

THE EFFECTS OF CROWN-LIFTING A TREE

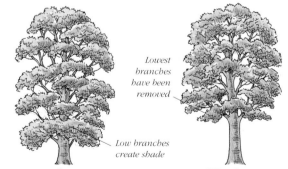

Lowest branches have been removed

Low branches create shade

An unpruned tree
This large tree may cause problems, especially if lower branches are shading a large area, and access beneath or around the tree is restricted.

A crown-lifted tree
This tree has been crown-lifted. The lower branches only have been removed, which will improve access and allow more light into the garden.

RENOVATING PATIOS

A NEGLECTED PATIO can look very dull. Common patio problems include weed infestation and loose, cracked slabs, which may be covered with slippery moss and algae. Even subtle alterations can have a surprising impact.

CLEARING AND CLEANING PATIOS

Before deciding how you want to change a patio, you should remove any debris that has accumulated, as well as stains and algal deposits. You will also need to eliminate weeds. This initial, basic work will go a long way toward improving the look of the patio.

CLEANING AND REPAIRING PATIOS

- **Debris** Place any organic debris in a compost pile for future use in the garden.
- **Drips** If you have an external faucet on a patio wall, make sure it is not dripping constantly. The algal growths that cause slippery, green patches are often caused by drips or leaks.
- **Green slime** Clean unsightly and dangerous slippery slabs with a stiff brush and soapy water, or use a commercial algae and moss killer.

- **Weeds** Always check the label before using a weedkiller, and perform a test on a small piece of slab in an obscure corner. Old or porous stone or concrete slabs may be stained by certain products. If in doubt, hand weed the area.
- **Repairs** If possible, repair or replace cracked slabs (see p. 167). If you cannot buy matching replacements, swap damaged slabs in prominent places with perfect ones from less obvious areas.

REMOVING WEEDS

Using weedkillers
Weeds may appear between patio slabs, or in cracks in broken slabs. Use a watering can with a special attachment to apply liquid weedkiller (see p. 97).

SOFTENING PATIOS

An established patio that is very angular can look harsh and uninviting. Slabs on a new patio that have not yet mellowed as a result of weathering can have a similar effect on the area as a whole. A few plants, and a variety of materials, can make all the difference.

COVERING A WALL

Planting in a patio
Bring color and shape to a bare patio wall by removing a nearby slab and planting a climber or wall shrub. Attach a support to the wall, and tie in young stems.

CHOOSING MATERIALS

Mixing and matching
Try combining different materials for a soft, interesting effect. Bricks, paving stones, and gravel – or bricks and cobblestones – look good together.

ADDING INTEREST

- **Containers** Use pots, barrels, and other containers to brighten up and soften a patio, particularly one that has no plants growing in it.
- **Focal point** Add a small statue or a water feature (see p. 133). Bubbling or cascading water, or a striking statue, will draw the eye away from plain, stark areas of a patio.
- **Wall shrubs** Choose shrubs that benefit from the protection of a wall. Wall shrubs will quickly add color and interest, and are generally more suitable for small patios than wide-spreading climbers.

PLANTING IN PATIOS

Broken slabs or sections of a patio can be removed with a spade or trowel, enabling you to plant directly in the soil beneath.

Undamaged paving may also benefit from selective planting, introducing new colors, shapes, and textures to liven up a bare patio.

PLANTING BETWEEN PATIO SLABS

● **Removing mortar** Use a chisel or a screwdriver to scrape out any debris, moss, or old mortar that remains between paving slabs.

● **Forking soil** Remove any crushed stone with a spade, and then lightly turn over the soil beneath with a hand fork to loosen it.

● **Adding scent** Try to include some plants with fragrant flowers or scented foliage. Choose plants that grow well in a confined space.

1 Insert the blade of a spade or trowel in a gap between paving slabs. Work the blade so that it digs in lower than the base of a slab, ease it beneath, and lever out the slab. Dig out any crushed stone or sand.

2 Loosen the soil around the edges of the hole, then remove it. Add plenty of good garden soil, along with compost or well-rotted manure and some general fertilizer. Mix together well.

3 Plant shrubs or perennials following as you would normally (see p. 47). Make sure they are at the correct depth, and loosen the roots, if necessary. Add a few bulbs if you wish, and water well.

CARING FOR PLANTS

Patio plants need special attention. Many patios are in sunny locations, which means that temperatures can be high during the summer. In addition, patio paving quickly depletes the area of moisture and nutrients.

● **Watering** To keep patio plants fresh, water them regularly and thoroughly. Add mulch to help retain moisture around the plants' roots.

● **Feeding** Feed patio plants throughout the growing season with a weak liquid fertilizer. Alternatively, apply a balanced granular fertilizer once a year (see p. 86).

● **Pruning** Occasional pruning may be necessary to keep a plant's growth in check once it is established.

TRANSFORMING A PATIO

● **Improving soil** Never skimp on soil preparation before planting in a patio. Any soil beneath a patio will probably contain very few nutrients or beneficial microorganisms (see p. 42). The soil may also be badly compacted.

● **Winter interest** Include a few evergreen plants with variegated leaves for added interest during winter.

● **Unsuitable plants** Do not choose plants that are invasive, or any that may create unwanted shade. Avoid plants with vigorous root systems, since the roots may start to push up the patio over time. Avoid using thorny plants, or those that are prone to aphid infestations, in places where people gather.

BRIGHT IDEA

Aging a patio
If you want to give your new patio a weathered look, paint the paving slabs with yogurt or liquid manure. This will encourage the growth of moss and algae on the surface of the slabs.

USING RAISED BEDS

Break up the monotony of a large patio area with a permanent raised bed. This can be planted with climbers and trailing plants to introduce both height and color. By selecting the appropriate soil, you will be able to grow plants that would not thrive in your garden soil.

MAKING RAISED BEDS ON PATIOS

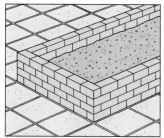

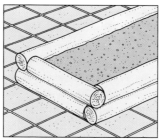

Using bricks
If you are building a raised bed out of bricks, make sure that they are frostproof. Choose bricks that match any others that are nearby so that the bed blends in well with its surroundings.

Using logs
Logs that have been pressure-treated with clear wood preservative make a long-lasting, rustic-style raised bed. Use rustproof galvanized nails to nail the logs together.

MAKING AND PLANTING
● **Using concrete** Make an inexpensive raised bed with concrete blocks. If you want to grow acid-loving plants, line the sides of the bed with rubber or heavy-duty plastic. Alternatively, paint the interior with several coats of sealant.
● **Drainage** Always make drainage holes at the bottom of a raised bed, and line the sides to prevent soil from spilling onto the patio.
● **Choosing plants** To disguise hard edges, select a number of plants that will trail down the sides of a raised bed.

ENHANCING SUNKEN PATIOS

Create planting areas around a sunken patio by building retaining walls and planting on top of them. Use materials that are the same as existing materials in that part of the landscape. Make sure that there is easy access between the sunken patio and the rest of the garden.

PLANTING AREAS AROUND SUNKEN PATIOS
● **Grass or flowers** Use a small, raised bed behind a retaining wall for planting annuals and perennials, or for laying out a grassy area.

● **Color** Use trailing plants to mask patio edges. Choose evergreens for interest all year around, and select other plants to provide seasonal color.

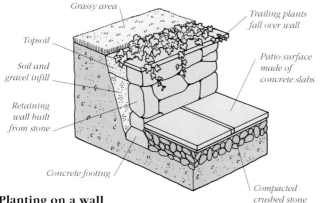

Grassy area

Trailing plants fall over wall

Topsoil

Soil and gravel infill

Patio surface made of concrete slabs

Retaining wall built from stone

Concrete footing

Compacted crushed stone forms solid bed for slabs

Planting on a wall
Use the top of a retaining wall to grow a range of plants, but first make sure that there is a fair amount of topsoil on top of the infill behind the wall. For best results, choose shallow-rooted plants.

TRADITIONAL TIP

Providing drainage
Retaining brick walls do not allow excess water from the soil to drain away. Prevent waterlogging by creating "weep holes" in the lowest layer of bricks. To do this, leave a few joints without mortar. Be sure to keep weep holes clear of debris.

CREATING TEMPORARY PLANTINGS

Containers of every size or shape – whether made from plastic, terracotta, stone, or lead – can be used to transform a patio instantly. Containers can be moved around each new season and planted up to provide color, interest, and fragrance (see p. 70–71).

PLANTING A TALL CONTAINER

Make good use of unsightly rubble to stabilize container

1 Stabilize a tall container by placing rubble or large stones at the bottom. This is important when a container will be used on a patio, where it is likely to be knocked over if not weighed down.

2 To conserve soil mix, find a separate plastic pot that fits snugly into the top of the container. Fill it with soil mix, and plant it up (see p. 66). The pot can be removed easily for replanting when necessary.

USING CONTAINERS

● **Maintenance** Most shrubs and some small, slow-growing climbers can be grown in containers on a patio. To keep them in good condition, water and feed them regularly (see p. 69). You may also need to prune the plants frequently.

● **Moving containers** As soon as the plants in a container are past their prime, move the container to an inconspicuous or hidden part of the patio. Place another container that is full of flowering plants in the same place.

● **Introducing water** Use a large, watertight half barrel to make a water feature that you can place in a corner of the patio (see p. 134).

USING BROKEN AND EMPTY POTS

There is no need to throw away broken containers. You can put them to good use by planting them up and using them on a patio or in the garden. If you plant them up correctly and use the right kinds of plants, cracks and missing chunks can be hidden.

CONCEALING DAMAGE

● **Positioning pots** Hide scratches, a missing piece, or a crack on a large pot by placing a smaller container of plants in front of it.

● **Trailing plants** Use trailing annuals such as *Lobelia erinus* or perennials such as *Aubrieta* to conceal any broken or chipped edges on pots. After planting up, apply a foliar feed (see p. 86) to encourage the plants to grow quickly.

USING EMPTY POTS

● **Decorated pots** Try grouping glazed, painted, or stenciled pots (see p. 79) together for an effective display of empty pots.

USING A BROKEN POT

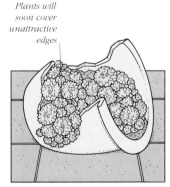

Plants will soon cover unattractive edges

Planting a broken pot
Lay a broken pot on its side, and plant it up with *Sempervivum*. These plants grow well in sparse, dry conditions and will soon grow over any broken edges.

GROUPING EMPTY POTS

Empty pot

Displaying empty pots
Use empty pots – either by themselves, or grouped with planted-up containers – to create an original display. Change the arrangement from time to time.

BUILDING A BARBECUE

A patio can be an ideal place for a barbecue. Although you can buy a barbecue from a store or garden center, building your own is a simple and cheap alternative. It also allows you to incorporate features that many barbecues do not have, such as a good-sized worktop.

CONSIDERING BARBECUE FEATURES

Level surface for stacking food and plates

Removable tray

Removable grill

Worktop

Charcoal storage

Concrete base can be used for burning trash in winter

Cupboard for storing barbecue tools and dishes

Constructing and siting a barbecue
A sturdily constructed barbecue is useful on any patio. Choose the right spot and the right materials so that it blends in with its surroundings.

DESIGNING A BARBECUE
● **Grill racks** Build your barbecue to fit standard-sized metal grill racks so that they can be replaced easily, if necessary.
● **Access** Locate a barbecue so that there is easy access to the house and to any seating area. Do not site it in the middle of a patio, where children may play.
● **Support** If you are not sure how well a patio was laid, build the barbecue on a concrete plinth to ensure that it will not sink into the patio.
● **Size** Always build a barbecue a little larger than you think you need it to be. A large barbecue will allow you to hold outdoor parties.
● **Built-in incineration** If your local ordinances permit outdoor burning, consider using your barbecue as an incinerator for trash and excess leaves. Put the grill rack in front to keep trash contained.

LOCATING A BARBECUE
● **Reducing smells** Do not build a barbecue close to the house; smoke and cooking smells may filter in.
● **Avoiding trees** Do not build a barbecue directly under a tree, which may be scorched if the heat becomes too intense. Also, trees may attract insects, which could also be attracted to your food.
● **Considering others** To avoid bothering your neighbors with smoke and noise, build the barbecue away from dividing walls or fences.
● **Seasonal use** Do not site a barbecue in a central location, since it will be used only for a small portion of the year.

ADDING LIGHTING
● **Electricity supply** Install an electricity supply from the house to a weatherproof, sealable socket on the patio. This will enable you to install lighting for a barbecue.
● **Safety** To avoid potential dangers, bury an electricity cable underground. If this is not possible, run the cable along an outside wall – do not string it along a fence or hedge.

WARNING!
Always take great care when lighting a barbecue. Follow instructions, and stand well back after lighting. Never use gasoline to light a barbecue.

MAINTENANCE

To keep a barbecue hygienic and in good condition, you need to clean it thoroughly after each use. Clean up ashes and any spilled fat, and throw away any debris that may attract vermin.

● **Removing fat** Scrub off fat deposits with a stiff brush and a strong solution of dishwashing liquid.
● **Caring for metal** As soon as the barbecue season is over, clean the racks and tools thoroughly. When dry, rub them with a rag soaked in cooking oil. Store them in a dry place to minimize rusting. Scrub well before reusing.

TRANSFORMING PATHS AND STEPS

Well-CONSTRUCTED PATHS AND STEPS should be maintained, since rebuilding them can be time-consuming. If they are unsightly, there are a number of ways to alter their appearance that do not require you to start from scratch.

SOFTENING EDGES

The severe edges and straight lines of some paths and steps can look out of place among the gentle, natural shapes of a garden. These structures may benefit from a fresh design or inspiring planting, transforming them into useful and attractive landscape features.

PERFUMING A PATH

Planting a lavender hedge
To add fragrance and shape to a garden path, plant a low hedge of lavender along its edge. If brushed against or crushed slightly, the foliage will perfume the air. Plant in a dry, sunny site.

PLANTING ALONG A PATH

Creating gentle shapes
Make a gentle, rippling path by planting bushy, sprawling plants in adjacent borders. Consider sinking terracotta pots at the edge of the path to break up straight lines further.

HIDING EDGES
● **Featuring stones** Conceal damage or alter the outline of a path by using large, rounded, or colored stones to create an attractive edging.
● **Planting seasonally** Plantings along a path's edge need not be permanent. Replace seasonal bedding at least twice a year to ensure constant color and to prevent plants from becoming too invasive.
● **Adding color** Lighten a dark, gloomy path or steps by filling the surrounding borders with evergreens that offer cream, yellow, and brightly variegated foliage year-round.

SUITABLE PLANTS FOR EDGING

Arenaria spp. (most),
Armeria maritima,
Aubrieta deltoidea and cvs.,
Aurinia spp.,
Campanula poscharskyana,
Dianthus deltoides,
Draba spp.,
Erinus alpinus,
Helianthemum spp.,
Iberis sempervirens,
Phlox (dwarf spp.),
Portulaca grandiflora,
Salvia officinalis,
Saxifraga (including
'Hi Ace' and 'Penelope'),
Sempervivum montanum,
Thymus spp. and cvs.
including *T. x citriodorus*
T. 'Anderson's Gold',
Viola odorata.

MAINTAINING EDGES
● **Repairing edges** Damaged paving can be dangerous, particularly if located in the center of a path or steps. Repair promptly (see p. 166).
● **Raising edges** Build a raised edge along a gravel path to prevent gravel from spreading onto a lawn and damaging a lawn mower. It will also keep soil from borders from spilling onto a path.
● **Planting edges** Path edges may become damaged with use. Remove the broken brick or slab, scoop out the soil beneath, add a new layer of compost, and plant a bushy, trailing evergreen in the space. The plant will spread and conceal the area below.

TRADITIONAL TIP

Laying brick edges
Make an inexpensive, striking edging to a path with bricks. Dig a small trench along both sides of the path. Place each brick in its trench on its side, so that it rests on the point of one corner and leans on the neighboring brick. Pack soil tightly around the bricks.

MAINTAINING GRAVEL PATHS

Gravel paths are inexpensive and easy to lay, and do not require special equipment to maintain. However, they can be difficult to walk on and are prone to invasion by weeds. Also, because of their loose surface, they are not suitable for a pronounced slope.

LAYING A NEW PATH

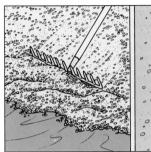

Laying a plastic base
Compact the soil, then create a raised edge with a strip of treated wood. Lay a plastic sheet over the soil to prevent weeds from appearing. Spread gravel over the plastic with the back of a rake.

RENOVATING A PATH

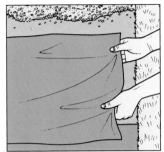

Removing gravel
Renovate an old path by laying sheets of plastic beneath the gravel: Work in sections along the path's length, raking the gravel away. Then position the plastic sheets so that their edges overlap.

WORKING WITH GRAVEL

● **Selecting gravel** If children are likely to use a path, be sure you use a smooth gravel that consists of well-rounded stones, such as pea gravel.

● **Creating drainage** Plastic underlay may prevent a path from draining properly, leading to waterlogging in wet weather. If this is a problem, replace the plastic with a layer of landscape fabric that acts as a barrier against weeds, but allows water to drain to the soil beneath.

● **Raking** Rake gravel regularly to level the surface of a path and redistribute the stones.

BRIGHTENING CONCRETE STEPS

Concrete forms a tough and resilient surface, making it a popular material for constructing steps. However, its bare, angular shape can look harsh and unattractive, and it rarely fits in well with surrounding garden features. Lighten this effect with clever planting.

IMPROVING STEPS

● **Featuring alpines** If steps are wide, sink a few pots of cushion-forming alpines into piles of gravel at intervals along the length of the steps. Planting in the pots ensures that growth is restricted and makes it easy to remove the plants.

● **Stacking terracotta** Break up a long, wide flight of steps by stacking planted-up, weathered terracotta pots in groups along the edge of the steps.

● **Creating form** Add an air of formality to the base of steps with two carefully chosen container plants placed on either side of the step. Spiral or cone-shaped box plants and standard bay or rose trees planted in Versailles tubs or large, terracotta pots, will make a striking, memorable display.

PLANTING FOR EASE

● **Using small pots** If steps are used infrequently, or if they are deep, add color with a number of small pots that are portable and easy to move.

Planting containers
Place seasonal bedding plants – such as bulbs, annuals, and tender perennials – on steps. Replace these at intervals for year-round interest. Alternatives are clipped shrubs and herbs.

PLANTING FOR EFFECT

● **Softening steps** Plant around steps to permanently soften their outline. Make sure that you choose plants that will not become too invasive.

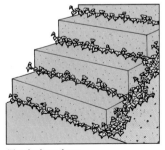

Training ivy
Plant small-leaved ivy in the soil adjacent to steps. Train the ivy along pieces of garden wire attached to the risers. Trim the ivy regularly to keep it from growing over the steps.

TRANSFORMING WALLS

WITH A LITTLE IMAGINATION, a wall can be transformed from a functional boundary marker into an exciting, vertical growing space, literally adding a new dimension to a garden. Train climbers and fruit trees for best results.

COVERING WALLS

The height and shape of the wall, as well as the choice of building material, affect how the structure fits in with its surroundings. If an old wall is unsightly, fruit trees, small flowering trees, or flowering shrubs can be trained to make an attractive, productive covering.

FAN-TRAINING A FRUIT TREE AGAINST A WALL

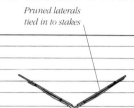
Pruned laterals tied in to stakes

Stems have been pruned out

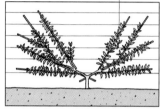
New side shoots tied to stakes and attached to wires

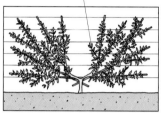
New side shoots are tied in

1 In early spring, select two laterals on a young fruit tree that are 12 in (30 cm) above ground level to form the main arms. Prune each one to 15 in (38 cm) and tie to a stake at a 40-degree angle. Prune the leader to just above the laterals.

2 The following year, in early spring, prune arms by one third to an outward-facing bud. In early summer, tie new side-shoots to stakes. Prune out any stems that develop below the two main arms or that point down or away from the wall.

3 In early summer, thin out excess stems to leave them 4–6 in (10–15 cm) apart. During summer, tie the sideshoots, and pinch out any that overlap the main framework of arms. Prune fruiting shoots back to a new shoot at the base of the tree.

CREATING WALL SPACE

Designing a wall
Be adventurous when planning a wall. Consider incorporating a porthole or a gate that is large enough to walk through. This will introduce light to new areas of the garden and could encompass distant views.

IMPROVING WALLS
● **Stains** Discolored bricks make a wall look unsightly. Scrub the surface (see p. 164) before deciding if any further action is necessary.
● **Tending climbers** Thin out and prune back climbers. If they are not responding to care, replace them.
● **Screening a wall** Cover a wall with more than one climber. Choose plants with different flowering times – evergreen and deciduous – to ensure that the wall is screened for as long as possible throughout the year.
● **Fruit trees** If a wall is in a shady site but you would like to fan-train a fruit tree, plant a sour cherry tree.

BRIGHT IDEA

Creating a new shape
To make a new climber that has put on uniform growth look more established and natural, trim it back unevenly to create an irregular, informal outline.

USING TRELLISES

Attaching trellises to a wall can be the answer to a variety of problems in a garden. Trellises provide privacy from neighbors, conceal eyesores, disguise damaged or discolored surfaces, and increase the potential planting space in a garden.

ATTACHING TRELLISES

● **Material** If using a trellis in a garden, choose a wooden frame. It will look good, is long-lasting, and can support more weight than most plastic or plastic-coated frames.

● **Supports** Use pressure-treated lumber to support a trellis. After cutting paint the surface with wood preservative safe for plants.

● **Hardware** Use galvanized nails, screws, and other hardware to prevent rust.

● **Paint** Before attaching a trellis to a painted wall, apply a fresh coat of paint to the surface, and make any necessary repairs.

PLANTING UP A TRELLIS

Main shoots tied to trellis

Stable container of enough depth

Supporting a climber

Use a triangular trellis to support a climber growing in a container. Before planting, place the trellis in the pot, then pack soil firmly around its base. Tie the top of the trellis to a wall, if necessary.

PROVIDING EASY ACCESS TO A WALL

1 To provide easy access to a wall for maintenance, attach narrow strips of wood to the trellis and the wall. Attach hooks to both ends of the wall strips, and eyes to the ends of the trellis strips.

2 To secure the trellis base to the wall, attach hinges to the bottom of the trellis. Alternatively, attach a pair of hooks and eyes to the lower wooden strips to make the removal of the trellis easy.

DESIGNING WITH TRELLIS

● **Adding color** Brighten up a standard, unpainted wooden trellis by painting it with a coat of colored wood preservative. Alternatively, mix together latex paint and clear wood preservative to create a unique color.

● **Selecting color** When painting a trellis, select a color that either complements or dramatically contrasts with the garden furniture and nearby plants and structures.

● **Choosing shape** Be adventurous when selecting new trellises; they are available in many different shapes and sizes. Alter the line of the top of a wall or screen with a concave or convex trellis, or use alternating square- and diamond-shaped pieces to bring variety to a garden.

● **Dividing trellis** Add an air of formality to a garden by using ornamental trellis posts.

COVERING A NEW TRELLIS

● **Annuals** Plant up a new, bare trellis with annual climbers the first year. These will provide a good covering while the permanent planting becomes established. Just one season's growth of sweet peas and morning glories will have the desired effect.

Using a temporary display
Screen a new trellis with a selection of containers filled with climbers, trailers, and tender perennials. These can be used elsewhere once any permanent planting has covered the trellis.

DESIGNING WITH SPECIAL EFFECTS

An ugly wall can be transformed by training climbers and fruit trees on it. Other clever devices can be used to make an area look different. Use colored paint, mirrors, and decoratively shaped trellises to create changes in a garden, both real and imaginary.

BRIGHTENING WALLS

- **Whitewash** If a garden is dark and gloomy, paint fences and walls with whitewash to lighten up the area.
- **Murals** Add another dimension to a garden by painting a mural on a flat, vertical surface. To add to the illusion, place a real pot by a painted one, and match the colors of the plant with those in the mural.
- **Mediterranean style** Put sunny walls and fences to use by planting climbers that require the protection and warmth they provide. Add terracotta pots of geraniums, pelargoniums, and nasturtiums to create a Mediterranean feel.

ADDING DEPTH

Attaching a decorative trellis
Add a sense of depth to a garden by attaching a trellis with a false perspective to a wall or other flat, vertical surface. Plant up the trellis with a sprawling climber, and position shrubs around it to add to the illusion of reality.

REFLECTING SPACE

Using a mirror
Attach a mirror to a wall or fence to increase light in a garden and give the impression of size and space. Be sure its position offers an attractive reflection. Cover mirror edges with wood, or plant with evergreen climbers.

USING ARCHES

An arch is often erected in the middle of a garden to link one area to another. It may also be placed randomly, acting mainly as a support for climbers. Attach an arch to a wall and create an arbor, to bring instant shade, seclusion, and privacy to a garden.

POSITIONING AN ARCH

Creating an arbor
Place a metal or wooden arch against a wall, and train climbers up it to make an attractive garden feature. Convert it into an arbor or secluded seating area by placing a bench inside.

WORKING WITH AN ARCH

- **Outside room** Convert part of a garden into an outside room by including seating space in a sheltered arbor. Consider adding a small table if space permits.
- **Selection** Choose an arbor carefully if it is to be located in a central site all year round. A wooden arch can look good by itself, and need not be covered with climbers. Treat regularly with wood preservative (see p. 162).
- **Position** Situate an arbor according to the amount of sun desired for the intended use of the garden – perhaps in the morning to eat a leisurely summer breakfast, or to enjoy the last of the evening sun.

TRANSFORMING AN ARCH

- **Fragrance** When planning an arbor, include scented climbers in your summer planting design. If you are likely to use the area only in the evening, be sure to select plants that remain fragrant during the evening.
- **Illusion** Place a mirror on the wall behind an arch to add a feeling of spaciousness.
- **Hiding place** Link two arches together to create a miniature hideaway or summer play area for children.
- **Using evergreens** If an arbor is to be used in early spring, late autumn, or winter, make sure that it has a covering of attractive evergreens as well as seasonal climbers.

CONSTRUCTING SCREENS

A BEAUTIFUL GARDEN can be spoiled by an ugly view or the intrusion of other houses. Necessary but unattractive items, such as trash cans, clotheslines, and sheds, can have the same effect. With planning, these can be screened from view.

CONCEALING UNSIGHTLY FEATURES

Take a careful and objective look at your landscape from a variety of positions, including inside the house, on the patio, and at the back door. Make a list of all the objects you would like to conceal or obscure; this can be achieved in a number of different ways.

DECORATING A DIVIDER

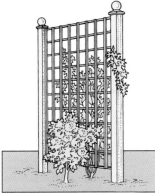

Covering a screen
Plant up both sides of a trellis or fence to make the most of the growing area and to create an effective and attractive screen.

CARING FOR PLANTS
● **Positioning** Stagger plantings along the two sides of a dividing screen to reduce possible interference between the root systems. This will also help to reduce competition for water and nutrients.
● **Maintenance** Feed the soil at the base of a densely planted screen, and make sure that it is always moist. Mulch regularly to provide the best possible soil conditions for plant growth.
● **Growth** Keep plant growth in check to ensure that a dividing screen does not become too wide and encroach upon adjacent areas.

SUITABLE PLANTS

Berberis darwinii,
B. thunbergii,
Corylus avellana,
Cotoneaster franchetii,
Cotoneaster lacteus,
Crataegus monogyna,
Euonymus japonica,
Forsythia x *intermedia,*
Fuchsia magellanica,
Garrya elliptica,
Ilex aquifolium,
Pittosporum tenuifolium,
Potentilla fruticosa,
Prunus spinosa, Pyracantha,
Rosa 'Nevada',
Rosa 'Roseraie de l'Hay',
Rosa rugosa,
Viburnum opulus
'Compactum'.

MONEY-SAVING TIP

Growing an annual screen
Plant a cheerful annual screen using sunflowers. Grow scarlet runner beans up the stems to add density and provide a source of fresh vegetables.

HIDING A TREE STUMP

Planting a climber
Always try to remove a tree stump, since it may encourage diseases such as root rot. If this is impossible, treat the stump with a commercial solution. After a few months, plant a climber to cover the stump with flowers and foliage.

CREATING A SCREEN
● **Appearance** Use sections of a trellis to make a screen around garbage cans and other unsightly objects (see p. 30). Make sure that the enclosed area is large enough for easy access once climbers have reached to their full size.
● **Scent** When screening potentially strong-smelling items, such as compost piles, wormeries, and liquid-manure containers, plant a selection of scented climbers to act as natural air fresheners.
● **Bamboo** To create a striking screen of foliage, plant clumps of bamboo. Their densely packed stems make them an ideal screen.

CONCEALING SERVICE AREAS

No matter how large a landscape is, you will probably want to fill every spare corner of it with plants. However, there will inevitably be items that take up valuable gardening space and are potential eyesores. Use temporary and permanent screens to conceal these objects.

POSITIONING AND PLANTING UP SCREENS

● **Using trellis** If you are using trellises to hide unsightly items, make sure they are strong enough to support climbers. To add strength, construct a frame around the structure using wooden strips.

● **Using evergreens** A trellis can be used on its own, but it is most effective and attractive if plants are climbing over it. Include evergreens in your planting design to ensure year-round concealment.

Partitioning
Use trellis panels and a trellis door to partition off a large, unsightly area in a garden. Plant up the trellis lightly so that the screen and the area beyond merge in with the rest of the landscape.

SELECTING A DISGUISE

● **Metal covers** Use containers to conceal metal service covers. Make sure they are lightweight so that they can be moved quickly in an emergency. If you would like to feature a heavy container, make it easy to move by fixing wheels to its base, or stand it on a wheeled platform.
● **Pipes** Group several different pots together to hide a cistern or septic tank pipes.
● **Large eyesores** Obtrusive oil tanks and gas cylinders are often situated close to houses. Use trellises, wattle hurdles, or fence panels as screens, and plant with climbers.

CONCEALING GARBAGE CANS

Most buildings have at least one garbage can. Both these and large, unsightly, wheeled plastic bins can be easily hidden. When using screens, avoid the temptation to conceal garbage cans and bins completely, since access must be unrestricted.

MAKING SCREENS

● **Small screen** To make a simple and effective screen, to hide a single garbage can from view, attach a trellis panel at right angles to an existing fence or wall.
● **Large screen** Use a trellis, willow panels, or fence panels to make an open-ended partition behind which garbage cans can be stored. Be sure the area is densely planted in the summer, to keep the sun off the garbage.
● **Scented screen** Plant up a garbage area with fragrant flowers. Mix strongly scented roses, honeysuckle, and jasmine with other climbers, and complete the colorful and perfumed effect with an annual sowing of sweet peas.

DESIGNING WITH BRICKS

Building for permanence
Construct a permanent garbage screen out of bricks, leaving holes for ventilation. Allow for access, but keep the top low to prevent animals from removing lids. Build a trough above, and plant up with trailing foliage.

USING A CONTAINER

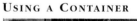

Using temporary color
To create an attractive, temporary display, use a large, planted-up container to partially hide a garbage can. Slip a section of a trellis panel between the container and the garbage can for additional concealment.

USING HEDGES AS SCREENS

In some cases, a natural, living screen or divider is more appropriate for a particular area than a constructed one. A hedge makes an attractive and long-lasting screen. However, for a hedge to look good, it must be planted, maintained, and clipped correctly.

CONCEALING THE SPARSE BASES OF HEDGES

● **Using a trellis** If the base of a hedge becomes sparse and leggy, construct a low trellis to hide the area. This can then be used as a support for climbers.

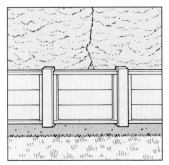

Positioning a screen
Position a fence so that it screens only the bare base of a hedge. When digging holes for the support posts, make sure that you avoid the roots of the hedge.

● **Partial screen** If you do not want to completely conceal the area beneath a hedge, partially obscure it with a selection of herbaceous plants.

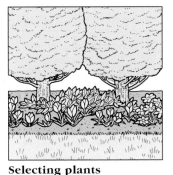

Selecting plants
If the soil beneath a hedge is dry, plant drought-tolerant plants and bulbs. Water and feed regularly to be sure that the plants and hedge do not compete for nutrients.

CARING FOR HEDGES

● **Maintaining** Feed and water hedges regularly, since they are constantly clipped and grow rapidly, using up large amounts of energy.
● **Trimming** To ensure that the top of a hedge is cut flat and level, keep shear blades parallel to the line of the hedge.
● **Roadside hedges** Before winter, place plastic screens around hedges that are planted along a road. This should prevent the roots from absorbing de-icing salt and also keep the foliage from being scorched.
● **Climbers** Erect a system of straining wires between posts along the length of a sparse hedge. Train twining climbers along them to create a curtain of color and foliage.

PROMOTING GROWTH

To promote even and sustained growth in a formal or informal hedge, it is important to trim it carefully on a regular basis.

● **Deciduous hedges** To create an attractive, dense deciduous hedge, trim it twice annually with shears or an electric hedge trimmer. (Be sure to keep the cord out of the way as you trim.)
● **Coniferous hedges** Treat conifers with care. When pruning in the first years, remove only the lateral branches until a hedge reaches its desired height. Do not cut back hard, since the inner brown foliage may be revealed. Because there is little replacement growth from these stems, it will be difficult to hide the damage.

TRIMMING HEDGES

● **Nests** Avoid trimming a hedge when birds are nesting. Wait until the fledgings have left the nest. The hedge will not suffer, and you will help to preserve the next generation of garden birds.
● **Shaping** Formal hedges look messy if cut unevenly or at the wrong angle. Use a taut piece of string tied between two upright posts to make sure that a hedge is level, and use a template to shape the top.
● **Clippings** Put clippings to good use by incorporating them in a compost pile. Do not do this if you know a hedge is diseased.
● **Shocking information** Never trim a hedge with electric shears in rainy weather: you could receive a severe shock.

MONEY-SAVING TIP

Restoring a hawthorn
To rejuvenate a hawthorn hedge that has become sparse and leggy at the base, bend a number of pliable stems downward. Hold these in the soil using small metal pegs. In time, these stems will root and fill out the base of the hedge.

SCREENING SHEDS

A shed is a practical – and often essential – addition to a landscape, offering a work area and storage space for tools, bulbs, seeds, and other items. However, even if it is in good condition, a shed is a potential eyesore and can detract from the overall effect of a garden.

CREATING A SCREEN USING A TRELLIS

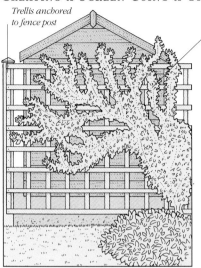

Trellis anchored to fence post

Climber trained to cover trellis

Building a screen
Erect a trellis to create an effective screen for a functional shed. Use fence posts to support the structure and to keep it away from the sides of the shed, allowing easy access for maintenance. When planting, choose a climber that will not outgrow the trellis.

MAKING SCREENS
● **Using chicken wire** Create a freestanding, column-shaped screen by rolling up a length of galvanized chicken wire. Train climbers over and through it.
● **Using natural materials** Use willow panels or hazel-wattle hurdles to make a functional and attractive screen. Although expensive, these are well suited to an informal or cottage-style garden.

PREVENTING WOOD ROT
● **Protecting screens** Be sure that the base of a wooden screen is raised 2–3 in (5–7.5 cm) above the soil to prevent wood rot.

ENHANCING SHEDS

Screening a shed can be impractical if access is limited. In such a situation, consider highlighting the shed rather than hiding it. With careful planting and grouped selections of decorative containers, an old shed can become an attractive, integral part of a landscape.

MAINTAINING SHEDS
● **Reroofing** Prolong the life of an old shed and improve its appearance by reroofing with new felt and fixtures and hardware (see p. 160).
● **Renovating** Scrub off algae and other debris from the surface, and allow the shed to dry thoroughly before applying a coat of wood preservative. Consider using a colored preservative or adding paint to camouflage discolored areas and to create a brand new look.
● **Cleaning** Check for wood decay, and treat and refill the wood, if necessary (see p. 162). At the same time, wipe the glazing with a commercial cleaning agent to remove the buildup of debris.

PLANTING FOR COLOR

Adding containers
Decorate a shed with hanging baskets and windowboxes packed full of annual flowers and trailing foliage. Strategically placed terracotta pots and other containers will help to hide damaged and discolored areas.

TRAINING CLIMBERS

Creating shapes
To create a striking effect, grow a climber up and over the roof of a shed. Since this method may encourage deterioration of the wood, it is best reserved for old sheds that have a limited function and life expectancy.

BLOCKING UNSIGHTLY VIEWS

Even when every effort is made to design, create, and maintain an attractive garden, the surrounding environment often presents an unsightly view. This effect can be countered by hiding and blocking unattractive objects with natural and constructed screens.

PLANNING A SECLUDED GARDEN

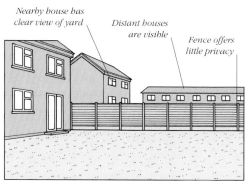

Nearby house has clear view of yard · *Distant houses are visible* · *Fence offers little privacy*

Assessing the surrounding area

Neighboring buildings sometimes overlook a house and have a clear view into the yard. These buildings may also be prominently visible from the yard, even with a high, wooden fence. Privacy and a sense of seclusion are important in a built-up area.

ADDING HEIGHT AND SHAPE

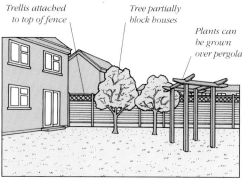

Trellis attached to top of fence · *Tree partially block houses* · *Plants can be grown over pergola*

Adding permanent structures

Trees give shape to a landscape and conceal unsightly views. A pergola and a trellis attached to the top of a fence bring shelter and seclusion to a yard. These permanent structures can be planted up for additional shape and color.

ADDING TRELLIS EXTENSIONS

Raising the height of a wall or fence is an inexpensive and relatively easy way to conceal unsightly views and ensure privacy. Trellis sections can be attached to the top of a wooden fence or brick wall, then planted up with annual and evergreen climbers.

PERMANENT EXTENSION

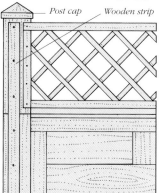

Post cap · *Wooden strip*

Using a strip of wood

To extend a fence using wood, remove the post cap, and nail the fence and an extension post together with a narrow strip of wood. Using galvanized nails, attach the trellis section to the post, and replace the cap.

REMOVABLE EXTENSION

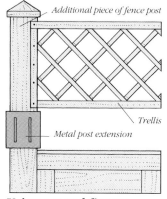

Additional piece of fence post · *Trellis* · *Metal post extension*

Using a metal fixture

Metal post extensions allow easy replacement of trellis panels. Remove the post cap, and slide the extension onto the post. Insert the additional piece of fence post, attach the trellis, and refit the cap.

WORKING WITH TRELLIS

● **Changing outlines** Alter the outline of a fence or wall by attaching concave or convex trellis sections to the top.

● **Limiting shade** Before extending the height of a fence or wall, assess how much light will be lost. Limit the amount of shade by attaching trellis sections, and planting a few small-leaved climbers. Avoid creating a wall of foliage.

● **Protecting wood** Once the trellis is in place, treat the fence with a coat of wood preservative to help blend the new wood with the old.

● **Planting** To conceal the joints connecting a fence and trellis, plant fast-growing climbers along with the permanent plantings.

PLANTING TREES

An established tree brings a sense of stability and permanence to a landscape. Its height can create shade and privacy, and its shape can significantly alter the overall look. When planting a tree, carefully choose a spot where it is least likely to cause damage.

USING TREES FOR SHADE AND PRIVACY

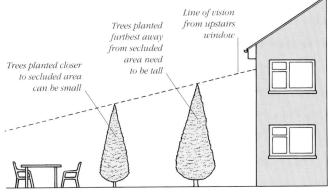

Line of vision from upstairs window

Trees planted furthest away from secluded area need to be tall

Trees planted closer to secluded area can be small

Planning the positions of trees for privacy

Carefully consider the position, shape, and overall design of your landscape before planting trees. Take into account the direction and path of the sun, and decide whether you want to divide one section of the landscape from another, create a secluded and shaded seating area, or conceal part of the landscape from the house. Conversely, you may want to screen certain rooms in the house, such as bedrooms or bathrooms, from general view.

SELECTING TREES

- **Seasonal use** Plant deciduous trees in an area that is used only in the summer. These will provide screening from late spring to autumn.
- **Size** Use small trees and shrubs to create a natural screen that partially blocks nearby objects from view.
- **Roots** Check the growth habit of a tree before purchasing it, particularly if your garden soil is clay-based. In certain conditions, tree roots can cause major damage to structural foundations.
- **Suckers** Some trees look good, but produce suckers. If you cannot spare the time required to remove suckers, avoid planting *Prunus* spp. and cvs., lilacs, and sumac.

USING PERGOLAS

A pergola adds height and diversity to a garden and can provide an attractive area for vertical planting. At the same time, it creates a decorative division that can also serve as a screen to conceal functional areas, damaged surfaces, and unsightly features.

CREATING COLOR

Planting climbers

Heavily plant a pergola with foliage and flowers. The climbers may take several years to become fully established but if they are given adequate attention and care, the wait will be worh it.

FEATURING PERGOLAS

- **Purchasing** When buying a pergola, make sure that its construction is strong enough to support the climbers in your planting design.
- **Constructing** Use pressure-treated wood for a pergola. The appearance of the completed structure can be altered with a coat of non-toxic, colored wood preservative, as long as it will not damage plants.
- **Renovating** When replanting an old pergola, take the opportunity to replace timber that is broken or rotten, and consider painting the repaired structure a different color.

SUITABLE PLANTS

Akebia quinata,
Berberidopsis corallina,
Campsis grandiflora,
C. radicans,
Celastrus,
Clematis spp. and cvs.,
Hedera,
Humulus lupulus 'Aureus',
Jasminum officinale,
Laburnum,
Lardizabala biternata,
Lonicera x *americana,*
L. x *brownii,*
Passiflora caerulea,
Rosa spp. and rambling and climbing cvs.,
Tropaeolum speciosum,
Vitis coignetiae,
Wisteria.

ADDING HEIGHT AND PERSPECTIVE

THERE ARE MANY DIFFERENT FACTORS to be considered when planning a landscape. Introducing height adds a new dimension to the landscape while adjusting the perspective can make a landscape appear narrow and long or wide and short.

INTRODUCING HEIGHT WITH ARCHES

Trees and large shrubs can be used to add height and shape to a landscape. Other permanent features, such as arches, pergolas, and decorative posts, can also be arranged to create points of interest. In a small landscape, just one feature can alter the overall look.

SELECTING AN ARCH STYLE

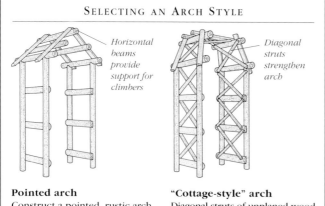

Horizontal beams provide support for climbers

Diagonal struts strengthen arch

Pointed arch
Construct a pointed, rustic arch from unplaned wood. Use galvanized nails or screws to fix the wood pieces to each other.

"Cottage-style" arch
Diagonal struts of unplaned wood add strength and support to an arch. Its "cottage-style" look is suitable for an informal garden.

PLANNING ARCHES
● **Height** When building an arch, make sure that it is tall enough for a person to walk through comfortably. Also, consider the types of flower that you are intending to plant; if they are pendulous, take this into consideration, and make the arch even taller.
● **Width** If a garden arch is to be walked through, make sure it is wide enough to allow two people to pass through side by side.
● **Planting** Use cross beams to increase the strength of an arch, making it suitable for supporting heavy climbers.

PLANTING A WALKWAY

Training climbers
Create an attractive walkway by training lightweight climbers over a series of wooden or plastic arches. Consider planting annuals or ornamental, runner, or edible pole beans.

CREATING NEW ARCHES
● **Building** To prolong the life of an archway, assemble with pressure-treated wood. Stabilize an upright arch post by setting it in concrete, or else use galvanized metal supports (see p. 163).
● **Transformation** Transform a new arch with fast-growing annuals such as *Eccremocarpus scaber, Ipomoea, Rhodochiton atrosanguineum*, and *Thunbergia alata*.
● **Planting beans** To make an "edible" arch, plant scarlet runner or pole beans with different flower colors.
● **Planting roses** When buying a rose for an arch, select a rambler; this has more flexible stems than a climbing rose.

TRADITIONAL TIP

Dividing an area
Use a trellis arch to divide an area into two distinct sections. Plant a screen of evergreen shrubs on either side.

USING PLANT SUPPORTS

Most climbing plants need to be trained on supports, such as tree trunks, bamboo-stake wigwams, and obelisks. Whether these supports occur naturally or are added to a landscape their height and shape can be used to create high points and enhance existing features.

USING A WIGWAM

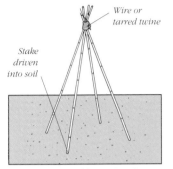

Wire or tarred twine

Stake driven into soil

USING AN OBELISK

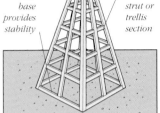

Wide base provides stability

Sturdy wooden strut or trellis section

MAINTAINING WOOD

● **Preserving** Treat a wooden structure regularly with a coat of wood preservative. Use pressure-treated wood and galvanized hardware for repairs to further extend its life.
● **Painting** Enhance a plant's appearance and help make its support attractive in winter by applying a brightly colored paint to the support.

Creating a pillar of color
Bamboo-cane wigwams are used traditionally to support pole beans. Plant up a wigwam with annual climbers to bring pillars of striking color to a border.

Supporting climbers
An obelisk looks good by itself and can be left outside through the winter. Use it to support climbers and create a permanent, attractive display.

CREATING SHAPES

● **Planting** Use a dense climber with attractive foliage, such as a variegated ivy, to create a solid, three-dimensional shape or screen.

PLANTING CLIMBERS

Evergreen and annual climbers can be used both to emphasize the height of an object and to conceal or alter the appearance of an eyesore. Some climbing plants need support in the form of a trellis or wires, while others can grow over an object without support.

COVERING A TREE

Transforming a dead tree
Try to remove a dead or dying tree, which may pose a hazard. If this is not possible, cut away the branches, leaving only the trunk standing. Grow a climber or two over the tree, adding wire supports, if necesssary.

CHOOSING SUPPORTS

● **Temporary** Form an arch from chicken wire, and use it to support lightweight, annual climbers for a colorful, temporary summer display.
● **Long-term** Use a sturdy wire frame to train climbers or to create unusual topiary shapes. Although not an instant or even quick effect, the frame will form a stylish, permanent plant support.
● **Using hose pipe** To support a lightweight plant, make a small arch using two wooden pegs and a piece of an old garden hose. Place a peg in one end of the pipe, and push it in so that only a third of the peg remains visible. Repeat with the second peg. Drive one end into the ground, form an arch with the hose, and secure the other end.

GREEN TIP

Transforming a post
If an old metal post or clothesline is embedded in concrete and cannot be removed easily, use it as a vertical support for a climber. The density of the climber's growth will hide the post.

DECEIVING THE EYE WITH DESIGN

When designing a garden, consider the effect you wish to create, and decide whether you would like to alter the shape and the perspective of the garden.

● **Divisions** To make a long garden seem wider and shorter, partially divide it up with trellis sections. Alternatively, use shrubs and other bushy plants to create a natural divider.

● **Rooms** Divide a garden into a series of different "rooms," each with a different theme or style. A garden will seem to be larger than it really is if it is not possible to see all areas from one spot.

● **Hedges** To alter the perspective in a short garden bordered by a hedge, cut the top of the hedge slightly lower along the back or far end of the garden. This will give the illusion that the hedge is farther away than it actually is.

● **Secret places** Create alcoves and arbors around walls or fences to increase the sense of hidden and unexplored areas.

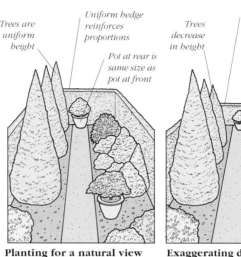

Trees are uniform height

Uniform hedge reinforces proportions

Pot at rear is same size as pot at front

Trees decrease in height

Back of hedge cut lower to emphasize sense of distance

Small pot makes path look longer

Planting for a natural view
Retain the natural perspective of a garden by considered repetition of heights and shapes. Lay a parallel-sided path, and flank it with trees of equal height. Place a planted-up container near the house, and place another at the end of the garden.

Exaggerating distance
To exaggerate the natural perspective of a garden, lay a tapering path, and plant it up with trees that are progressively shorter toward the back of the garden. Place a pot in the background the same style as – but smaller than – a pot in the foreground.

USING PLANTS TO SUGGEST SIZE

The design of a garden can create illusions, and the apparent size of an area can be altered at little cost with careful planting. When purchasing a plant, make sure that you consider its color and shape, since these characteristics can increase or decrease the sense of space.

INCREASING LENGTH

Working with color
To increase the apparent length of a border, position brightly colored flowers and foliage in the foreground, and frame these against darker colors. Plant pale colors at the back of a garden.

CREATING SPACE

Featuring foliage shapes
To suggest space in a small garden, place plants with large, flamboyant foliage and bold outlines at the front of a border. Where possible, vary the colors for additional emphasis.

CHOOSING PLANTS

● **Pastels** Choose pale or pastel colors for the back of a border to create a sense of distance.

● **Grays** To make a border seem larger, include a variety of plants with gray foliage.

● **Hot colors** Make a garden seem shorter by planting fiery, hot-colored flowers. This will bring these plants to the foreground.

● **Glossy foliage** Brighten a dull corner with glossy foliage that reflects the light, such as that of *Ajuga, Fatsia,* and *Mahonia.*

● **Strategic planting** Scatter distinctive plants through a border to draw it together and make the area appear smaller.

Plants & Planting

IF A PLANT IS TO SUCCEED, *you need to do your homework before planting it. Is the plant suited to the type and texture of soil present in the site you have chosen for it? Will it receive the right amount of sun or shade? Is the plant the right size for the site, or will it grow too large? Will it look good alongside its new neighbors, or would its size, shape, and flower color be more suitable elsewhere? When you know you have the right plant, invest time and care in preparing the soil.*

SOIL CONDITIONERS

Digging and turning the soil will improve its texture to some extent, but to improve the texture, nutrient content, drainage, or moisture retention considerably, you need to incorporate suitable materials before you begin to plant.

● **Soil texture** Use coarse sand and gravel to loosen the soil and improve its texture. Always use horticultural sand and gravel, since builder's materials sometimes contain contaminants that are harmful.

● **Soil pH** Lime and peat can be used to alter a soil's acidity or alkalinity. Lime will raise soil pH and help to break up a heavy or compacted soil. Peat or a peat alternative lowers soil pH and improves moisture retention, which makes it especially useful for light soils.

● **Soil improvers** Cocoa fiber, organic matter, composted bark, and leaf mold all improve moisture retention, texture, and drainage. Manure improves soil texture and fertility because of its nitrogen content. Always use well-rotted manure (see p. 49).

Peat   Cocoa fiber   Organic matter

Leaf mold   Manure   Composted bark

Lime   Coarse sand   Gravel

BASIC EQUIPMENT

Before you buy any tools, test them for size and weight, and make sure they are comfortable to handle. Stainless steel tools will not rust, but are more expensive than other tools.

● **Cultivation** A hand fork and trowel are excellent for planting, weeding around, or moving small plants. Use a Dutch hoe for weeding between young and established plants and vegetable rows, and for marking off rows for planting. A garden fork and spade are essential for digging and turning over the soil. Use a garden rake to collect debris, to break up the soil surface, and to rake the soil level before sowing seed.

● **Pruning** Use pruners for most pruning jobs. A sharp knife is good for light pruning tasks and is useful for cutting string. Wear gloves to protect your hands.

● **Watering can** Choose a watering can that is large enough to carry a useful amount of water, but not so large that it is too heavy when full of water.

Watering can

Pruners

Hand fork

Trowel

Sharp knife

Gardening gloves

Garden fork

Spade

Dutch hoe

Garden rake

PLANTING PREPARATION

Good preparation saves you time and effort later, so find out about your garden before planting up beds and borders. Plants that are planted under optimal conditions perform well and are equipped to resist attack from pests and diseases.

DETERMINING THE TEXTURE OF SOIL

You can find out a lot about your soil simply by feeling it. Its texture affects the amount of work you need to do on it, as well as the types of plants you can grow successfully. The ideal soil is loam, which is a mixture of the two extreme soil types – sand and clay.

CHECKING SOIL
● **Local research** To get a general idea of your soil type and the plants you will be able to grow most successfully, find out what is growing in your neighbors' gardens. Make a note of the plants that are doing well and those that are struggling.
● **Soil compaction** Check for localized areas of compaction, such as a path in a lawn, or an area next to a barbecue or under a child's swing. These compacted areas need to be prepared by spiking (see p. 131) or digging over.

CLAY SOIL

Clay soil feels smooth and sticky

Sticky and smooth
Clay soil is made up of tiny particles, making it heavy, sticky, and moisture-retentive. Although clay soils are often difficult to work, they are usually fertile.

SANDY SOIL

Sandy soil feels dry and gritty

Dry and loose
Sandy soil can dry out rapidly and does not retain nutrients well. It usually needs more maintenance than clay soil, but is easy to work initially.

TESTING THE pH OF SOIL

The acidity or alkalinity of your soil (the soil pH) is one of the factors that most influences the plants you can grow. Some plants will suffer, and may even die, if grown in an unsuitable soil. Use a testing kit to find out which kind of soil you have, and grow plants suited to the pH.

COLOR TESTING KIT

Yellow-orange indicates acid soil

Acid result

Bright green indicates neutral soil

Neutral result

Dark green indicates alkaline soil

Alkaline result

Using a color testing kit
Take a small sample of garden soil, and mix it with the chemical solution in the kit.

Allow the mixture to stabilize. Match the resulting color against the pH chart in the kit.

ADJUSTING SOIL pH

● **Alkalinity** Increase the alkalinity of your soil by applying lime at the recommended rate. Mushroom compost, which usually contains a lot of lime, can have a similar effect.
● **Acidity** Making soil more acidic is difficult. Add ammonium sulfate or sulfur.
● **Treatments** Try to change the acidity of your soil before you start planting. Recheck the pH. frequently to see how much it has changed.

CHOOSING THE RIGHT PLANTS

Putting the right plant in the right place is essential to your success as a gardener. When deciding on a design, consider your soil texture and pH, as well as the site's exposure (see p. 44). Use the chart below to help you to decide which plant to put where.

SOIL TEXTURE	SUITABLE PLANTS	
CLAY SOIL A clay soil is able to retain moisture and nutrients efficiently. However, during very dry weather it may crack, while during wet periods it can become waterlogged. The erratic moisture levels can harm plants.	*Acer* spp., *Aucuba, Bergenia, Campanula* spp., *Celastrus scandens, Clematis, Cornus* spp., *Cotoneaster, Euonymus fortunei, Forsythia,* hardy herbaceous geraniums,	*Helleborus* spp., *Hosta* spp., *Kerria, Laburnum, Lathyrus, Lonicera* spp., *Malus* spp., *Philadelphus, Prunus* spp., roses, *Rudbeckia, Sedum* spp., *Syringa, Viburnum, Vitis coignetiae, Wisteria.* *Syringa*
SANDY SOIL A sandy soil is light and drains quickly. It is prone to drying out and generally does not remain as fertile as a clay soil. A sandy soil is much easier to dig. However, because it does not retain nutrients well, plants may need extra attention, especially during dry weather.	*Abutilon* (some), *Achillea* spp., *Artemisia, Ceanothus, Cercis siliquastrum, Cistus, Cotinus, Cytisus, Elaeagnus, Jasminum*	(hardy types), *Kerria, Laburnum, Lavandula, Mahonia, Perovskia, Rosmarinus, Sorbus, Verbascum, Wisteria.* *Verbascum*

SOIL pH	SUITABLE PLANTS	
ALKALINE SOIL The types of plants you can grow in alkaline soil are limited, largely because of the effect that the high soil pH has on nutrient availability. Unsuitable plants often show deficiencies in iron and manganese, resulting in a distinct yellowing between the veins on the new leaves.	*Acanthus, Acer* (some), *Achillea, Aesculus, Alcea, Alchemilla, Allium, Alyssum, Anemone, Aquilegia, Arabis, Artemisia, Aubrieta, Bergenia, Campanula, Caryopteris, Ceanothus,*	*Ceratostigma, Chaenomeles, Clematis, Crataegus, Crocosmia, Fuchsia, Gypsophila, Kerria, Lavatera arborea, Lonicera, Matthiola, Pyracantha, Silene, Syringa, Tulipa, Verbascum, Viburnum, Weigela.* *Tulipa*
ACID SOIL An acid soil may have a sandy, clay, or loam (a mixture of sand and clay) content. Most plants are able to survive in a typically acid soil, while some plants will not flourish in any other kind of soil.	*Arctostaphylos, Berberidopsis corallina, Calluna, Camellia, Daboecia, Enkianthus, Eucryphia, Fothergilla, Gaultheria, Hamamelis, Kalmia,*	*Lapageria rosea, Lithodora, Magnolia* spp. (some), *Nomocharis, Nyssa, Pernettya, Philesia magellanica, Phyllodoce, Rhododendron, Trillium, Vaccinium.* *Rhododendron*

IMPROVING SOIL

Before planting your garden, take the time to work on the soil. Both its texture and its fertility can be improved considerably, and this is easy to do before the beds are full of plants. Exactly what you need to do depends on the kind of soil you have.

ADDING ORGANIC MATTER TO SOIL

● **Adding life** Bring your soil to life by adding organic matter (see p. 38), which contains a whole host of microorganisms that help to keep garden soil in good condition.

● **Different types** Each type of organic matter has slightly different properties. These may alter the moisture retention, pH, aeration, and nutrient levels of the soil (see p. 40).

Saving time Instead of digging in organic matter, spread it evenly over the soil in autumn. Winter temperatures help to break it down, enabling worms and other organisms to incorporate it into the soil for you.

(see p. 38)

MAKING LEAF MOLD

Collect fallen leaves, and pack them loosely into a large, black plastic bag. Make a few holes in the bag. Loosely fold over the top and secure with a brick. The leaves should be thoroughly decomposed after 6 to 12 months, when the leaf mold will be ready to use.

WORKING THE SOIL

● **Using frost** Dig heavy clay soils in late autumn. Frost will help to improve the soil's texture by breaking the soil down into small pieces.

● **Wet weather** Try to avoid digging heavy soil when it is very wet, since this causes compaction of the soil. Reduce soil compaction by standing on a board to spread your weight (see p. 142) across a large area.

● **Even surface** After the soil is dug or turned, the surface may be rough and lumpy. To produce a fine tilth before planting or sowing, dig or turn the soil over again, breaking up any lumps of soil on the surface with a rake.

● **Organic matter** You can compost virtually any organic garden waste to make organic matter. Leaves, grass clippings, shredder by-products, prunings, and annual weeds can all be used (see p. 43).

CLAY SOIL

● **Improving drainage** Always use a fork for a clay soil. A spade may seal the edges of the holes as it is driven in, making it even harder for water to drain through.

Opening up clay soil Incorporate horticultural gravel into a clay soil to a depth of at least 12 in (30 cm). This helps to improve drainage, but does not affect nutrient levels. Do not use builder's gravel (see p. 38) which may contain contaminants.

STONY SOIL

● **Root crops** Remove as many large stones as possible before planting, especially if you intend to grow root crops. Their shape and development can be spoiled by stones.

Enriching stony soil Fork in leaf mold or compost to enrich a dry, stony soil. Choose a dry day to do this work, if possible. Start at one end of the bed and work backward so that you do not step on the soil you have just turned over.

MAKING COMPOST

Making your own compost is an easy, quick, and environmentally friendly way to dispose of organic garden and kitchen waste. It also provides you with a very inexpensive, high-quality material that will greatly improve the quality of your garden soil.

COMPOST INGREDIENTS

Almost any organic kitchen or garden waste can be composted, but avoid diseased material or perennial weeds. Natural-fiber pillows, carpets, and knitted items can be composted, as can old, shredded newspapers. Avoid meat and strong-smelling waste, since these attract vermin. Turn the compost once a week.

Grass
Grass clippings should be used sparingly.

Clippings
Pruning clippings are made from chopped twigs.

Weeds
Mix annual weeds with drier materials.

Waste
Kitchen waste, such as peelings, can be used.

Knitted items
Cut up natural-fiber items and add to compost pile.

Carpets
Old carpet should be cut up into small squares.

Feather pillows
Old feather pillows are a useful ingredient.

Newspapers
Newspaper should be shredded or cut into strips.

GOOD COMPOST

- **Layering** Add material to the pile in thin layers; never use very much of any one ingredient at once. Try to intersperse moist, leafy material with drier ingredients such as shredded twigs.
- **Nitrogen** Green material has a high nitrogen content, which helps to speed up the composting process. Avoid using too much moist greenery, since it can turn into strong-smelling slime rather than good, well-rotted compost.
- **Hot weather** Add water to the compost pile during very hot, dry weather, or if you are using lots of dry material. Moisture encourages the materials to break down.
- **Cold weather** Keep the compost pile well insulated during cool weather so that the rotting process does not slow down too much.

MAKING YOUR OWN CONTAINER

- **Barrel bin** Use a plastic barrel to make a compost bin. Cut off the top and bottom, drill 1-in (2.5-cm) holes around the sides, and use one end as a lid.
- **Recycled wood** Make a compost container from sturdy corner posts and old floor boards nailed together with galvanized nails.

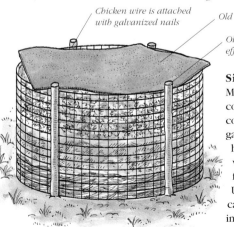
Chicken wire is attached with galvanized nails

Old carpet used as lid

Old tool handles make effective stakes

Simple container
Make a low-cost compost or leaf mold container using galvanized chicken wire held in place with wooden stakes driven firmly into the ground. Use a piece of old carpet to form a warm, insulating lid.

EASY ACCESS

Removable panel
Choose a compost container that has a removable front panel. This allows easy access to the compost so you can turn it regularly or remove some of it for use in the garden. Always make sure that the compost is well rotted before using it.

EXPOSURE

The exposure of a garden is the direction it faces, and this determines how much sun or shade various areas in the garden will receive. Other factors to consider include the soil type, as well as any overhanging trees, high walls, slopes, or nearby buildings.

ASSESSING A GARDEN

● **Careful planning** Study your garden before planting. Notice where shade falls throughout the day, and remember that evergreens cast shade all year. Determine whether shady areas are moist (at the bottom of a slope) or dry (at the top), and choose appropriate plants.

● **Sunny walls** Soil at the base of a sunny wall is particularly prone to being hot and dry. Improve the soil's ability to retain moisture (see p. 38), and choose drought-resistant plants (see p. 89).

DEALING WITH A SLOPING FLOWER BED

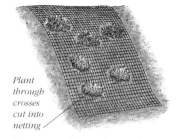

Plant through crosses cut into netting

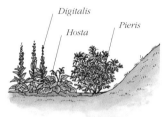

Digitalis

Hosta

Pieris

Planting through netting

Groundcover plants stabilize the soil on a slope. On a steep slope, plant through plastic netting secured with pegs. This will retain the soil in place.

Choosing the right plants

Choose plants that prefer a moist site for the base of a slope, since water will run off the slope down to the bottom. *Digitalis, Hosta,* and *Pieris* are all suitable.

PLANTS FOR DIFFERENT EXPOSURES

EXPOSURE	SUITABLE PLANTS		
SUNNY AND DRY Many plants are well suited to a fairly dry, sunny site. However, even these plants will need plenty of water in their first year to encourage healthy, sturdy growth and to help them become fully established.	*Achillea* spp., *Arabis* spp., *Aster* spp. and cvs., *Aubrieta, Campsis radicans, Cistus, Cytisus* spp., *Eryngium, Fremontodendron, Genista* spp.,	*Hypericum* spp., *Iberis* spp., *Phlomis* spp., *Rosmarinus, Santolina, Sedum* spp., *Senecio* spp., *Tamarix, Vitis coignetiae, Weigela, Yucca gloriosa.*	*Aster novae-angliae*
DRY SHADE Dry shade is common in areas with light soil, and beneath trees and hedges. Walls or fences can shelter an area so that it receives little or no rain. A brick wall will absorb moisture from the soil. Fortunately, a number of plants will tolerate dry shade.	*Alchemilla mollis, Anemone nemorosa, Aucuba, Cyclamen* spp., *Daphne laureola, Epimedium* spp., *Euonymus* spp., *Hyacinthoides non-scripta, Hypericum* x *inodorum* and cvs.,	*Ilex aquifolium* and cvs., *Iris foetidissima, Lonicera japonica* 'Halliana', *Mahonia* spp., *Pulmonaria* spp. and cvs., *Ranunculus* spp. and cvs., *Ruscus aculeatus, Vinca* spp.	*Ilex aquifolium*
MOIST SHADE This occurs in gardens that have a naturally moisture-retentive soil. It can also occur at the base of a shaded slope or in areas that are overshadowed by trees. Many plants will not flower well in shade, so foliage is an important consideration.	*Anemone blanda, Aucuba, Camellia japonica* and cvs., *Convallaria majalis, Digitalis, Eranthis, Erythronium, Fritillaria* (most), *Galanthus nivalis, Helleborus* spp.,	*Hosta* spp. and cvs., *Lonicera* spp., *Paeonia suffruticosa, Pieris* spp. and cvs., *Primula* spp. (most), *Rhododendron* spp. and cvs., *Skimmia japonica, Vinca* spp.	*Primula vulgaris*

CHOOSING PLANTS

SELECTING THE BEST POSSIBLE PLANTS is one of the surest ways of increasing your chances of success. Whether you buy your plants from a local store or from a reliable garden center or nursery, always make sure they are in good condition.

USING A PLANT LABEL

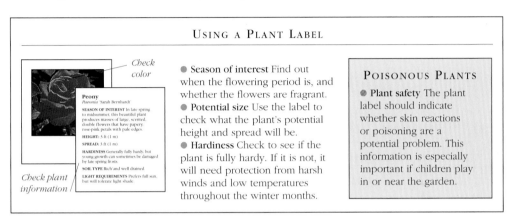

Check color

Check plant information

Peony
Paeonia 'Sarah Bernhardt'
SEASON OF INTEREST In late spring to midsummer, this beautiful plant produces masses of large, scented, double flowers that have papery, rose-pink petals with pale edges.
HEIGHT: 3 ft (1 m)
SPREAD: 3 ft (1 m)
HARDINESS Generally fully hardy, but young growth can sometimes be damaged by late spring frosts.
SOIL TYPE Rich and well drained.
LIGHT REQUIREMENTS Prefers full sun, but will tolerate light shade.

● **Season of interest** Find out when the flowering period is, and whether the flowers are fragrant.
● **Potential size** Use the label to check what the plant's potential height and spread will be.
● **Hardiness** Check to see if the plant is fully hardy. If it is not, it will need protection from harsh winds and low temperatures throughout the winter months.

POISONOUS PLANTS

● **Plant safety** The plant label should indicate whether skin reactions or poisoning are a potential problem. This information is especially important if children play in or near the garden.

CHOOSING PLANTS FOR YOUR GARDEN SOIL

BEFORE buying a plant, be sure that it is suitable for the spot you have in mind. Knowing the range of different growing conditions in your garden will help you decide what to buy. You should also consider what the plant will look like with its neighbors.

BUYING GOOD PLANTS

● **When to buy** Avoid buying plants during or just after an extremely cold spell. Even the root balls of hardy plants may freeze if unprotected, and this can prove fatal. Delay buying until spring, when a plant's state of health is apparent from the foliage.

● **Clean soil mix** Select plants with soil mix that is free of weeds, algae, moss, or liverworts. These all indicate that the plant may have been in its pot too long.

● **Damaged plants** Avoid wilting plants and those with blotched leaves. If plants have been underfed, or have suffered from drought or waterlogged conditions, they may be permanently damaged.

● **Fragrance** Try to choose some plants specifically for their scented blooms.

CHOOSING FOR A SPECIFIC SITE

● **Narrow bed** Choosing plants suitable for a narrow bed can be tricky. If the bed is adjacent to a wall or fence, choose plants that can tolerate dry shade. If the bed is next to a path, avoid plants with thorns or prickly leaves.

● **Island bed** If the bed is wide, choose tall plants that require little maintenance for central areas where access is difficult. If the bed is in a lawn, choose plants that will not flop over the grass.

Corner bed
This type of bed often needs plants that can thrive in a relatively dry soil. Choose tall plants for the back and small, trailing plants for the edges.

● **Easy border** Choose shrubs that require little pruning, and combine these with perennials that need no winter protection. Avoid plants that must be supported, and try to buy drought-resistant plants (see p. 89). Bulbs are useful, but plant only hardy ones that do not need to be lifted and stored during the winter.

Tall plants at back of bed

Small, trailing plants at edges

STORING PLANTS

Always try to transfer plants into the ground as soon as possible after purchasing them. If extremes of cold or wet make the soil totally unsuitable at the time, or if you cannot plant everything in one day, you may need to store plants. Do this for as short a time as possible.

STORING PLANTS OUTDOORS

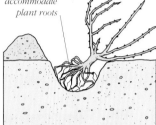

Hole must be large enough to accommodate plant roots

Heeling in
Heel in bare-root shrubs and trees to keep the roots moist and in good condition. Place the plant at an angle in a hole in the ground. This reduces the effect of wind on the stems, which can rock the roots.

Planting in a pot
Sink a container-grown plant into the ground while it is still in its pot. This will help to protect the plant's roots from extremes of temperature. It will also help keep the soil mix from drying out.

BRIGHT IDEA

Short-term storage
Put evergreen shrubs and conifers in a sheltered spot, where they will be protected from the sun, wind, and freezing temperatures.

CARING FOR STORED PLANTS
● **Protecting roots** The roots of a stored plant are very susceptible to damage. Extremes of temperature can kill roots. Protect the root ball by insulating it with soil, burlap, or plastic bubblewrap.
● **Preventing growth** Never feed a plant while it is being stored. This could stimulate growth at a time when the plant needs a resting period.

● **Moist roots** Keep roots moist, but do not overwater them. Roots that are confined to a sunken pot or to a temporary planting hole are easier to overwater than those that are in open ground.
● **Dormant plants** Plants that are dormant adapt to storage conditions much more successfully than plants that are still actively growing.

STORING PLANTS INDOORS
● **Sheds and garages** Do not allow temperatures to rise high enough to encourage growth. This will make it difficult for a stored plant to become established once it is planted outside.
● **Rodents** Keep mice away; they will eat plants in storage.

STORING BULBS

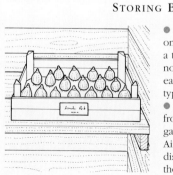

● **Dry conditions** Place bulbs on dry sand or newspaper in a tray, and make sure they are not touching each other. Label each tray with the date and the type of each bulb.
● **Circulating air** A cool, but frost-free shed, greenhouse, or garage is ideal for storing bulbs. Air circulation helps to prevent diseases, but avoid exposing the bulbs to drafts.

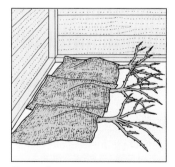

Covering roots
Store bare-root plants temporarily in an unheated garage or shed. Cover the roots loosely with plastic or moist burlap to prevent them from drying out.

PLANTING KNOW-HOW

Provided you choose well and follow the correct planting technique, your plants should have a healthy and promising start. Follow up with good care to ensure that your plants stay vigorous and healthy (see p. 80).

KEEPING A PLANT MOIST

Do not risk putting a potbound plant in the ground without first improving its condition. Gently loosen any circling roots, and use pruners to prune back damaged or very tangled roots. After planting, water your plants regularly until they are well established (see p. 92).

BEFORE PLANTING
● **Planting hole** Prepare a planting hole before you take a plant out of its container.
● **Tangled roots** If tangled roots are difficult to loosen, first soak the root ball in a bucket of water for several hours, or even overnight. Soaking the roots makes it easier to move them, and limits the damage you cause in the process.
● **Soil conditions** Whenever possible, choose suitable weather conditions for planting. Do not plant when the soil is excessively dry, waterlogged, or frozen.

WEED CONTROL

Removing weeds
Remove any weeds from a pot. This limits their spread and prevents them from competing with the plant for water.

DIRECT WATERING

Positioning a pipe
Place a section of drainpipe or wide-bore hose in a planting hole. This will allow you to direct water straight to a plant's roots.

BASIC PLANTING TECHNIQUE

Whatever you are planting, treat it with the care it deserves, and it will respond positively. One of the most common mistakes is to plant too deeply. Always make sure that the top of the planting hole is level with the top of the soil mix.

CORRECT PLANTING PROCEDURE

Soak plants thoroughly

Leave stem area clear

1 Dig a planting hole about twice the size of the plant's root ball. Water the hole well to ensure that it is thoroughly moist, and make sure the soil drains freely (see p. 42).

2 Place plants waiting to be planted in a bowl of water. Position each plant at the correct depth in its hole, then backfill the hole with a mixture of compost, fertilizer, and soil.

3 Firm the soil, and water the plant thoroughly to settle the soil around the roots. Lay 2–3 in (5–7 cm) of mulch all around the root area, leaving the stem area clear.

PLANTING SHRUBS

Sʜʀᴜʙs ꜰᴏʀᴍ ᴛʜᴇ permanent structure of the garden. Choosing the best specimens and making sure they get a good start is very important, and well worth your investment of time, money, and care in the long run.

CHOOSING SHRUBS

Yᴏᴜ can buy shrubs container-grown, containerized, balled-and-burlapped, or bare-root. If you buy them when not in leaf, examine the roots and the general shape. Each plant should have a healthy, well-developed root system and evenly distributed stems.

CONTAINER-GROWN SHRUBS

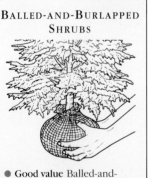

Shrub should have healthy, well-spaced top-growth

Foliage should not be yellow or withered

Stems should be free of damage, pests, and diseases

Roots should be firm and white or pale brown

CONTAINERIZED SHRUBS

Soil mix falls away when pot is removed

Roots have been cut before potting

Slow to establish
Containerized shrubs are shrubs that have been lifted and potted up just before sale. They may be slow to establish.

Checking roots
Remove the pot carefully to check the root system. If the soil mix falls away as you remove the pot, the root system is poorly developed. If there is a mass of tangled roots, the shrub is potbound.

BALLED-AND-BURLAPPED SHRUBS

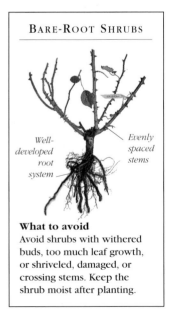

● **Good value** Balled-and-burlapped shrubs may be less expensive than container-grown shrubs, and often grow better than bare-root specimens.
● **Squeeze the soil** Gently squeeze the soil to be sure it is moist and firmly packed.

TIPS ON CHOOSING
● **Good buy** Small, young shrubs are usually easy to establish. In general, they grow more rapidly and more successfully than larger, more expensive specimens.
● **Unnecessary pruning** Avoid plants that have been strangely or unnecessarily pruned. This is often a sign that the plants have been damaged or that they have suffered from dieback.
● **Careful inspection** It is a waste of your time and money to buy a plant that has an inadequate root system. Do not hesitate to remove the pot to check the condition of the roots, if necessary.

BARE-ROOT SHRUBS

Well-developed root system

Evenly spaced stems

What to avoid
Avoid shrubs with withered buds, too much leaf growth, or shriveled, damaged, or crossing stems. Keep the shrub moist after planting.

WHEN AND HOW TO PLANT A SHRUB

Always try to plant shrubs during autumn or spring so they have time to become established before the dry summer weather arrives. Container-grown shrubs can be planted all year round, but even these shrubs often perform best after autumn or spring planting.

BEFORE PLANTING

● **Loosening roots** Soak the roots in tap water before planting. This helps to ensure that they are really moist, which makes it easier to loosen them when tangled.

● **Dry site** If planting in a dry spot, make a slight depression in the soil around the shrub. This ensures that water runs toward the plant rather than off the soil surface.

● **Heavy soil** If planting in a heavy soil, do not put moisture-retentive organic matter in the planting hole. This may act like a sump and draw water from the wet soil, making a dangerously wet area around the roots.

PLANTING TECHNIQUES

● **Replant sickness** Never use the same, or a closely related, plant to replace one that you have removed. If planted in the same spot, the new shrub may suffer replant sickness and fail to thrive.

● **Correct depth** Make sure that all the roots are covered, but that the stem base is no deeper than it was before.

PLANTING A BARE-ROOT ROSE

Graft union

Checking depth
Place a stake across the planting hole, and hold the rose in the center of the hole with its roots well spread. The graft union should be a maximum of 1 in (2.5 cm) below the stake.

Pruning out dead wood
Use sharp pruners to prune out any dead, diseased, damaged, crossing, or straggly stems. Cut back to a healthy, outward-facing bud. Make sure that the remaining stems form an even shape.

● **Planting hole** Make sure the planting hole is at least twice the size of the root ball, and prepare it well with organic matter and fertilizer.

● **Underplanting** Underplant new shrubs with small bulbs for seasonal interest, or choose bulbs to coordinate with the form and color of the shrub's foliage or flowers.

USING MANURE

● **Root damage** To avoid damaging the roots, always mix fertilizer and well-rotted manure into the planting mix. This prevents direct contact of "hot" materials with the roots.

GREEN TIP

Planting roses
Add roughly chopped banana skins when planting roses. This improves the texture and moisture retention of the soil, and also adds potassium to it.

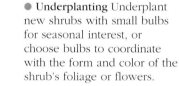

Soil must be moist before applying mulch

Cover mulch with soil to prevent rapid evaporation and to disguise it

Mulching
Use newspaper as a low-cost, efficient mulch. Make sure the soil is moist, then lay very wet newspaper on the soil surface around the shrub. Spread soil over the newspaper to disguise it.

PLANTING PERENNIALS

Although perennials are available throughout the year, it is best to buy them in autumn or spring, when they will become established rapidly once planted. If your soil is heavy and wet, delay buying and planting perennials until spring.

CHOOSING A PERENNIAL

Small perennial plants are generally a better value than large specimens, though larger plants are useful for providing more immediate results. You will be getting very good value for your money if you choose large plants that are ready to be divided (see p. 60).

HEALTHY CONTAINER-GROWN PERENNIALS

Top-growth is green and healthy

Crown has sturdy new shoots

No weed growth visible on soil mix surface

Strong roots with no signs of dieback

Checking a crown
When choosing a perennial plant, look for signs of new growth at the crown. If the plant is dormant, be sure the crown is firm and undamaged.

TIPS ON CHOOSING
● **Wilting plants** Before buying plants, be sure the surface of the soil mix is neither too wet nor too dry. Never buy wilted perennials; if they have been allowed to dry out once, they have probably been without water before and suffered considerably.
● **Moss-free** Choose plants that do not have any surface growth of algae, moss, weeds, or liverworts. This is a sign that they have been in their pots too long.
● **Cracked containers** Check to make sure the container is intact. If it is cracked, the roots may be damaged.

ROOTS IN MESH

Some perennials have a mesh bag around their roots. The roots should be able to grow out of the mesh and become established in the soil. However, if the plant is not vigorous, this may not happen, in which case the roots will remain restricted.

Mesh may be visible at surface of soil near base of stem

Cutting mesh
Before planting, carefully cut through the mesh in several places with sharp scissors, a knife, or pruners, taking care not to cut through the plant's roots. This will make it easier for the roots to grow out into the surrounding soil.

MONEY-SAVING TIP

Making new plants
Take cuttings from tender perennials in late summer to ensure that you have plenty of plants the following year
(see p. 153).

WHEN AND HOW TO PLANT A PERENNIAL

Perennials can be planted at any time of the year, except during extreme weather conditions. They should grow rapidly, and usually perform well within their first year. Use the chart below as a guide to the ideal planting distances for perennials.

REMOVING A PLANT

Slide your fingers between stems

Tapping a pot
Turn the pot upside down, and firmly tap the bottom with your hand or the handle of a trowel. The plant should slip out of the pot quickly and easily, with the root ball still intact.

REDUCING STRESS

Use pruners to remove large leaves and flowers

Preventing moisture loss
To reduce stress on the plant during dry or hot weather, prune off flowers and large leaves before planting. Cover the plant with a "tent" of netting supported by sticks.

GREEN TIP

Adding ferns
Incorporate a handful of coarsely chopped ferns into a planting hole to improve the texture of the soil. Do not use ferns with lime-loving plants, since they are slightly acidic.

PLANTING DISTANCES FOR PERENNIALS

PLANT	DISTANCE	HEIGHT
Acanthus mollis	24 in (60 cm)	36 in (90 cm)
Ajuga reptans	12–18 in (30–45 cm)	4–12 in (10–30 cm)
Alchemilla mollis	15 in (40 cm)	12–18 in (30–45 cm)
Anaphalis spp.	12–18 in (30–45 cm)	12–24 in (30–60 cm)
Aruncus sylvester	12–18 in (30–45 cm)	4–6 ft (120–180 cm)
Coreopsis grandiflora	18 in (45 cm)	12–18 in (30–45 cm)
Dicentra spectabilis	18 in (45 cm)	12–30 in (30–75 cm)
Doronicum spp.	12 in (30 cm)	24 in (60 cm)
Geranium endressii	18 in (45 cm)	12–18 in (30–45 cm)
Geum chiloense	12–18 in (30–45 cm)	18–24 in (45–60 cm)
Gypsophila elegans	12 in (30 cm)	24 in (60 cm)
Gypsophila paniculata	24–36 in (60–90 cm)	3 ft (90 cm)
Helenium autumnale	12–18 in (30–45 cm)	4–6 ft (120–180 cm)
Heuchera sanguinea	18 in (45 cm)	12–18 in (30–45 cm)
Liatris spicata	18 in (45 cm)	2–3 ft (60–90 cm)
Lupinus	24 in (60 cm)	36 in (90 cm)
Lychnis coronaria	9–12 in (22–30 cm)	18–24 in (45–60 cm)
Lysimachia punctata	18 in (45 cm)	2–3 ft (60–90 cm)
Monarda didyma	15 in (37.5 cm)	2–3 ft (60–90 cm)
Penstemon barbatus	24 in (60 cm)	36 in (90 cm)
Potentilla cvs.	12–18 in (30–45 cm)	12–24 in (30–60 cm)
Pulmonaria saccharata	12 in (30 cm)	12 in (30 cm)
Rudbeckia fulgida	18 in (45 cm)	12–36 in (30–90 cm)
Tiarella cordifolia	12 in (30 cm)	6–14 in (15–35 cm)
Verbascum	18–24 in (45–60 cm)	3–5 ft (90–150 cm)
Veronica spicata	12–24 in (30–60 cm)	6–18 in (15–45 cm)

PLANTING DISTANCES
● **Width and height** Check the potential height and spread of plants before planting. Refer to plant labels, and use the chart on the left as a guide. Remember, different cultivars can vary considerably.
● **Filling in gaps** A newly planted herbaceous border can look very sparse. If necessary, use bulbs and temporary seasonal bedding to fill in any gaps (see p. 17).

FOLIAGE AND FLOWERS
● **Winter appearance** Consider the season of interest of each perennial, and its appearance in winter. Most perennials die back in winter, but some retain many of their leaves.
● **Grouping plants** For a stunning display, try planting several of each type of plant together, rather than dotting individual plants throughout the whole border.

SUPPORTING A CLIMBER

Covering walls and fences with perennial climbers gives a new dimension to a garden. Some climbers are self-clinging and need no support, but most need a trellis or wires to keep them in place. Before planting, make sure the support is both stable and strong.

NETTING AND STAPLES

● **Light support** Use plastic or wire netting to support lightweight or annual climbers. Bird netting or plastic fruit-tree netting is ideal.

Using netting
Galvanized stock netting is suitable for lightweight, permanent climbers. Use rustproof galvanized U-shaped staples to hold the netting slightly away from the fence.

WIRE AND EYE SCREWS

● **Strong support** Galvanized wire makes a good supporting structure for vigorous climbers. A system of horizontal wires works best for heavy climbers.

Using wire
Use eye screws to hold heavy-duty wire in place on a fence or wall. Screw in an eye screw, wind one end of the wire around its head, pull the wire tight, then secure it to another eye screw.

TRELLIS ON WALLS

● **Wooden support** A trellis makes a good support for light- or medium-weight climbers, and can be cut to size.

Attaching the trellis
Attach the trellis to narrow strips of wood with hinges on the lower section (see p. 27). You can then swing the trellis down to repair or maintain the wall behind without damaging the trellis.

LOOSE FITTINGS

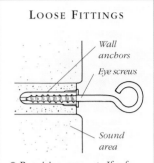

Wall anchors

Eye screws

Sound area

● **Repairing supports** If a few eye screws, nails, or staples are loose, drill a new hole in a nearby area, and reattach the hardware. Always try to repair plant supports with the plant in place.

● **Broken wire** If one of the supporting wires breaks, it is probably a good idea to replace all of them, since other wires may break soon after the first one.

BASIC EQUIPMENT

Always buy good-quality fittings; they are durable and save a lot of time, money, and frustration in the long run. Do not skimp on the number you use; too few may cause the support to fail.

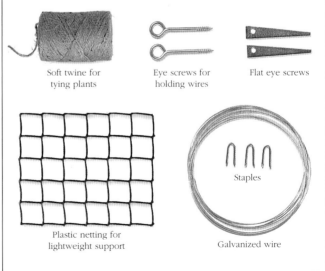

Soft twine for tying plants

Eye screws for holding wires

Flat eye screws

Plastic netting for lightweight support

Staples

Galvanized wire

PLANTING A ROSE

Most roses are bought bare-root in late autumn or winter and should be treated like any other bare-root plant (see p. 49). A much smaller selection of container-grown roses is available throughout the year; treat these like container-grown shrubs (see p. 48).

PROVIDING SUPPORT

Soft twine

Tying new stems
Container-grown roses may have some leafy stems. Tie these to supporting wires with soft twine or use commercial ties to ensure that the stems are not damaged by the support.

CLIMBERS ON WALLS
● **Flaky walls** Avoid planting self-clinging climbers against a wall that has a flaky surface or loose mortar. These plants are likely to make the problem worse and may cause extensive damage to the wall.

CLIMBER COVER
● **Temporary cover** Newly planted climbers may take a few years to grow to a useful size. Create a temporary covering with rapid-growing annual climbers such as *Ipomoea purpurea* or *Lathyrus*. You may end up liking them so much that you decide to keep them – even when the permanent climbers are larger.
● **Leggy climbers** Many climbers become rather sparse at the base as they get older. If they do not respond to feeding or other maintenance (see p. 86 and p. 102), plant decorative shrubs at the base to hide the straggly stems.

CONSERVING MOISTURE

Using mulch
After planting, water the rose well. Apply a 2–3 in (5–7.5 cm) layer of mulch over the moist soil. Keep the mulch away from the base of the support and the rose stem, since it can rot both.

DISTANCE FROM WALL
● **Avoiding the rainshadow** Dig the planting hole for a wall-trained climber 12–18 in (30–45 cm) away from the wall or fence so that the plant's roots are not in an area of ground sheltered from the rain.

Stake provides temporary support for young stems

Planting at an angle
Plant a climber at an angle to encourage it to grow toward the support. Use a stake as a temporary support for young, fragile stems. Train a few of the larger stems into position on the lower end of the support.

COMPANION PLANTING

Deterring pests
Try planting marigolds around the base of your roses. Although not scientifically proven, this technique is worth trying and may deter several rose pests, such as nematodes.

PLANTING CLEMATIS

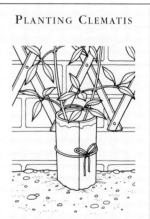

● **Protecting the base** Plant clematis several inches deeper than it was in its container. Place strong cardboard or plastic around the base of the plant to protect it from slugs and snails. Secure with twine.
● **Extra precaution** Smear grease around the top of the cardboard or plastic. Slugs and snails will not be able to climb over this, so they will not reach any young stems and cause them damage.

PLANTING ANNUALS

Annual bedding plants bring color and shape to a garden, and are relatively easy to grow from seed. If you lack time, space, or equipment, choose from the many plants available through local or mail-order companies.

CHOOSING ANNUALS

Most annuals are grown for the colorful displays they provide during the summer months. They are available from midspring. Some, such as *Viola* x *wittrockiana* and *Bellis*, are grown as annuals for winter color and are best bought in late summer or autumn.

IDENTIFYING HEALTHY ANNUALS

Sturdy growth

Good-quality plants in center of tray

Compact, green foliage

QUALITY AND COLOR
● **Quality** Be sure you are buying a full and healthy tray of annuals. Do not purchase poor-quality plants.
● **Color and type** You can brighten up your garden at minimal expense by buying annuals in bulk. For best results, limit the number of colors you use to two or three.

Buying plants
Choose plants that are strong and sturdy, with no signs of diseases, pests, or nutrient deficiencies. Avoid old plants, which rarely transplant satisfactorily and have less flowering potential.

MAIL-ORDER BUYING
● **Saving time** Save both time and windowsill or greenhouse space by ordering annuals from mail-order companies. Annuals are available at various growth stages, from seedlings to plantlets, and they should arrive with protective packaging and full planting instructions.

FRAGRANT ANNUALS
● **Providing scent** Most annuals are only slightly scented. Plant one of the exceptions, *Matthiola bicornis,* for a strong scent in the evening. Try training *Lathyrus odoratus* among other border plants, or use the dwarf forms in pots.

BUYING SEEDS
● **Catalogs** Most garden centers stock a good selection of seeds. However, it is worth looking through the catalogs produced by major seed suppliers, which usually offer a wide range of choices.
● **Early ordering** Whether you buy your seeds from garden centers or catalogs, make sure you do your seed shopping early. New kinds are available starting in winter, and the most popular varieties are likely to sell out quickly.
● **Damaging heat** Garden centers can become very hot during the summer. Avoid buying seeds at this time, since extreme temperatures can damage seeds.

SEEDLING PLUGS

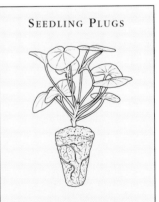

Many annuals are available as seedling "plugs," each with its own plug of soil mix. When planted, the well-developed root system suffers little damage and grows rapidly, helping to ensure growth of stems, leaves, and flowers.

ESTABLISHING ANNUALS

The lifespan of an annual is no more than a year. In order for these plants to look their best during the short time they are in flower, they must be well planted. A moist soil, a good supply of nutrients, and regular deadheading are the keys to success.

REMOVING ANNUALS

Hold firmly, and push bottom with thumb

Root ball

Releasing root balls
Water trays well before removing the plants. Release the root balls by pushing up from the bottom of the tray and easing the plants out. Plant on cool days or when the area is shady. Early evening is best, since the plants can settle before the midday heat.

FEEDING ANNUALS

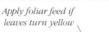

Apply foliar feed if leaves turn yellow

Applying foliar feed
Shortly after planting, spray the leaves with a foliar feed. This stimulates the roots to grow and speeds their establishment. Apply another foliar feed if the plant leaves begin to turn yellow; this is an indication of nutrient deficiency.

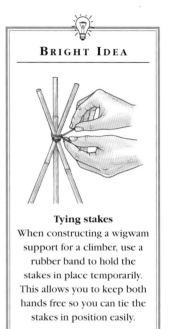

BRIGHT IDEA

Tying stakes
When constructing a wigwam support for a climber, use a rubber band to hold the stakes in place temporarily. This allows you to keep both hands free so you can tie the stakes in position easily.

CONSIDERING HEIGHT AND COLOR

The charm of an annual flower bed often depends on an irregular planting plan, with one color flowing into another. Vary the plant heights, introducing as many levels as you can, and – unless you have a very large flower bed – stick wtih two or three colors.

PLANTING ANNUALS IN A FLOWER BED

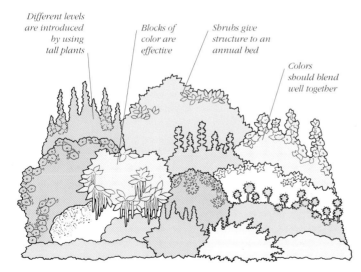

Different levels are introduced by using tall plants

Blocks of color are effective

Shrubs give structure to an annual bed

Colors should blend well together

SELECTING COLORS
● **Blocks of color** Group bold blocks of annuals in a limited range of colors together to show this kind of planting off to best advantage.
● **Combinations** Soft pinks and mauves, rich blues toned with pinks, and warm yellows, reds, and oranges are all good color combinations.

Foliage and texture
A variety of textures and shapes make an eye-catching display. Use different plants and foliage to add texture to your design. Annual foliage plants can also be used to provide contrasting or harmonizing colors.

PLANTING BULBS

ALTHOUGH MOST BULBS are fairly inexpensive, those that are fully hardy can provide a regular display of flowers for many years. All they need are an adequate supply of food and water, and a little maintenance (see p. 57 and p. 156).

CHOOSING BULBS

Always try to choose bulbs that show no signs of new root development. However, if they have started into growth, make sure the growth tips are firm and healthy. If you choose double-nosed bulbs, remember that the smaller of the two may not flower for a year or two.

HEALTHY BULB

Undamaged tip has not started to grow

Examining a bulb
A healthy bulb feels firm. It has no patches of mold, obvious blemishes, or signs of insect attack on its surface. The tunic (outer skin) should be intact.

No damaged outer scales or soft areas

Tunic is intact, with no loose layers

Firm base, with no new root growth

No blemishes or signs of disease

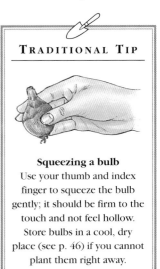

TRADITIONAL TIP

Squeezing a bulb
Use your thumb and index finger to squeeze the bulb gently; it should be firm to the touch and not feel hollow. Store bulbs in a cool, dry place (see p. 46) if you cannot plant them right away.

PLANTING BULBS IN A BASKET

Flowering bulbs look good until the flowers and foliage start to fade. Removing the foliage too soon prevents the bulbs from performing properly the next year. Plant bulbs in a basket, then lift the basket and put it in an inconspicuous place while the leaves die down.

BULBS IN CONTAINERS
● **Recycle containers** You can use many suitable household containers for planting bulbs. A pond basket is also ideal.
● **Extra holes** Good drainage is essential. If the container does not have many holes, make extra holes in the bottom.
● **Tender bulbs** Basket planting is an easy way of dealing with tender bulbs. When temperatures fall, lift the basket and put it in a cool, but frost- and mouse-proof shed or garage for the winter.

PREPARING AND PLANTING A BASKET OF BULBS

Place bulbs at random

1 Fill the bottom third or quarter of the basket with garden soil. Plant the bulbs as you would normally (see p. 57), and fill the basket to the top with soil.

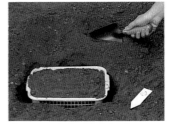

2 Dig a hole slightly deeper than the basket, and lower the basket into it. Backfill the hole with soil, then water. Hide the plant label in the basket so that it stays with the bulbs.

PLANTING BULBS IN BEDS

Most bulbs need sun, but a few prefer shade, so be sure to select the right bulbs for the spot you have in mind. Choose small bulbs for the front of beds and for planting next to paths or a lawn. Their small size does not cause problems with other plants' foliage.

WET SOIL

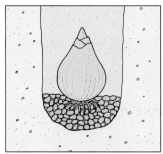

Improving drainage
Most bulbs prefer a well-drained site. To improve drainage if planting in a heavy soil, put a 1-in (2.5-cm) deep layer of coarse grit in the bottom of each planting trench or individual planting hole.

GROUPING BULBS
● **Odd numbers** Bulbs look best planted in groups of odd numbers. Most will start to multiply after a few years, creating a miniature drift.
● **Set patterns** As a general rule, avoid set patterns and straight lines. However, some bulbs, such as gladioli, look fine in a formal planting.

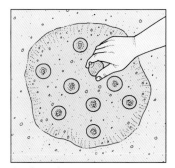

Saving time
Plant several bulbs in one large hole to save time and effort. Bulbs planted in this way look less formal than those that have been planted individually.

DRY SOIL

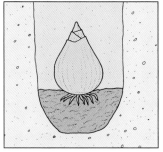

Retaining moisture
Bulbs may not flower properly in very dry soil, and they may even die. To improve the soil's moisture retention, place a 1.5-in (3.5-cm) deep layer of moist compost in the bottom of each planting hole or trench.

BULB MAINTENANCE
● **Regular watering** Adequate moisture throughout the year is essential if flower buds are to form properly. Be sure to water bulbs regularly during dry spells in summer.
● **Unsuitable conditions** Do not risk planting bulbs if weather conditions are not suitable and the ground is very wet or frozen. Store the bulbs (see p. 46) until conditions improve, or plant them loosely in boxes filled with compost their first year.
● **Tulip fire** To avoid this fungal disease, wait until late autumn to plant tulip bulbs.
● **Pot bulbs** Plant hardy pot bulbs in the garden when they have finished flowering. These bulbs are often crammed together, so make sure you divide the clump into individual bulbs.
● **Bulb boost** Apply a foliar feed to dying foliage (see p. 56).

PLANTING DEPTHS

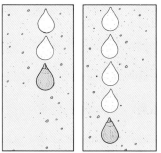

Checking depth
Always check the instructions on the packet; most bulbs are planted at a depth of three to five times their height. If winter temperatures are very cold or summers are very dry, plant the bulbs slightly deeper.

LILY BULBS

● **Drainage** Use a 1-in (2.5-cm) layer of gravel in the planting hole when planting lilies. This will encourage any excess water to drain away.
● **Planting on their sides** Lily bulbs are notoriously prone to rotting in damp weather conditions. If water gathers around the scales, the bulbs die off rapidly. If you plant each lily bulb on its side, water is less likely to remain around the crown, and the chance of rotting is reduced.

MOVING PLANTS

DON'T BE AFRAID TO MOVE a plant that is not thriving because it is in the wrong place. It probably has a better chance of survival if it is moved than if it is left in its original site. Spring and autumn are the best seasons for transplanting.

CHOOSING PLANTS TO TRANSPLANT

The most important factor in transplanting is to avoid damage and disturbance to plant roots as much as possible. Small, young plants are invariably easier to transplant than older, more established ones. Use the tables below to help you decide which plants to transplant.

EASY TO MOVE	RISKY TO MOVE	DIFFICULT TO MOVE
Most herbaceous perennials and shrubs that have not been planted in open ground for more than two or three years can be moved easily and successfully. Good aftercare is essential, however.	Old, well-established plants are generally harder to move than young plants because they have wide-spreading roots. Specimens only three or four years old have a reasonable chance of success, but moving them is risky.	Generally speaking, plants of Mediterranean origin have a very fine and wide-spreading root system, and do not transplant successfully. The following plants are best left where they are, if possible.
Azaleas Bamboos *Camellia* *Gaultheria* Heathers *Kalmia* *Pieris* *Rhododendron* *Vaccinium*	*Buddleia,* *Chaenomeles* Peonies* *Rosa* spp. and cvs. Most conifers All climbing plants (unless they are very young, with little root development) *To increase your chances of transplanting peonies successfully, try undercutting them (see p. 59).	*Cistus* spp. *Cytisus* *Eucalyptus* *Lavandula* *Magnolia* spp. *Mahonia* spp. Poppies Rosemary

TRANSPLANTING CHECKLIST

● **Time of year** Move plants in autumn or early spring, never when they are growing actively and growth is soft.
● **Time of day** Whenever possible, move plants late in the day, when temperatures have dropped. This reduces the possibility of moisture loss.
● **Weak plants** Avoid transplanting a plant that is already showing signs of distress. Try to improve its growing conditions before moving it.
● **Insurance** In case of failure, take several cuttings from the plant before moving it.

● **Stems** Tie back foliage and stems before transplanting. The process is much easier if you do not have to contend with floppy branches. This also reduces the risk of damage to the plant.
● **Spreading roots** The roots of shrubs and trees usually extend past the outermost spread of the branches. Try to move as much of the root system as possible, even if this means persuading several friends to help.
● **Watering** Water the ground thoroughly before starting work. If possible, do this for several days before transplanting.

● **Soil level** Position a transplanted plant so that the soil level in its new planting hole is the same as the soil level in its original position.
● **Water loss** After transplanting, consider using an anti-transpirant spray to reduce water loss from the leaves. This is especially effective on large leaves.
● **Pruning** If possible, prune back the foliage to reduce stress from moisture loss.
● **Mulch** After transplanting, water, mulch with a deep layer of organic material, and protect the plant from sun and wind.

TRANSPLANTING A SMALL SHRUB

Small shrubs are usually fairly straightforward to move. Their root balls are compact and are easy to lift with minimal disturbance. If the plants have wide-spreading roots, they are more difficult to move. Keep shrubs well watered and mulched after they have been replanted.

IDEAL CONDITIONS
● **Check the ground** Do not attempt to transplant a shrub if the ground is either waterlogged or frozen.

PREPARATION
● **New position** Prepare a new planting hole before lifting the shrub. Transfer the plant as quickly as possible.

CONSERVING MOISTURE
● **Moisture loss** If a delay between lifting and planting is unavoidable, wrap the root ball in plastic or damp burlap.

TYING AND DIGGING UP A SMALL SHRUB

Use string or raffia to tie branches

Tie lower branches to aid digging

Ease roots out of the ground

Support top-growth when moving plant

1 Loosely tie up the branches. This makes the shrub easier to dig, and reduces the risk of stems being broken.

2 Dig a circle around the root ball. Angle the spade at about 45 degrees so that you can dig out the lowermost roots.

3 Lift the plant onto a sheet of plastic to transport it. Steady the top-growth to minimize root damage.

TRANSPLANTING A LARGE SHRUB OR TREE

Moving a large shrub or tree is risky, but it is often worth the effort and may be the only chance you have of saving a particularly valuable specimen. If you are able to plan a few months ahead, a two-step process called "undercutting" is the most reliable method.

UNWANTED SHRUBS
● **Making a screen** If digging up specimens you no longer need, group them together to screen a shed or compost pile.

PLANT CARE
● **Evergreens** Spray the foliage of evergreens every day for two weeks after transplanting.
● **Securing** If a shrub seems loose in its new location, drive three stakes into the ground around the planting hole. Secure the shrub's main stem to each stake with plastic rope. To protect the shrub's bark, thread the rope through a piece of old garden hose.

UNDERCUTTING A LARGE SHRUB

Branches are tied together

Dig trench outside root ball

New, fine roots will grow into compost circle

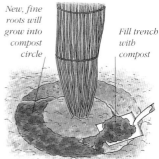

Fill trench with compost

1 Tie all the branches together firmly with twine or garden wire. The autumn before you want to move the shrub, dig a circular trench around the outer edge of the root ball.

2 Fill in with compost, and water thoroughly. Keep this area moist at all times. Next autumn, dig around the outer edge of the circle and lift the plant with its new roots.

TRANSPLANTING PERENNIALS

Although most perennials are easier to transplant than trees or shrubs, it still pays to transplant them with care, and at a time when they are least likely to resent disturbance – in autumn or spring. When lifting a plant, check to see if the clump also needs dividing.

MOVING AND DIVIDING A WELL-ESTABLISHED PERENNIAL PLANT

Use thumbs to split plant

1 Choose as cool a day as possible, and try to wait until early evening. Use a garden fork to dig up a well-established clump. To minimize damage, dig deeply and lift as much of the root system as you can.

2 Divide the plant (see below). Make sure that each section has its own piece of the root system. Discard sections that are weak or badly damaged. The center of the clump often contains the older, less vigorous parts of the plant.

3 Replant divided sections immediately. Considerable moisture can be lost through the leaves. To minimize this, trim off any old, damaged, or very large leaves, but make sure you do not cut into the crown of the plant.

MOVING PERENNIALS

● **Ideal conditions** Autumn and spring are the traditional times for moving and dividing perennials. However, if your soil is particularly heavy and wet, reserve this job for the spring. If subjected to very wet soil, newly transplanted perennials are likely to suffer over the winter.

● **Summer transplanting** If a plant has to be moved or divided in the summer, choose as cool a day as possible. Water the plant thoroughly beforehand. Move it late in the day, preferably just before dark, so that it has time to recover before being subjected to midday temperatures.

● **Division points** Take a close look at the clump; you should be able to see where to separate it. Using your fingers, you can feel where the natural division points are. Divide the plant at these points.

DIVIDING METHODS

The most appropriate way to divide a perennial plant depends on the type of plant it is. Small, fibrous-rooted perennials can be divided by using two hand forks back-to-back. You may need to use a spade for tough, fleshy-rooted plants.

Be sure each section has at least one visible bud

Dividing with forks
Drive a garden fork into the clump. Then drive a second fork in so that the two are back-to-back. Ease the forks up and down before pulling them apart gently and slowly. Repeat this method to divide the plant up into a number of pieces.

Dividing with a spade
Cut through the center of the mass of roots with a spade to divide them into sections. Some roots and buds will be damaged in the process, but this is unavoidable. Use a sharp knife to neaten the cut surfaces before replanting.

CARING FOR A NEWLY PLANTED PLANT

All too often, newly planted plants are abandoned to the elements. The care and attention provided up to this point are soon wasted if not followed by good care. Anything that is newly planted, or recently replanted or divided, needs special attention.

SHADING A PLANT

Shading on sunny side only

Erecting a shelter
A new plant does not have a well-established root system, so it is unable to replace lost moisture easily. Provide temporary shading using netting stapled around bamboo stakes.

RETAINING MOISTURE
● **Mulching** Regular and thorough watering is essential. Mulch to reduce moisture loss from the soil surface and competition from weeds.

Leave stem area clear

Mulching with carpet
Old carpet makes an excellent mulch. Cut a square or circle of carpet slightly larger than the root system. Cut a slit in it, then position the carpet around the plant. Disguise the carpet with a thin covering of mulching material, such as bark chips or soil.

STAKING A PLANT

Making a twig support
Twigs make unobtrusive supports for tall, multistemmed plants. Drive them into the ground early in the year, before the plant has made much growth. Tie them together with soft twine.

THE FIRST YEAR
● **Critical period** Lavish attention on a transplanted or new plant during its first year. During this period, a new plant is more prone to problems and less able to cope under adverse conditions than at any other time in its life.

WATERING AND FEEDING
● **Organic matter** Improve the moisture retention of light soil by incorporating bulky organic matter before replanting (see p. 38).
● **Small areas** Polymer granules may help to improve moisture retention in a small area. These absorb a large quantity of water and slowly release it as conditions become drier.
● **Fertilizers** Regular feeding of newly planted plants is essential. Never let granular fertilizers or manure touch the plants directly, or the leaves may be scorched (see p. 49).

TYING A PLANT

Tie string loosely

Tying a tall plant
Tall flower spikes or stems often require support, especially in exposed places. Attach them to stakes using string tied loosely in a figure eight, plant ties, or strips cut from old panty hose.

DEADHEADING

● **Rhododendrons** At regular intervals, remove faded flower clusters cleanly, but carefully to limit damage to surrounding buds and new growth. Remove any dry, dead, or diseased buds at the same time.
● **Long stems** When deadheading plants that have long stems, cut each stem back to the next growth point or set of leaves.
● **Reducing stress** After planting, minimize the stress to plants by removing any faded flowers, as well as several of the new buds.

CONTAINER GARDENING

*C*ONTAINER GARDENING *is understandably popular. Not only does it give you the freedom to create and control your planting environment, it also makes it possible for each plant to have the most suitable growing medium, as well as the best position for healthy growth. Containers can be used for long-term plantings in permanent locations, or moved around depending on the season.*

TYPES OF CONTAINERS

Containers are available in several materials: plastic, terracotta, cast stone, and wood. Weight is an important factor, especially if the container is for a balcony or roof. Size is another consideration; small pots dry out quickly, but large ones are harder to move around.

● **Plastic containers** These are relatively inexpensive and very easy to maintain. They are lightweight and weather-resistant. Plastic is available in a range of colors that can be coordinated with buildings, garden furniture, and plants.
● **Terracotta and cast stone** For year-round use, choose frost-resistant containers. Cast stone pots are generally heavier and more expensive than other containers. They may not be suitable for acid-loving plants.
● **Wooden containers** These need regular maintenance and are heavy, but they provide good insulation for plant roots in cold weather.
● **Hanging baskets** These are available in a range of sizes and are best suited to seasonal plantings. Carefully planted, they look equally good from all angles. They can be used on all kinds of vertical surfaces.

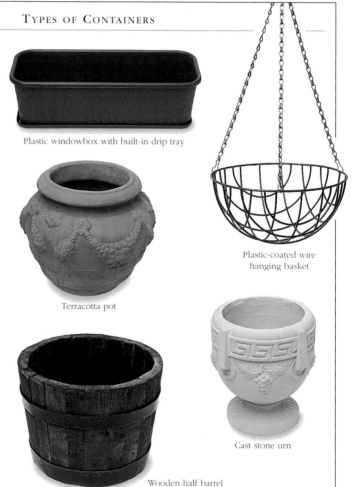

Plastic windowbox with built-in drip tray

Plastic-coated wire hanging basket

Terracotta pot

Cast stone urn

Wooden half barrel

EQUIPMENT

The items shown here are useful for planting up, maintaining, and decorating containers.

● **Planting up** All you need are a few key items: a good-quality trowel for filling and emptying containers, and for planting; a watering can for watering the plants before and after planting; pot feet or bricks to help prevent drainage holes from becoming blocked; and a layer of broken pots or broken-up styrofoam to provide good drainage (if the pot has no drainage holes).

● **Maintaining** A hand fork is good for weeding the surface of established containers. You will need sharp pruners and scissors for trimming and deadheading plants.

● **Decorating** Use a paintbrush to paint your containers with oil-based, matte, or latex paint, or a water-based preservative, depending on the material.

Hand fork

Trowel

Reversible rose for fine and heavy sprays

Watering can

Pruners

Scissors

Broken flower pots

Paintbrush

Windowbox feet

Pot feet

Broken-up styrofoam plant trays

Bricks

PLANTING MATERIALS

It is essential to choose the correct growing medium for your plants and their containers.

● **Soil mixes** Peat-based mixes are suitable for short-term use. Soil-based mixes are useful for stabilizing pots, but only when weight is not a factor.

● **Granules** Slow-release fertilizers gradually release nutrients according to soil temperature. Water-retaining granules release water when the soil mix dries out.

Peat-based mix

Soil-based mix

Peat-substitute mix

Slow-release fertilizer granules

Water-retaining granules

CONTAINER KNOW-HOW

WHATEVER TYPE OF CONTAINER you choose, the preparation, planting up, and maintenance are basically the same. All containers require adequate drainage, suitable soil mix, and an appropriate selection of plants.

MAKING THE MOST OF A CONTAINER

By choosing plants carefully, you can create a display that will last throughout the year. Shrubs, perennials, and bulbs can be left undisturbed to come up year after year. You can complete the planting with seasonal plants around the edges of your container.

SOIL MIX AND PLANTS
● **Soil mix** Use a peat-based, or peat-substitute, soil mix for large containers. It is lighter than soil-based mixes.
● **Permanent plants** Permanent container plants need regular feeding and watering. You should also repot them if their roots become crowded.

Seasonal planting
The larger the container, the more you can plant in it, especially if bulbs are planted at different depths. Put a shrub or perennial in the center of the container, where it has more room to spread its roots, and add seasonal bedding plants around the edges.

Permanent plant in center of pot

Trailing plants are planted around edges of pot

Small bulbs are planted toward top of pot about three times as deep as their height

Large bulbs are planted toward bottom of pot about three times as deep as their height

DRAINAGE FOR CONTAINERS

Adequate drainage is just as important to healthy container plants as adequate watering. If the container has no drainage holes, add a layer of broken pots or broken-up styrofoam before planting. If the container has holes, keep them completely clear.

CHECKING HOLES

Use a high-speed drill to create holes

Making drainage holes
Check to be sure the drainage holes in your container have been drilled properly. If they have not, use a drill to do this yourself.

TEABAGS

Drainage layer
Try using a layer or two of used teabags instead of broken flower pots. Teabags are readily available and are easy to recycle.

DRAINAGE FEET

Keeping holes clear
Prevent drainage holes from becoming blocked with garden debris by placing your container on bricks or pot feet.

SEASONAL PLANTING

A ll too often containers are full of plants during the summer, but empty the rest of the year. Use this chart to help you choose plants that will thrive in all seasons, and that can be either part of a permanent display or planted during the appropriate season.

SEASON	SUITABLE PLANTS		
SPRING Brighten up walls, patios, and gardens with a cheerful spring container or two. The warmth from your house may cause spring flowers in hanging baskets and windowboxes to bloom even earlier than similar plants in open ground.	*Azalea, Bellis* ('Pompette Mixed'), *Chiondoxa,* crocus, *Erica,* variegated *Hedera helix* cvs.*, hyacinths, dwarf irises, *Muscari azureum,* dwarf narcissus ('Hawera', 'Tête-à-Tête', 'Peeping Tom', 'February	Gold', 'February Silver'), *Primula, Scilla siberica* and cvs., dwarf tulips including *Tulipa kaufmanniana, Vinca minor* 'Variegata', *Viola* x *wittrockiana,* wallflowers. * = Trailing	 *Tulipa*
SUMMER There is almost no limit to the range of plants that are suitable for planting up in summer containers. New species and cultivars are available every year, so the variety is unbeatable. There are so many different colors to choose from that you can design your container almost any way you want.	*Anisodontea capensis, Argyranthemum frutescens* and cvs., *Brachycome, Cineraria* x *hybrida, Convolvulus sabaticus* cvs.*, *Dianthus chinensis, Fuchsia* (some*), *Helichrysum petiolare, Heliotropium,*	*Impatiens, Lobelia erinus* (some*), *Nicotiana alata* cvs., *Osteospermum, Pelargonium, Petunia* x *hybrida, Portulaca grandiflora, Thunbergia alata*, Tropaeolum, Verbena* x *hybrida, Viola.* * = Trailing	 *Helichrysum petiolare*
AUTUMN Some summer plants will still be going strong in early autumn, but all the plants listed here can be used either on their own or combined with large plants that have good autumn color.	*Ajuga reptans* cvs., *Callistephus chinensis, Chrysanthemum koreanum, Chrysanthemum morifolium, Chrysanthemum rubellum, Cyclamen cilicium,* dahlias (bedding cvs.), *Euonymus fortunei*	cvs., *Gazania, Hedera* cvs.*, *Lamium maculatum* cvs., *Lobelia siphilitica, Oxalis floribunda, Sedum spectabile.* * = Trailing	 *Cyclamen*
WINTER Although the choice is more limited for winter than for other seasons, it is still possible to create splashes of color with what is available. You can enjoy fragrance, too, by including some winter-scented shrubs such as *Daphne odora, Lonicera fragrantissima,* and *Hamamelis.*	*Buxus,* conifers, *Cotoneaster, Cyclamen* cvs., *Eranthis hyemalis, Erica carnea* cvs., *Euonymus fortunei* cvs., *Euonymus japonica, Galanthus nivalis, Hedera helix* cvs.*, *Helleborus, Ilex, Iris unguicularis,*	*Laurus, Mahonia* cvs., *Ophiopogon planiscapus, Phormium* cvs., *Pieris, Senecio maritima, Solanum capsicastrum, Vinca minor, Vinca major* cvs., *Viola* x *wittrockiana* cvs. * = Trailing	 *Daphne*

PLANTING UP CONTAINERS

IT IS SURPRISING HOW MANY bedding plants you can squeeze into a container. Generally, the more you use, the better the end result. For best results, buy good-quality plants, and keep the container well fed and watered.

CONTAINER SUCCESS

Use a combination of upright, trailing, and bulky plants to create a full effect. For a more dramatic look, try a single larger plant, such as a shrub or small tree. After planting, leave the container in a sheltered spot for a few days before putting it in its final location.

PREPARING AND PLANTING UP A CONTAINER

Soak container with water

Use an upside-down plastic flower pot

Experiment with arrangements before planting

Soaking a container
Terracotta and stone absorb water. To keep the soil mix from drying out, water both container and plants well before planting.

Saving soil mix
Deep pots are not necessary for shallow-rooted plants. Put an upside-down pot inside your container to save soil mix.

Positioning a pot
If a plant is prone to drying out, place a plastic pot near it, and water into the pot. The water will go directly to the plant's roots.

BASIC PLANTING METHOD

Once you have chosen a suitable soil mix and container for the types and number of plants you want to use, the basic planting method used for all containers is the same. Remember to bury the plant labels in the soil mix next to the plants so that you have a record of your successes and failures.

Mix well before planting

Firm soil mix between plants

Loosen compacted root ball with your fingers

1 Make maintenance easier by mixing slow-release fertilizer and water-retaining granules with the soil mix before you plant up your container.

2 Start in the center and work outward, planting your largest plant first. Make sure the plants are level, and gently loosen any compacted root balls.

3 Use your fingers to firm the soil mix between plants, leaving no spaces. Water well, and leave the plants in a sheltered spot for a few days.

MAKING AN HERB GARDEN

A container allows you to have a miniature herb garden full of the herbs you use the most in a convenient place. It also makes it possible for you to move the herbs around so that they receive the summer sun and the winter protection they need in order to thrive.

HERB CONTAINERS

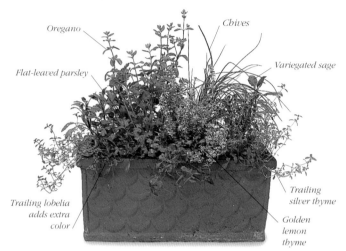

Oregano

Chives

Flat-leaved parsley

Variegated sage

Trailing silver thyme

Golden lemon thyme

Trailing lobelia adds extra color

Decorative planting
Herbs in containers look attractive and smell delicious. Use variegated or colored varieties for added interest.

CARING FOR HERBS
● **Tender herbs** Plant tender herbs in their own small pots within the container so that you can replace them easily if they become damaged.
● **Pesticides** Avoid pesticides whenever possible. If you have no choice, use only those that are suitable for edible crops. Check for pests and diseases regularly, and deal with them immediately.
● **Large herbs** Herbs such as rosemary and bay need to be planted in their own containers, since they can grow much larger than other herbs.

MAINTAINING HERBS

Clip regularly
To prevent small plants from being crowded out, clip vigorous herbs with sharp scissors to remove straggly growth.

STORING HERBS

Add chopped herbs to water in ice cubes

Freezing to preserve
Store herb clippings in ice cubes or entire trays for use in winter when herbs are scarce. Thaw them before using.

BRIGHT IDEA

Controlling mint
Mint is an invasive herb that can quickly crowd out other less vigorous plants in the same container. Restrict its root growth by planting it in its pot when it is still small.

SUITABLE HERBS

Most herbs are suitable for containers, provided they have a well-drained soil mix and plenty of sun. Small herbs, such as chives, basil, marjoram, oregano, parsley, and sage, are particularly well suited to container cultivation. Larger herbs, such as bay and rosemary, need regular trimming. Tender herbs, such as cilantro and basil, are fairly easy to grow in a container, but must be brought indoors before frost in colder climates. Generally, it's best to just resow them annually to ensure a new crop of vigorous plants.

Rosemary

COMBINING FRUITS AND VEGETABLES

Pots, windowboxes, and even hanging baskets can all be used for growing vegetables and fruits, provided you feed and water them well. You do not need to restrict a container to just fruits or vegetables – some fruits and vegetables can be combined.

FRUIT AND VEGETABLE COMBINATIONS

Early cropping lettuces are most suited for growing with strawberries

Plant strawberries around edges of container

Looking good
Strawberries and lettuce grow well together in a container. For visual impact, plant red and frilly-leafed lettuce with the strawberries.

IDEAL FRUITS

Strawberries grow well in containers, and most other fruits can be grown successfully in containers as long as they are maintained. Choose apples, pears, plums, nectarines, or other tree fruit on a dwarfing rootstock.

IDEAL VEGETABLES

Green beans, tomatoes, zucchini, radishes, beets, eggplant, peppers, carrots, lettuce, and scallions can all be grown in containers.   Peppers

MONEY-SAVING TIP

Homemade grow bags
Save money by making your own grow bags from plastic trash bags filled with inexpensive soil mix. Water before inserting the plants. These work especially well for crops that prefer their own container.

CONTAINER CROPS

● **Attracting pollinators** Create a mixed container with scarlet runner beans and sweet peas trained up the same support. The sweet peas will help to attract pollinating insects. The container must be large and deep, and will need regular and thorough watering.
● **Intercropping** Grow quick-maturing crops, such as lettuce or radishes, between slower crops that are more demanding later in the season.
● **Water loss** Avoid windy sites for your fruit and vegetable containers, since wind causes rapid evaporation. Make sure that rainfall is not blocked by any overhanging trees or nearby walls and roofs.
● **Mulching** Mulch containers with a 2-in (5-cm) deep layer of cocoa bean shells, gravel, stones, or similar material to conserve moisture.

STRAWBERRY JARS

● **Jar size** Choose large jars; they are much easier to maintain than small ones.

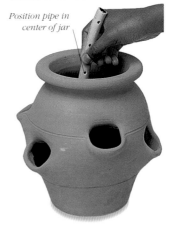

Position pipe in center of jar

Watering strawberry jars
Make some small holes in a length of hose, and put it in the jar before planting. Water through the hose to make sure that all the strawberry plants get their share of water.

MAINTAINING YOUR PLANTS

Maintenance for container-grown plants is far more intensive than that for plants grown in the open ground. Because container plants do not have access to the garden soil, they are completely dependent on you for all their food and water requirements.

PLANT MAINTENANCE

● **Feeding** Start fertilizing six to eight weeks after planting, and continue for as long as the plants are still growing. Choose a high-phosphorus fertilizer to encourage flowering. For immediate results, use a foliar feed.

● **Pests and diseases** Deal with pests and diseases promptly. The close proximity of plants in a container can cause a minor infestation to rapidly become a serious outbreak.

● **Pruning** Large plants may need regular pruning so they don't outgrow their containers. It's also a good idea to repot plants occasionally into slightly larger containers.

RENEWING SOIL MIX

Use trowel to remove soil mix

Maintaining fertility
Top-dress permanent plantings in spring to maintain soil fertility. Carefully scrape away the top layer of soil mix, making sure you do not damage any plant roots, and replace it with new mix or well-rotted manure.

DEADHEADING

Encouraging flowers
Pinch out - or use pruners to cut off - faded flower heads or any that are beginning to form seedpods. This will stimulate the plant to produce more flowers of a larger size, and over a longer period of time.

TRIMMING PLANTS

● **Controlling growth** Some plants tend to take over the whole container. Trim vigorous plants regularly to keep them in check.

REMOVING LEAVES

● **Falling leaves** Remove leaves from overhanging trees and other plants promptly, since they encourage rotting and may exclude air.

Encouraging bushy growth
Use sharp scissors to prune any straggly stems; this will encourage bushy growth. Cut any flower heads off trailing plants to encourage the growth of new foliage.

Pinch out with thumb and fingers

Keeping plants healthy
Remove diseased leaves – or even entire plants – regularly to prevent the problem from spreading further. Always cut plants back to perfectly healthy, sound growth.

GREEN TIP

Saving water
Keep water and liquid fertilizer from being wasted by putting pots or other containers directly underneath your hanging baskets. Any overflow from the baskets will then drip into the containers below.

POTS AND BARRELS

THERE IS AN EVER-INCREASING range of pots and barrels available, from the very basic and cheap to the extremely elaborate and expensive. Some can hold only one small plant, while others are suitable for a good-size shrub or tree.

TYPES OF POTS AND BARRELS

Pots and barrels come in different colors, shapes, sizes, and materials. Make sure that your pot is the right size for the plant or plants selected, and that it has good drainage.

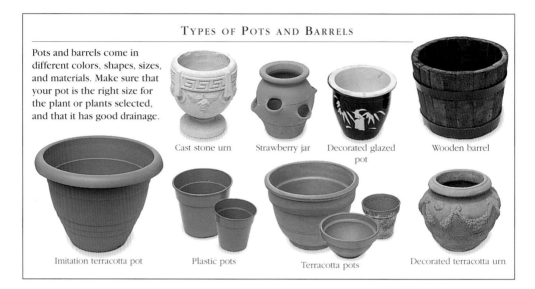

Cast stone urn   Strawberry jar   Decorated glazed pot   Wooden barrel

Imitation terracotta pot   Plastic pots   Terracotta pots   Decorated terracotta urn

---

USING POTS AND BARRELS

An unattractive container can be hidden by clever planting, but always try to use pots, barrels, and windowboxes that complement their surroundings for a pleasing, coordinated look. These containers should also be the right size and style for the plants you choose.

SINGLE SPECIMEN

Creating a focal point
Make an eye-catching focal point in your garden by planting a single specimen in a large container. For year-round interest, choose an evergreen or shrub that has colorful leaves or berries in autumn.

GROUPING POTS

Softening hard edges
Group pots together to hide ugly, hard edges or to liven up a boring part of your garden. Plant tender plants in small pots so that they can be easily moved to a sheltered area for protection during the winter months.

BRIGHT IDEA

Plastic insulation
In milder areas, before planting up, line the sides of a pot with bubblewrap to prevent the root balls from freezing over winter.

DISPLAYING POTS AND BARRELS

Pots and barrels are normally used to soften and brighten up paved areas, but they can also add a whole new dimension to established gardens. You can move your pots wherever they are needed in order to create different focal points throughout the season.

IN THE GARDEN

● **A friendly garden** Brighten up a new garden, or one that you are renovating, with temporary pots and barrels. They will make the garden a friendlier place to work in.

● **Rotating pots** Make a flower bed full of color and interest throughout the year by introducing pots and barrels that are packed with flowers. As soon as these displays are past their prime, replace the pots with others that are in full flower.

● **Hiding eyesores** Use a carefully positioned, colorful pot or barrel to hide an eyesore in your garden (see p. 30), or to protect a damaged area of lawn edging (see p. 130).

POSITIONING POTS AND BARRELS

Stacking pots
Create a living statue of plants by stacking several pots on top of each other. This arrangement forms a dramatic garden ornament and looks especially striking if you restrict yourself to a limited range of colors.

Filling gaps
Rather than overplanting a new border, use pots to fill gaps temporarily until the border plants have matured. Using pots also allows you to experiment with many different plant and color combinations.

BALCONIES AND ROOFS

Gardening above ground level usually means gardening in pots and barrels. This need not be too restricting, though, since a wide range of plants can be grown in suitable pots, allowing you to fill even the bleakest balcony or roof with color and fragrance.

MAKING A WINDBREAK

Protecting tender plants
Create a windbreak on a balcony or roof by growing climbers or wall shrubs up a trellis. Besides providing shelter for less hardy plants, it looks very attractive, especially if painted to match the overall color scheme.

LIGHTWEIGHT POTS

Use broken-up plant trays

Lessening the load
To keep weight to a minimum, use lightweight plastic pots and pieces of broken-up styrofoam instead of broken pots or stones. If you are planting shallow-rooted plants, you can fill up to a third of the pot with styrofoam.

STRENGTH AND SAFETY

● **Suitability of area** Always check the suitability and load-bearing capacity of a balcony or roof before using it to create a garden. Use lightweight soil mix and pots to be safe.

● **Container size** If space is limited and weight is restricted, use a few large containers rather than many small ones. Large containers support just as many plants, but they do not dry out as quickly.

FRESHENING THE AIR

● **Fragrant plants** Include fragrant plants in your selection so that you can enjoy their scent from inside or outside the house.

ALPINE TROUGHS

Make your own trough with hypertufa – a mixture of cement, sand, and peat. Use two boxes as the mold – one inside the other – and place the inner box on small wooden blocks to allow the base to form. When these are removed, they will form drainage holes.

MAKING A HYPERTUFA TROUGH

Wear gloves

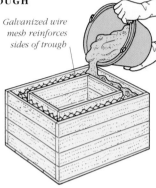

Galvanized wire mesh reinforces sides of trough

1 Mix 1 part cement, 1 part coarse sand, and 1–2 parts peat, or peat substitute, in a large plastic bucket. Using a sturdy tool, stir in water until the mixture thickens.

2 Pour the mixture into the space between the boxes, which should be about 2 in (5 cm) wide. Cover the top with plastic, and allow the mixture to set for one week.

MAKING ROCKS

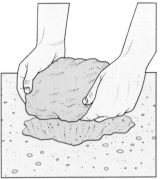

Hypertufa rocks
Dig a small, unevenly shaped hole in the ground. Fill it with hypertufa, and allow it to set. The hypertufa will form a realistic-looking rock for your trough.

PLANTING AN ALPINE TROUGH

Choose mound-forming plants, since these are less invasive than the sprawling types. For continuous seasonal interest, visit your local garden center or nursery throughout the year to see what is in bloom. The trough will need replanting when the available nutrients in the soil have been depleted.

● **Drainage** Place the trough on bricks. Place fine, galvanized mesh over the drainage holes, and add broken pots, keeping the holes clear. Cover the bottom with a layer of coarse grit.

Slow-growing plants will not deplete soil nutrients too quickly

Place trailing plants near edges

Take care not to damage roots

In hot weather, soak hypertufa regularly

Plant rosette-forming succulents

Mulch with a layer of gravel

Protecting roots
Wrap the delicate roots of small alpines in moist tissue paper before planting them in a crevice. This minimizes root damage and helps the plants become established.

Trough maintenance
A well-planted trough will look good throughout the year and be easy to maintain. Plant trailing plants around the edges, and mulch with a layer of gravel to prevent the leaves from rotting under wet conditions.

WINDOWBOXES

Planted up carefully, windowboxes can look stunning from both inside and outside the house. Use a selection of upright, trailing, and gap-filling plants, and include some fragrant plants to enjoy when the windows are open.

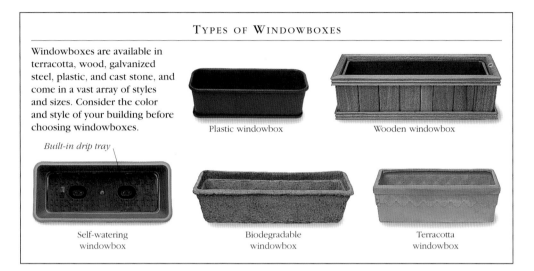

TYPES OF WINDOWBOXES

Windowboxes are available in terracotta, wood, galvanized steel, plastic, and cast stone, and come in a vast array of styles and sizes. Consider the color and style of your building before choosing windowboxes.

Plastic windowbox

Wooden windowbox

Built-in drip tray

Self-watering windowbox

Biodegradable windowbox

Terracotta windowbox

PLANNING A WINDOWBOX

Unless you have a sturdy window ledge to support the box, it is best to use a lightweight peat or peat-substitute soil mix.

Before finalizing your planting plan, make sure you can open your window and that you can reach the box to maintain it.

SHAPES AND COLORS
● **Foliage** Use foliage plants to add shapes and colors to your planting throughout the year. These form a framework to which you can add flowering plants at different times during the year.

CHOOSING PLANTS
● **Tender plants** Include a few tender plants in your planting. They will thrive better in the shelter of a wall than if planted in open ground.
● **Tall plants** Avoid using very tall plants unless the box is in a sheltered location. Tall plants may make the windowbox top-heavy and therefore unstable. Look for compact forms of your chosen plants.

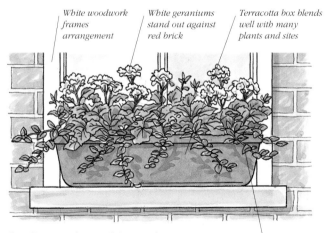

White woodwork frames arrangement

White geraniums stand out against red brick

Terracotta box blends well with many plants and sites

Trailing silver foliage blends well with geraniums

Blending and matching colors
Consider the background color of your building when selecting your plants and choosing or decorating your windowbox. Also, make sure your box is a suitable size for the window ledge.

USING A WINDOWBOX

Windowboxes can be invaluable when it comes to brightening up gray, uninspiring buildings. They can also be used successfully in many other places. The bleakest of surroundings can be brought to life by an imaginatively planted windowbox.

DISPLAYING A WINDOWBOX

Attaching to railings
You need a sturdy windowbox with a strong base for hanging on railings, since there is little, if any, support from below. Use strong metal hooks or brackets to attach the windowbox to the horizontal top rail. You will also need a lightweight soil mix.

Tumbling down walls
Used like an elongated planter on top of a wall, a windowbox like this should include trailing plants to tumble down the wall. Make sure it is firmly attached with brackets or galvanized screws, and that your neighbor has agreed to the idea.

WINDOWBOX SITES
● **Balconies** Windowboxes that are attached to a balcony railing, or are placed on a balcony floor so that the plants can cascade through the railings, do not use up too much precious floor space.
● **Culinary box** A sunny window ledge is the ideal place for a windowbox planted up with herbs. Small cherry tomatoes also grow well in a windowbox.
● **High up** If you live in a high-rise building, choose only low-growing plants for your windowboxes, and plant them firmly to protect them from the wind. Be sure to stake any fragile plants.

MAINTAINING A WINDOWBOX

Wooden windowboxes may need to be treated with a water-based preservative every few years. Painted boxes may require stripping and repainting. It is not just the box that needs attention; the hardware may also need to be repaired or replaced.

PRESERVING WOOD

Apply at least one coat

Applying preservative
Be sure that the surface of the wood is clean and dry before applying paint or preservative. Remove the windowbox from its position so that you can paint the bottom and sides as well as the front.

PAINTING A WINDOWBOX
● **Renovating a box** Brighten up a dull windowbox by painting the visible surfaces. Use an oil-based (gloss) paint or a water-based wood preservative for wooden windowboxes, and a latex paint for discolored, shabby plastic boxes. Be sure that the painted surface is dry before adding plants.

INSURANCE COVERAGE
● **Damage** Make sure your insurance policy covers windowboxes, as well as any damage they might do to people or property if they fall. If you do not own the building you live in, make sure you are allowed to use windowboxes.

SECURING BOXES

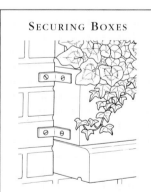

● **Supported box** Screw galvanized L-shaped brackets into wall anchors in the wall. Screw a bracket to each side of the windowbox.
● **Hanging box** If the box hangs below the window, support it with brackets attached to the wall and base.

HANGING BASKETS

ONE OF THE MOST popular types of containers, hanging baskets can be used very effectively in the smallest areas. Choose as large a basket as possible, as well as a good-quality liner, to ensure that the plants do not dry out quickly.

TYPES OF BASKETS

Hanging baskets are available in many different styles and sizes, so you can choose exactly what you want. A good-quality basket will last a long time and look attractive for many years.

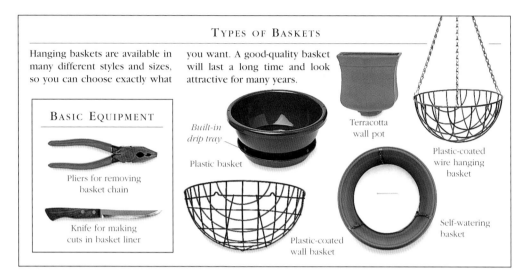

BASIC EQUIPMENT

Pliers for removing basket chain

Knife for making cuts in basket liner

Built-in drip tray

Plastic basket

Terracotta wall pot

Plastic-coated wire hanging basket

Plastic-coated wall basket

Self-watering basket

PLANTING UP A HANGING BASKET

For a really full effect, pack as many plants as you can into your basket, and plant up the sides as much as possible to hide the liner (see p. 76). With trailing plants such as lobelia, alternate one trailing and one upright plant to prevent the basket from looking straggly.

PLANTING TRAILING PLANTS

Wrap from leafy end

Cover roots with wide end of cone

Ease plant through slit

1 Wrap any trailing plants in small pieces of plastic shaped into narrow cones. This protects the root balls when they are pulled through the sides of the basket.

2 Use a sharp knife to cut a slit in the lining, then ease the plant through. Remove the plastic immediately. Always plant up in the shade to minimize stress on the plants.

BRIGHT IDEA

Disguising chains
Hide ugly basket chains by training trailing plants to cover them. Wind the stems around the chain gently, or tie them loosely with garden string or plastic ties.

HANGING BASKET LININGS

TRADITIONAL LININGS
● **Felt and foam** These liners are not too expensive, and are unobtrusive if green.
● **Coconut fiber** These bulky liners provide winter insulation.
● **Recycled wool** Woolen liners are backed with plastic.
● **Sphagnum moss** This is a popular lining material, but is not always environmentally acceptable.
● **Cardboard** These liners are designed to fit the basket, but are difficult to fit properly.

ALTERNATIVE LININGS
● **Newspaper** Cut several sheets of newspaper into circles to use as a liner. However, it is not very attractive.
● **Old sweaters** Recycle a wool sweater by cutting it up and using it as a liner. Although not very attractive, it is efficient.
● **Blanket weed** Try using a dense layer of blanket weed as a moss substitute.

Felt liner   Foam liner   Coconut fiber liner

Premarked holes for trailing plants

Recycled wool liner   Sphagnum moss   Cardboard liner

Newspaper   Old sweater   Blanket weed

USING HANGING BASKETS

Most hanging baskets are suspended from brackets attached to buildings. However, they lend themselves to far more exciting uses. A porch, sunroom, conservatory, and garage are all suitable sites for hanging baskets, as are arches, pergolas, and garden walls.

DISPLAYING A HANGING BASKET

Baskets for arches
Brighten up a wooden arch or pergola with a few hanging baskets. Choose shade-tolerant plants such as impatiens, begonias, and fuchsias if the arch is well established and covered with dense foliage.

Baskets for walls
Half-baskets are especially well suited to garden walls, and the protection from the wall may prolong their growing season. Winter baskets attached directly to a building wall benefit from the extra warmth.

COLORFUL BALL
● **Hanging ball** Create a sphere of color using two baskets planted up with bushy plants through the sides only. When the plants have settled tie the baskets together – flat surface to flat surface – to form a ball.

WINTER PROTECTION
● **Extra warmth** Winter baskets benefit from a very dense liner to protect their roots from freezing. Use an attractive, but thin liner that is lined with a cheaper, less attractive liner for additional insulation. A piece of wool from an old sweater or a few sheets of newspaper are both suitable.

HANGING A BASKET

Hang your planted basket where you can still reach it. If it is too high, it may be difficult to maintain. Before you hang the basket, be sure the bracket is firmly in place, and rotate the basket so that its most attractive sides are showing.

PULLEY SYSTEM

Lower basket for watering and feeding

Lowering a basket
To make watering a high basket easy, buy a special bracket and basket hanger that incorporates a pulley system so that you can lower and raise the basket.

SUCCESS WITH BASKETS
● **Checking brackets** Use wall anchors and galvanized screws to attach a bracket to a wall. Make sure the bracket is long enough to hold the basket away from the wall.
● **Suitable site** In sunny gardens, avoid siting baskets on the sunniest walls. Plants benefit from some shade.
● **Saving plants** If you run out of plants, leave one side of your basket more sparsely planted than the others, then hang the basket in a corner so that the sparsely planted side is hidden.
● **Keeping a record** Photograph any baskets you are particularly pleased with so that you have a permanent record of your successes.

PRESSURE SPRAYER

Make sure bracket will take weight of watered basket

Direct spray close to plant roots

Pumping water
Use a long tube attached to a spray-pump container to water and feed hanging baskets that are too high to reach easily.

MAINTAINING A HANGING BASKET

Of all containers, hanging baskets are the most difficult to keep looking good. Because they are often located in windy, sunny areas, they need watering at least once a day in summer. Once a basket has dried out, it can be difficult to revive the plants.

CONSERVING MOISTURE

Remove chain before planting up

Making a water reservoir
When planting up, place an old saucer or an aluminum pie pan in the bottom of the basket before adding the soil mix. This will act as a water reservoir.

REWETTING SOIL MIX

Add only a couple of drops of dishwashing liquid

Using a wetting agent
If the soil mix becomes so dry that water runs off, add a couple of drops of mild dishwashing liquid to the water so that it can penetrate the surface.

EMERGENCY ACTION

Rescuing a dry basket
Lower a very dry basket into a bowl of water, and leave until the soil mix looks moist. Remove the basket, then leave it in the shade until the plants perk up.

RECYCLING CONTAINERS

Wֿ ITH A LITTLE IMAGINATION, you can transform something quite unexpected into an attractive planter. If you use household items creatively, you can have plenty of pots at a fraction of the cost of traditional containers.

CONTAINER IDEAS

Aֿ lmost any remotely suitable item can be used as a plant container. To be usable, it must be large enough to hold sufficient soil mix for proper root growth and to prevent it from drying out rapidly. Good drainage is also essential.

USING AN ALTERNATIVE CONTAINER

Disguise sides of colander with trailing plants

● **Catering containers** Catering food containers can often be obtained inexpensively. Made from plastic or metal, they are not very attractive, but – if carefully planted with plenty of trailing plants – the sides of the containers can be completely hidden.

● **Car tires** For a container that you can make as deep or as shallow as you like, try stacking a few old car or tractor tires on top of each other.

● **Old bathtub** Use an old bathtub as a planter. The depth of the soil allows you to grow large plants successfully.

Tall plant is supported by stake

Holey basket
A colander comes complete with drainage holes. All you need to do is attach a set of basket chains. You can also use a large sieve, as long as it is lined first.

Ornamental pot
An old ceramic pot can make an ornamental pot that is suitable for seasonal displays of annuals. Be sure to create a drainage hole in the bottom.

BRIGHT IDEA

Keeping insects out
Put a piece of open-mesh fabric or fine-gauge wire mesh under a bottomless container to keep pests out.

MAKING DRAINAGE HOLES

Proper drainage is absolutely essential. Without it, water will accumulate and kill the plant roots. Use any suitable, safe method to make drainage holes, and always wear goggles.

Use a high-speed steel drill bit

Push point through carefully

Metal container
Use a drill bit to make several drainage holes in the bottom of a metal container.

Plastic container
A metal awl should pierce plastic. You may need to heat the tool first to penetrate thick surfaces.

DECORATING A CONTAINER

Ugly, shabby, or dull containers can be transformed instantly with a coat of paint or wood stain. New terracotta, hypertufa, or stone can be artificially aged, too. Well-weathered containers look softer than new ones, and fit in better with their surroundings.

USING WOOD STAIN
● **Colors** Subdued colors are usually best, because they do not detract from the beauty and style of the plants.

Try using an old wooden crate as a windowbox

Staining wood
Change the look of a wooden container by painting it with a wood preservative or stain. Stains come in a wide range of colors.

PAINTING CONTAINERS
● **Matching** Try linking your containers with your garden furniture by painting them in matching colors.

Paint the rim in a contrasting color

Painting terracotta
Create a subtle, but effective look by painting just the rim or raised pattern of a container, leaving the rest its original color.

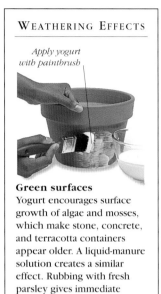

WEATHERING EFFECTS

Apply yogurt with paintbrush

Green surfaces
Yogurt encourages surface growth of algae and mosses, which make stone, concrete, and terracotta containers appear older. A liquid-manure solution creates a similar effect. Rubbing with fresh parsley gives immediate results, but requires more time.

REPAIRING A CONTAINER

It is sometimes possible to repair a cracked, chipped, or slightly broken container. However, you should repair any cracks as soon as they appear. A neglected crack can fill with water, which expands as it freezes during the winter, causing even more damage.

SEALING SHALLOW CRACKS IN POTS

Apply mixture with putty knife

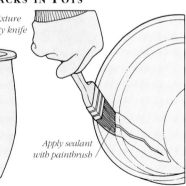

Apply sealant with paintbrush

Outside cracks
Shallow cracks may develop if a pot is knocked over or as a result of a heavy frost. Apply a mixture of white glue and sand to fill cracks in concrete or cast stone containers.

Inside cracks
Cracks on the inside can be repaired simply by applying a sealant with a paintbrush. This rather obvious kind of repair cannot be seen from the outside of the pot.

CONTAINER CARE
● **Frost-resistant pots** Always make sure your containers are frost-resistant. A pot that is not frost-tolerant may be reduced rapidly to a crumbling mass.
● **Damaged pots** Use damaged or repaired pots for temporary, seasonal plantings of annuals or herbaceous plants. These plants exert little, if any, pressure on the sides of containers.
● **Barrel-shaped pots** Never put a potentially large plant in a barrel-shaped pot; it will be impossible to remove without breaking the pot.
● **Repotting** Woody plants may outgrow a small container. Repot them regularly to prevent pots from shattering.

PLANT CARE

*O*NCE YOU HAVE CHOSEN *and planted the ideal plants for your garden, you must continue to look after them according to their needs. Regular maintenance and aftercare, especially during the first year, are vital to their long-term success. Plants that are well cared for will perform well, look attractive, and resist attack from pests and diseases.*

AVOIDING PROBLEMS

Most problems in the garden can be avoided, or at least their impact kept to a minimum, by good aftercare. A plant should thrive if it is kept well watered, fed, and pruned. Some tasks, such as feeding, watering, and mulching, should be carried out as required throughout the year. Others, such as pruning and deadheading, may need to be done at specific times. Even problems with pests and diseases can be kept to a minimum if plants are well cared for; a vigorous, healthy plant is, in most cases, well equipped to fight off a problem and to compensate for any damage that does occur.

FLOWERS

Flower buds may require adequate sunlight and warmth to form. A regular supply of moisture to plants is necessary for the continuing development of healthy buds. Use a high-phosphorus fertilizer (see p. 86) to encourage flowering.

STEMS

Check plant stems for diseases and pests; prune out, if necessary, or apply other control measures. Prune to encourage flowering and to maintain an open structure. This will allow air to circulate, making the plant less prone to attack from diseases.

LEAVES

Protect young foliage from late frost; once it is damaged, dieback may occur. Check foliage for pests and diseases, and take prompt action to deal with problems (see p. 108). Apply a foliar feed during the growing period to stimulate growth.

ROOTS

Keep roots well fed and watered. Avoid drought and waterlogged conditions, since both can prevent roots from taking up nutrients in the soil. Do not restrict roots by poor planting, planting in a cramped position, or planting in compacted soil.

FRUITS

To ensure good size and quality, supply adequate moisture to plants during fruit development. Regular watering prevents fruits from cracking and developing disorders. Feed with a high-phosphorus fertilizer (see p. 85) to encourage fruiting.

BASIC EQUIPMENT

Caring for your garden with good-quality tools will help you perform tasks efficiently and will prove cost-effective. The tools you need will depend on the size and type of your garden.

● **Comfort** Make sure your tools, pruners, hand forks, and hand trowels are comfortable to hold and easy to grip. A molded plastic handle is comfortable, even in cold weather, and is easy to clean.
● **Weight** You may prefer to use lightweight tools. Many tools traditionally made of metal are available in plastic, including wheelbarrows and watering cans.
● **Length** It is important to use spades, forks, hoes, and rakes with the correct shaft length.
● **Tread** Choose a spade with lined or checkered tread at the top of the blade. This will relieve pressure on your instep and improve your grip.
● **Reach** Choose a hose that reaches all parts of the garden.
● **Small areas** Use a hand sprayer to apply pesticides to plants in a small area.
● **Protection** Protect your hands with gardening gloves.

Tread

Spade

Garden fork

Watering can

Dutch hoe

Garden rake

Hose-end attachment

Pruners

Wheelbarrow

Hand sprayer

Hand fork

Trowel

Gardening gloves

Hose

PROTECTING PLANTS

WEATHER CONDITIONS VARY not only from season to season, but also from day to day. Many plants are able to withstand changing temperatures, but some will need special care and attention during extreme weather conditions.

PROTECTING FROM FROST

Frost is potentially very damaging. Its arrival may be unexpected, and it often follows or precedes fairly mild weather, when plants are particularly vulnerable. Early-winter frosts, and the late frosts that occur once plants have started growing again in spring, are the most damaging.

PROVIDING INSULATION

Protecting plant and pot
Protect the root ball of a container plant – and the pot itself – by wrapping the container in burlap, newspaper, or bubblewrap. Tie in place.

COVERING OVERNIGHT
● **Row covers** Drape plants with horticultural fleece or film, or old net curtains, to protect flower buds and soft, new growth. Remove as soon as frost is no longer a danger.

Using newspaper
For simple and inexpensive overnight frost protection, cover vulnerable plants with a layer or two of newspaper held in place with bricks or large stones.

PROTECTING ROSES

Mounding soil
Mound up soil around rose stems during very cold weather. Remove the soil when the weather warms up. If the soil is heavy or wet, use compost.

FIGHTING FROST
● **Insulation** Protect the crowns of herbaceous plants and shrubs by surrounding them loosely with chicken wire. Anchor the wire to the ground, and pack it with dry leaves, hay, or straw.
● **Air circulation** Make sure that air can circulate around insulated plants. Stagnant air allows moisture to accumulate, which can lead to rotting.
● **Fertilizers** Soft growth is prone to frost damage, so do not use high-nitrogen fertilizers late in the season (see p. 84–85). Feed with potash to encourage strong growth.

PROTECTING FROM SNOW

A covering of snow on hedges, shrubs, and trees is potentially damaging, since snow will weigh down stems. The greatest danger is from snow that has partly thawed and then frozen again.

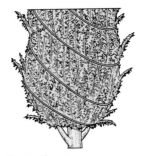

Protecting trees
Protect trees that have dense branch structures, such as conifers, by tying the branches together with galvanized wire.

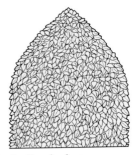

Protecting hedges
Clip hedges so that their upper surfaces slope. This will prevent snow from settling on them and causing them to lose their shape.

PROTECTING FROM HEAT

Excessive heat can be damaging to plants at all stages of growth. High temperatures can cause too much moisture loss, scorching, poor nutrient uptake, and wilting. Temperatures that fluctuate are potentially more damaging than those that are consistently too high.

PREVENTING WILTING

● **Vulnerability** Protect young plants, as well as any that have been transplanted recently. These are particularly prone to damage from wilting.

Using a flower pot
Protect a small, vulnerable plant with a temporary sun shield such as a flower pot. Position the pot early in the day, before temperatures start to rise. Choose as large a pot as possible so that air can circulate inside it.

KEEPING TEMPERATURES DOWN IN A GREENHOUSE

Paving slabs absorb heat during daytime

Water away from plants

Damping down
Reduce greenhouse temperatures in very hot weather by wetting the floor with water several times a day. This will increase the humidity and lower the overall temperature. Avoid splashing the plants, since this may cause scorching.

CONTROLLING PESTS

● **Maintaining humidity**
Spider mites thrive in hot, dry environments. Damp a greenhouse down regularly to maintain high humidity and deter these pests (see above).

KEEPING AIR FRESH

● **Ventilation** Be sure that there is good ventilation in a greenhouse. Install blinds or use paint-on shading to reduce high temperatures and the scorching effect of bright light.

PROTECTING FROM WIND AND POLLUTION

Within any garden, plants need to be protected from a wide range of potential problems. Some, such as strong winds, occur naturally. Others, such as pollution, result from industry and automobiles. Take steps to minimize the effects of some of these problems.

PREVENTING DAMAGE

● **Exposed areas** Permeable windbreaks are suitable for large, exposed areas. Erect them around the affected area, and secure them with stakes.
● **Wind tunnels** Wind rushes through gaps between buildings. When siting a new shed or greenhouse, do not create a wind tunnel by putting it too close to another building.
● **Suitable plants** Choose plants that suit the conditions. Plants with small, thick, or waxy leaves are more resistant to wind than those with thin, delicate, or large leaves.

MAKING A WINDBREAK

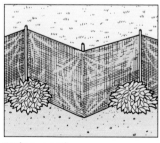

Using netting
Young plants are especially prone to damage from strong winds. Protect susceptible plants with a temporary windbreak made from netting or burlap secured with stakes.

BUILDING A BARRIER

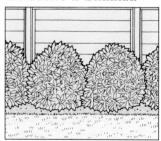

Using a hedge
A garden near a busy road is exposed to high pollution levels. Help keep excessive lead out by erecting a barrier of panel fencing. Plant with a pollution-tolerant hedge such as privet.

FEEDING PLANTS

To perform properly, plants almost always need additional feeding. In any garden, but especially one in which plants are packed together, use either a complete fertilizer or specific nutrients. For more details, consult the chart.

BASIC FERTILIZERS

Some fertilizers contain a range of nutrients. Others provide a selection of nutrients tailored to specific plants, deficiencies, or growing conditions.

● **Compost** Usually formed from a combination of garden and kitchen waste, compost is a good source of nitrogen.
● **Manure** This is a good source of nitrogen and trace elements.
● **Mushroom compost** Use this to improve soil texture. It also contains a range of nutrients.
● **Liquid seaweed extract** Apply this to soil, or use it as a foliar feed. It contains nitrogen, potassium, and phosphate.
● **Bone meal** This is a good source of phosphate.
● **Fish, blood, and bone meal** Use this as a general fertilizer. It contains phosphorus, nitrogen, and potassium.
● **Amonium sulfate** This contains concentrated nitrogen.
● **Potassium sulfate** A good source of potassium, this fertilizer is readily available.
● **Wood ashes** These contain a small amount of potassium.

Compost

Manure

Mushroom compost

Liquid seaweed extract

Bone meal

Fish, blood, and bone meal

Ammonium sulfate

Potassium sulfate

Wood ashes

SAFETY

● **Protecting skin and lungs** Always wear gloves when using fertilizer, and do not breathe in vapor or dust. Read the instructions, and use the recommended amount.
● **Storage** Store fertilizers in a cool, dry, and preferably dark place. Make sure that all containers are tightly closed and that they are out of the reach of children and animals.

USING FERTILIZERS

● **When to use** Correct timing of application is essential. Feeding late in the season may promote soft growth, which will be vulnerable to early frost. Late feeding may also cause bud failure on ornamental shrubs such as camellias.
● **Avoiding scorching** Keep all fertilizers – except for foliar feeds – off leaves, flowers, and stems (see p. 86).

● **Appropriate choice** Choose a fertilizer that is formulated for the specific needs of the plants you are feeding, and for the time of year you are planning to apply the fertilizer.
● **Watering in fertilizers** Always keep a separate watering can specifically for applying liquid and foliar feeds. Never use this can for watering or for applying chemical pesticides to plants.

FORMS OF FERTILIZER

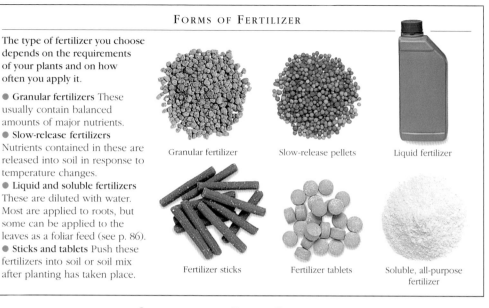

The type of fertilizer you choose depends on the requirements of your plants and on how often you apply it.

- **Granular fertilizers** These usually contain balanced amounts of major nutrients.
- **Slow-release fertilizers** Nutrients contained in these are released into soil in response to temperature changes.
- **Liquid and soluble fertilizers** These are diluted with water. Most are applied to roots, but some can be applied to the leaves as a foliar feed (see p. 86).
- **Sticks and tablets** Push these fertilizers into soil or soil mix after planting has taken place.

Granular fertilizer

Slow-release pellets

Liquid fertilizer

Fertilizer sticks

Fertilizer tablets

Soluble, all-purpose fertilizer

SELECTING THE RIGHT FERTILIZER

NUTRIENT	PLANTS MOST IN NEED	SOILS MOST IN NEED	SIGNS OF DEFICIENCY
NITROGEN	All plants, but especially those grown for their foliage.	Most soils following heavy cropping, but especially poor soils.	Pale leaves and generally unhealthy-looking growth.
PHOSPHATE	All plants; especially useful for root development and for newly planted plants and bulbs.	Most soils following heavy cropping, but especially sandy or poor soils.	Poor root development and establishment, which is indicated by stunted growth.
POTASSIUM	All plants, especially those grown for their flowers or fruit; use to harden plants before a harsh winter.	All soils, especially those that have had lots of high-nitrogen fertilizer or manure incorporated.	Poor flowering, poor fruiting; plants may also be prone to frost or general winter damage.
MAGNESIUM	All plants, since this is a major component of chlorophyll.	Sandy, acid, wet soils, or those with a high potassium content.	Yellow or brown patches around edges and between leaf veins.
IRON	All plants, especially those intolerant of alkaline soils, e.g. *Rhododendron*.	All soils, but especially those with a high pH caused by chalk, limestone, and lime.	Yellowing between leaf veins, especially on younger growth.
OTHER NUTRIENTS	Various minor nutrients and trace elements are needed in small amounts by plants.	Most light soils, and any soil that has been used heavily.	Poor general growth; symptoms may indicate a deficiency of a particular nutrient.

APPLYING FERTILIZERS

Fertilizers can be applied using one of many different methods, depending largely on the type or formulation of the fertilizer you use. Choose the type best suited to the size of your garden, the results you wish to achieve, and the amount of time you have available.

DILUTING FERTILIZERS
● **Quick absorption** Use a liquid fertilizer for quick results. This type is usually applied with a watering can.
● **Large areas** If you are fertilizing a large area, use a hose-end applicator that dilutes the fertilizer.

Watering fertilizer in
Apply liquid fertilizer directly to roots by getting as close to the base of the plant as possible. Any liquid that is not absorbed by the soil is wasted, or may even feed nearby weeds.

APPLYING FOLIAR FEED

Spraying leaves
Apply foliar feed with a hose-end applicator, or use a fine-rosed watering can. Most of the fertilizer will be absorbed by the leaves; any excess will be absorbed by the plant roots.

SCATTERING FERTILIZER
● **Saving time** Scatter fertilizer granules over the entire soil surface to benefit the greatest area of soil and to minimize the risk of overfeeding.
● **Individual feeding** Apply fertilizer granules around the bases of individual plants.

Forking in fertilizer
Take great care not to damage plant roots when forking granules into the soil around the base of a plant. Water the granules in well afterward unless heavy rain is forecast.

TIMING FOLIAR FEEDS
● **When to apply** Dusk is the best time to apply a foliar feed. Never use a foliar feed in bright sunlight, or leaves and petals may be scorched.
● **Late application** Foliar feeds can be used relatively late in the growing season because they will not continue to promote plant growth during the cold winter months.

PHOSPHORUS FERTILIZERS
● **High flower yield** Encourage flowers by applying a high-phosphorus fertilizer – the type used on tomato plants This is most beneficial to bedding plants (see p. 87).

USING FERTILIZER
● **Watering in** Always water fertilizer in thoroughly. Plants can absorb nutrients only if they are dissolved in liquid.
● **Adjusting soil pH** If your soil has a high pH, or if you are growing acid-loving plants, choose a fertilizer formulated especially for this kind of soil or these plants (see p. 85).
● **Applying lime** Do not apply lime at the same time as manure. Lime reacts with the nitrogen in the manure, releasing nitrogen in the form of ammonia. This can cause damage to plants and is a waste of nitrogen.
● **Avoiding scorch** Do not let concentrated fertilizer come into direct contact with leaves, flowers, or young stems, or they may be scorched.
● **Drastic action** Combine a quick-acting foliar feed with a long-lasting general fertilizer applied at the roots for a plant in urgent need of feeding.

MIXING FERTILIZER

Avoiding scorching
When planting, mix the fertilizer with soil or compost before backfilling the hole. This makes the fertilizer available to all parts of the root system, and minimizes the risk of scorching.

TIMING THE APPLICATION OF FERTILIZERS

Fertilize during a period of active plant growth, but not when it could promote new growth too late in the season. The precise timing of applications depends on the type of fertilizer you are using as well as on the individual requirements of the plant.

FEEDING SEEDLINGS
● **Seedling boost** If your seedlings look unhealthy, it is possible that the nutrients in the soil mix have been depleted. Unless you are able to transplant the seedlings immediately, apply a combined foliar and root feed.

Be careful not to drench seedlings when applying fertilizer

Applying fertilizer
Use a small watering can or plant mister to apply a liquid fertilizer to seedlings that are waiting to be pricked out. Make sure that you dilute the fertilizer to half its normal strength.

FEEDING A SHRUB
Keep feed away from stem

Boosting a pruned shrub
Encourage new growth in an extensively pruned shrub by applying a complete fertilizer. Sprinkle the fertilizer around the base of the shrub, and fork it in without damaging the roots.

FEEDING BULBS
● **Promoting flowering** The flowering capacity of bulbs can be improved by applying a foliar feed to the leaves. This especially benefits naturalized bulbs, and bulbs that have been growing in the same place for some time.

Feeding after flowering
Once flowering is over, apply a foliar feed every 10–14 days. Continue doing this until the foliage starts to turn yellow and die back. Do not tie or cut down any leaves for at least six weeks.

FEEDING A LAWN
● **Dry weather** If your lawn needs feeding during a hot, dry summer, and it is not possible to water in a granular fertilizer, use liquid fertilizer on the lawn instead. Inadequate feeding often encourages disease.
● **Application** To feed a lawn, weigh the correct amount of fertilizer, and divide it in half. Apply the first half in one direction, up and down the lawn, apply the second half across, at right angles to this.
● **Yellow grass** If the grass begins to turn yellow and is generally lacking in vigor, apply a nitrogen-rich fertilizer.

REGULATING FEEDINGS
● **Dry weather** Do not feed plants if they are suffering from lack of water. They will not be able to absorb the fertilizer properly and may be damaged in the process.
● **Overfeeding** Late in the season, avoid using more high-nitrogen fertilizer than plants require. This could promote soft growth, which is particularly prone to frost damage (see p. 82).
● **Encouraging flowers** To increase the flower yield, apply a dressing of potassium sulfate to a flower bed in autumn and in early spring.
● **Vegetables** Leafy plants that are in the ground for a long time, such as cabbage, may need an extra feeding of nitrogen before harvest.
● **Liquid seaweed** Feed tomatoes, eggplant, and zucchini with liquid seaweed every two weeks during the growing season.

BRIGHT IDEA

Converting weights
To calculate how many handfuls of fertilizer are needed for an area, weigh one handful and divide the total weight needed by this figure.

USING NATURAL FERTILIZERS

Some gardeners may prefer to use fertilizers of a natural origin; others use only chemical fertilizers. The best results are usually achieved by using a combination of both for different purposes. Whichever type you select, there are plenty of fertilizers from which to choose.

UTILIZING NITROGEN

Cut plants close to ground level

Nourishing the soil
Peas and beans have bacteria in their roots that allow them to convert nitrogen into a usable form. Cut the plants down to ground level after harvesting, and leave the roots to break down and nourish the soil.

ADDING NUTRIENTS
● **Peas and beans** Always include these and other legumes in a crop rotation (see p. 109). They will help to increase nitrogen levels in the soil – even if their roots are not left in the ground at the end of the season.
● **Compost** Start a compost pile immediately if you do not already have one (see p. 43). Compost contains many natural plant nutrients and helps to improve and condition the soil.
● **Wood ashes** Collect wood ash from a cold bonfire after burning plant material, and use it as a fertilizer. Wood ashes contain useful nutrients, particularly potassium sulfate.

GREEN TIP

Using eggshells
Add a layer of crushed eggshells to the bottom of a planting hole to provide calcium and to improve drainage. Use for all plants, except those that prefer an acid soil, because eggshells are alkaline.

MAKING YOUR OWN FERTILIZER

Make your own totally organic liquid fertilizer from plants such as stinging nettles (or comfrey). The process is very simple and, provided that you have somewhere to store a quantity of fertilizer, is a cheap and satisfying way of providing your plants with good-quality, effective nutrients.

Pour water over nettles in bowl

Use wooden spoon to stir nettles

Strain liquid into plastic bucket

Plastic wrap

Leftover nettles can be used on compost pile

1 Collect freshly picked stinging nettles, and press them into a large bowl or bucket. Start with as many nettles as you can, since they decrease in volume once they start to rot down. Add water, allowing roughly 18 pints (10 liters) of water to about 2 lbs (1 kg) of nettles.

2 Mix the stinging nettles and water thoroughly, making sure that all the nettles are covered with water. Cover with plastic wrap or a tight-fitting lid. Stir several times with a wooden spoon over a period of several weeks. Always replace the plastic wrap or lid.

3 In a few weeks, after the mixture has rotted down, strain it into a bucket. Before using the liquid fertilizer, dilute it with water about ten times. The remaining solid matter can be incorporated into a compost pile for future use.

WATERING PLANTS

A REGULAR SUPPLY OF WATER IS ESSENTIAL for your plants. Without it, plants suffer moisture stress and may wilt and die. Established shrubs and trees can last without water longer than plants with shallow roots, such as annuals.

KEEPING A GARDEN WATERED

Water is often in short supply, particularly during long dry spells in summer, and is a precious resource we should try not to waste.

The watering technique you use – that is, how, when, and where the water is applied – is important if you are to avoid wasting water.

WATERING CORRECTLY

Directing water
To be sure water is able to penetrate right down to the roots, position the hose or watering can spout at the base of the plant, and water gently.

WATERING INCORRECTLY

Watering too strongly
Never direct a strong stream of water at the base of a plant. This washes away the soil from the roots and prevents the water from seeping down into the soil.

ASSESSING CONDITIONS

● **When not to water** Avoid watering during the heat of the day. Watering in bright light can cause scorching, especially on flowers, buds, and petals. The resulting humidity may also encourage fungal diseases such as powdery mildew, scab, and botrytis, to develop.
● **Watering twice** Water the surface of very dry soil lightly to prevent water from running off the surface. Water again once the initial water has been absorbed into the soil.
● **Pot watering** To water a large plant, sink a pot with a drainage hole into the nearby soil, and fill with water.

PLANT-WATERING CHECKLIST

There are some situations in which soil is particularly prone to drying out. Use drought-resistant plants for these areas. Some plants and planting situations always need plenty of water.

SITUATIONS THAT ARE DROUGHT-PRONE
● Free-draining, light, sandy soil.
● Some alkaline soils.
● Soil adjacent to walls (the walls absorb soil moisture).
● Plants growing against a house wall (rain falling onto the soil is restricted by overhanging roofs and gutters).
● Plants on steep slopes, especially if they face the sun.
● Plants in windy areas.

PLANTS THAT ARE RESISTANT TO DROUGHT
● Silver foliaged plants such as *Helichrysum* and *Stachys lanata*.
● Shrubs such as *Abelia* x *grandiflora, Azara, Ceanothus, Cistus, Cotinus coggygria, Genista, Hibiscus syriacus, Olearia, Potentilla fruticosa, Senecio,* and *Weigela*.
● Perennials such as *Alyssum, Armeria, Aubrieta, Coreopsis verticillata, Crassula, Dianthus, Oenothera, Phlox douglasii, Sempervivum,* and *Thymus*.

PLANTS THAT NEED PLENTY OF WATER
● Newly planted trees, shrubs, climbers, and perennials.
● Seedlings and transplants.
● Young trees, shrubs, and perennials.
● Leafy vegetables, which may flower and seed early if deprived of water.
● Peas, beans and other legumes, as well as sweet corn – particularly during and just after the flowering period.
● Fruiting crops such as eggplant, zucchini, and tomato – particularly during and just after flowering, and when fruiting.
● Tree, bush, and cane fruit, from flowering until harvest.
● Shrubs such as *Camellia* and *Rhododendron*, the buds of which form at the end of the summer and flower in spring.

CONSERVING AND SAVING WATER

Water may be in short supply at any time of the year. However, a long, hot summer is most likely to put plants at risk, and this is just the time when restrictions on garden watering are often in force. It therefore makes good sense to conserve water in any way you can.

IMPROVING MOISTURE RETENTION IN SOIL

● **Organic matter** Improve the water retention of soil by incorporating plenty of organic matter (see p. 42). This is especially important for sandy or light soils that drain very quickly.

● **Mulch** Apply a layer of mulch to the soil to retain moisture. An organic mulch should be applied in a 2–3 in (5–7.5 cm) deep layer. Keep the stem area free of organic mulch, since it can cause rotting.

Digging in compost
In all but the heaviest of soils, dig compost into the soil before creating a bed. When planting, incorporate compost into each planting hole and the soil used to backfill them.

Using plastic
Black plastic is a useful and inexpensive moisture-retaining material. Once it is in place, cover it with a layer of garden soil or a traditional and attractive mulching material.

USING CONTAINERS

● **Water-retaining granules** These are especially useful for plants in containers. You can either mix them with the soil mix and water thoroughly, or mix them with water and allow them to swell thoroughly before incorporating them into the soil mix (see p. 66).

● **Positioning** Containers are usually displayed in the sunniest part of the garden, since this is where most plants flower best. During very hot weather, move them to an area that is sometimes in shade.

● **Avoiding waste** Check outdoor containers daily during very hot weather; they may need watering once or even twice a day.

● **Self-watering** Use planters that are designed to supply water on demand. They are particularly suitable for use on balconies and verandahs.

CONTROLLING WEEDS

Use hand fork to remove weeds

Removing competition
Pull weeds from around plants regularly. Weeds grow rapidly and absorb a surprising amount of water from the soil in the process. As you weed, try to minimize disturbance to the soil.

WEEDING IN DROUGHT

● **Cutting weeds** In extremely dry conditions, cut off weeds at soil level instead of pulling them. This method reduces disturbance to the soil and prevents further moisture loss from the soil.

● **Wilting weeds** In very hot weather, leave uprooted or decapitated annual weeds on the soil surface to die, forming a "mini-mulch" layer.

MULCHING A LAWN

● **Using grass clippings** During drought conditions, do not rake up or collect grass clippings. Leave them as a mulch on the surface of the lawn after mowing.

TRADITIONAL TIP

Making a windbreak
Wind, especially from the sea, has a drying effect on plants and soil. Create a windbreak of trees and shrubs to protect an exposed garden.

COLLECTING AND RECYCLING WATER

Inside any house, a huge quantity of water is used every day. Much of it could be recycled for use in a garden with little effort. Not all water is suitable, however, so it is important to be selective. Use containers to collect and store as much water for recycling as you can.

COLLECTING WATER FOR GARDEN USE

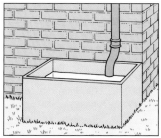

Using a container
Position any clean, watertight container under a downpipe to collect and store water for a garden. Make sure that you will be able to lift it when it is full. If it is too heavy, siphon off the water with a section of hosepipe.

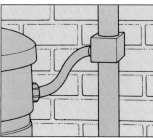

Diverting water
The downpipe that carries water from a bathroom sink or tub is an excellent source of water throughout the year. To collect the water, attach a section of pipe to divert it from the downpipe into a suitable container.

USING RECYCLED WATER
● **Safe water** Use water from the bathtub (it must not contain very much bubble bath) and the bathroom sink for recycling. Suction pumps are available to drain bathwater through a hose to the garden.
● **Unsafe water** Do not use excess water from a washing machine or from a dishwasher. Some of the chemicals contained in detergents could be damaging to plants and soil in the long run. The water from water-softening units can also be very damaging to garden plants because it contains salts.

USING A WATER BARREL

A water barrel is ideal for collecting and storing rain and suitable waste water. If possible, install several water barrels in different places. Position them to collect rainwater from a greenhouse, shed, or other outbuilding, and from gutters on a house and garage.

RAISING ON BRICKS

Adjusting height
If the faucet on your water barrel is difficult to operate because it is too close to the ground, raise the barrel by placing it on several bricks. The extra height will also make it easier to fill a watering can.

MAINTAINING HYGIENE
● **Preventing algae** Clean water barrels regularly to prevent a buildup of algae and debris. Scrub the interior with a stiff brush and soapy water, and rinse thoroughly. Use a long-handled broom to reach inside.
● **Keeping water clean** Add some crystals of potassium permanganate to the water at regular intervals. These help to keep the water "sweet," and have no adverse effect on young or established plants.

USING THE WATER
● **Preventing disease** Use water collected from gutters on open ground only. It may contain harmful organisms that cause fungal diseases in seedlings, young plants, or plants in containers.

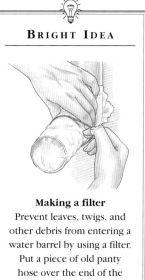

BRIGHT IDEA

Making a filter
Prevent leaves, twigs, and other debris from entering a water barrel by using a filter. Put a piece of old panty hose over the end of the downspout, and secure with a rubber band. Clean regularly, especially after heavy rain.

WATERING BEDS AND BORDERS

Successful flowering and fruiting, as well as healthy vegetable growth and development, are dependent on a regular and adequate supply of water. Applying the right amount of water at the right time and in the right way, while wasting as little as possible, is important.

WATERING EFFICIENTLY
● **Frequency** Water plants thoroughly from time to time rather than applying too little water too often.

Making a basin
To make sure that water goes down to the roots instead of lying on top of the soil, scoop out soil from around the base of the plant. Fill the hollow with water and let it soak in slowly.

SAVING WATER
● **Dry areas** Select drought-resistant plants, such as those from Mediterranean countries (see p. 89), for dry sun.
● **Grouping plants** Keep plants that need a lot of water together so that when watering, you will not waste water on nearby plants that do not need as much.
● **Directing a hose** Always point the end of the hose beneath the foliage when watering beds and borders. This will prevent water from being wasted, and will reduce the risk of leaf scorch.
● **Positioning plants** Do not put plants that prefer shade in a sunny spot. They will wilt very quickly, and large amounts of water will be needed to revive them.

BRIGHT IDEA

Protecting plants
A hose pipe may drag over flower beds and squash the plants as you pull it from place to place in the yard. To prevent this, drive short wooden posts into the corners of each bed, or at intervals along the edges.

WATERING VEGETABLES IN BEDS AND BORDERS
● **Cloches** The soil inside a cloche dries out faster than the open ground; use a leaky hose to water in a cloche.

● **When to water** Water vegetables regularly, preferably in the evening. If crops are wilting, water immediately.

● **Helping pollination** Apply plenty of water to the roots of runner beans at flowering time to encourage pollination.

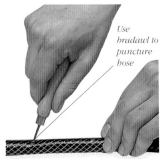

Use bradawl to puncture hose

Making a leaky hose
Take a length of hose – preferably one that is already leaky, and make small holes along it. Tightly tie up or block one end. Lay the hose along a row of plants, attach the open end to a tap, and turn the faucet on very gently.

Making trenches
Use a hoe to make shallow trenches between rows of vegetables. Be sure to leave plenty of room for normal root development. Water into the trench, thus allowing the water to seep down to the roots.

Watering long rows
To water long, inaccessible rows, first make small holes along a length of plastic guttering. Lay this between two rows, and pour water into one end. The water will run along the guttering so that each plant receives water.

WATERING LAWNS

During a dry summer, the grass in a lawn turns brown and growth slows down. An established lawn generally resists drought well. If there are no water restrictions in force, water your lawn as soon as you notice that the grass does not spring back after it is walked on.

IMPROVING DRAINAGE

Spiking a dry lawn
Before watering a dry lawn, use a garden fork to spike the soil. Drive the prongs in to make drainage channels. This will encourage the water to penetrate the soil, rather than run off the surface.

LOOKING AFTER A LAWN
● **Watering** After watering, the soil should be moist to a depth of 4–6 in (10–15 cm). Dig a small hole to see if the soil is damp to the required depth. If it is, note how long it took to water.
● **Feeding** Never use a granular fertilizer on a lawn during drought conditions, since grass needs thorough watering both before and after the fertilizer is applied. Use a specially formulated liquid lawn fertilizer instead.
● **Dry weather** Allow grass to grow slightly longer than usual in very dry weather. Moisture is retained in the blades, and excessive cutting will deplete a lawn's store of moisture.

BRIGHT IDEA

Using a sprinkler
Determine how long to water an area with a sprinkler by putting a straight-sided jar by the sprinkler. When the jar has collected 1 in (2.5 cm) of water, move the sprinkler.

WATERING GREENHOUSE PLANTS

However well a greenhouse is shaded, the plants inside will be more vulnerable to heat or drought stress than those growing outside. Plants in pots will be in particular need of attention. Always choose a greenhouse that has adequate vents, windows, and doors.

USING CAPILLARY MATTING

Matting soaks up water

Plant is above the water so that it can draw water as needed

Constant watering
To ensure that plants are well watered, place them on one end of a piece of capillary matting. Submerge the other end in a water trough or other reservoir of water.

WATERING EFFICIENTLY WITH CAPILLARY MATTING
● **Rapid action** Wet capillary matting before using it. This allows the capillary action of the fibers to work more rapidly and efficiently.
● **Wick** To help a plant in a large pot absorb water, insert a small matting wick through a drainage hole to protrude onto the matting below.

WATERING A GROW BAG

Bottle tied to plant support with string

Using a plastic bottle
Cut off the bottom from a plastic bottle, take the cap off, and insert this end into the soil mix in the grow bag. Water through the bottle so that the water does not run straight off the top of the soil mix.

WEEDING

A S WEEDS GROW, THEY COMPETE WITH PLANTS for water, light, and nutrients. Weeds are invasive and set seed quickly if you do not act promptly. The first, and most important, step in eradicating weeds is to identify them (see p. 95).

BASIC EQUIPMENT

Weeds can be controlled using a variety of different methods and equipment. A combination of cultivation and chemical methods is usually effective.

● **Suppressing weeds** Use a 1–2-in (2.5–5-cm) layer of gravel or grass clippings to prevent weeds from growing. Black plastic, though less attractive, has the same effect.
● **Choosing a hoe** Use a Dutch hoe to cut through weeds without damaging plant roots. An eye hoe is good for chopping weeds in half. Use an onion hoe for weeding between onions and other closely grown plants.
● **Crevices and lawns** For narrow crevices in a hard surface, use a pavement weeder. Use a dandelion weeder or an old kitchen knife for removing weeds such as dandelions, docks, and daisies from lawns.
● **Applying weedkiller** Prevent spray from drifting onto nearby plants by using a dribble bar attached to a watering can. This also makes it possible to apply weedkiller accurately.

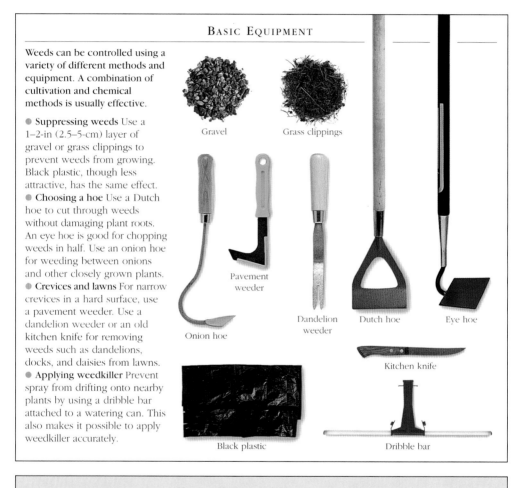

Gravel

Grass clippings

Pavement weeder

Onion hoe

Dandelion weeder

Dutch hoe

Eye hoe

Kitchen knife

Black plastic

Dribble bar

USING WEEDKILLERS SAFELY

● **Protection** Wear protective clothing such as rubber gloves and old clothes when mixing and applying weedkillers.
● **Mouth and skin** Never eat, drink, or smoke while mixing or applying chemicals. Wash you hands thoroughly after use.
● **Dilution** Dilute soluble weedkillers according to the manufacturer's instructions on the label.

● **Correct use** Always use each product only for the purpose recommended on the label.
● **Amount** Apply weedkiller at the rate stated on the label.
● **Wind** Never use weedkillers in windy weather, when spray can blow onto nearby plants.
● **Storage** Keep weedkillers safely out of reach of children and animals, preferably locked away in a cupboard or in a garden shed.

● **Containers** Store weedkillers in their original containers. Make sure they are clearly labelled.
● **Watering cans** Do not use the same watering can for watering and applying liquid weedkillers. Keep one watering can and dribble bar, or sprayer, solely for applying weedkiller.
● **Disposal** Always dispose of leftover diluted weedkiller. Never store and reuse it.

COMMON WEEDS

ANNUAL	HOW TO TREAT	PERENNIAL	HOW TO TREAT
HAIRY BITTER CRESS	This is a common annual weed that develops quickly. It often grows on the soil mix of potted plants; check new purchases before planting. Hoe regularly before it sets seed. Hand weed, or cover with mulch.	HORSETAIL	Underground stems of horsetail can penetrate 10 ft (3 m) below the soil surface, so digging out is rarely successful in the long run. Use repeated spot treatments with glyphosate or other systemic weedkillers.
ANNUAL MEADOW GRASS	Usually found in lawns, this may also appear in poorly maintained borders. It can be prevented by good lawn cultivation, including regular mowing, appropriate feeding, watering, and aeration.	BINDWEED	Bindweed regenerates from sections of underground stems or roots, which can be spread by digging and caught up in new plants. Repeated digging out is necessary. Apply glyphosate to leaves.
ANNUAL NETTLE	Annual nettle grows in beds, borders, and vacant spaces between plants. Hand weed, or spot treat it with a suitable weedkiller such as glyphosate or similar product.	QUACK GRASS	Quack grass is common in beds, borders, vacant ground, and lawns. It spreads by creeping roots. Try forking it out from light soils, or smother it with plastic. Treat with glyphosate, and mow the lawn regularly.
GROUNDSEL	This annual is found in borders, beds, and vacant spaces between plants. Hoe or hand weed regularly before the weeds can set seed. Cover affected ground with a deep mulch.	DOCK	Dock grows in lawns beds, and paths. It regenerates from small root sections and spreads by seed. For docks in lawns, use a weedkiller containing 2,4-D or MCPA. On vacant ground, use a glyphosate weedkiller.
COMMON CHICKWEED	Common chickweed grows in borders, beds, and vacant spaces between plants. Hoe or hand weed regularly before weeds set seed. Cover with a deep mulch.	PERENNIAL NETTLE	This regenerates from a creeping root system and spreads by seed. Eradicate before mid summer, when plants set seed. In light soils, dig it out. Use glyphosate spray in uncultivated areas.

PREVENTING WEEDS

Try to prevent weeds from invading your garden whenever possible. Once weeds are established and have started to set seed, they can be extremely difficult to eradicate. Depriving weeds of light is one of the best natural ways of suppressing weed growth, and it is easy to do.

DEPRIVING WEEDS OF LIGHT TO INHIBIT GROWTH

● **Weeds in crops** Use black plastic as an inexpensive way of inhibiting the growth of weeds in a vegetable plot.

● **Uncultivated ground** Cover the ground with black plastic or old carpet to suppress perennial weeds.

● **Mulch** Before applying a weed-suppressing mulch, make sure the ground is moist, and apply a fertilizer.

Using groundcover
Plant dense-growing plants close together to suppress weed growth attractively. Use a suitable mulch until the plants become sufficiently established to do the job on their own.

Using matting
Fruit bushes and many other plants cannot be planted very close together. If regular hoeing is impossible, deprive weeds of light by placing polypropylene matting around the plants.

Using grass clippings
Use a mulch of fresh grass clippings around plants. Do not use composted grass, since it may form an impenetrable barrier through which water and air cannot pass.

USING GRAVEL
● **Gravel mulch** Use a 2-in (5-cm) layer of coarse gravel around ornamental plants to suppress weed growth.

Preventing weeds and rot
Gravel is a particularly suitable mulch for alpines. It keeps weeds at bay and prevents rotting caused by moisture build up around the crowns of the plants.

STOPPING THE SPREAD
● **Before mulching** Remove all annual and perennial weeds from the soil before putting down weed-suppressing mulch or matting. Weed seeds in the soil will still germinate once the mulch is in place, but these seedlings will be far easier to deal with than large, well-established weeds.
● **New plants** Before planting new purchases, remove any seedlings that are growing on the surface of the soil mix.
● **Weed regeneration** Never compost noxious weeds, since many of them can regenerate from underground roots or stems, even if they have been chopped up. Do not incorporate weeds that have set seed into a compost pile; some seeds may survive the composting process.

BRIGHT IDEA

Plastic lines one side of trench

Trench needs to be 30 cm (12 in) deep

Making a weed barrier
Prevent the creeping roots of weeds in a neighbor's garden from finding their way under a fence. Dig a 12-in (30-cm) deep trench, line one side with heavy-duty plastic, then replace the soil.

USING CHEMICAL WEEDKILLERS

U sed with care, chemical weedkillers are a useful and labor-saving way of dealing with weeds. They offer a means of eradicating weeds when cultivation methods are not feasible. You can combine chemicals with other control methods, or use just the chemicals.

TYPES OF CHEMICAL WEEDKILLER

Weedkillers are available in several forms, including powders, gels, liquids, and ready-to-use formulations, such as sprays.

WARNING!
Wear rubber gloves and old clothes when mixing and applying weedkillers. Always follow the instructions carefully.

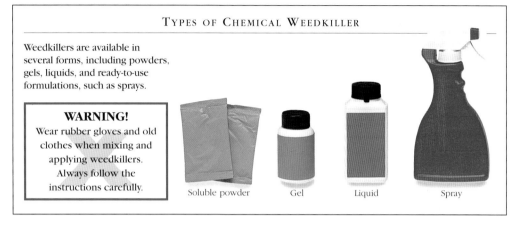

Soluble powder   Gel   Liquid   Spray

WEEDING IN BORDERS

Using paint-on gel
Paint a gel-formulation weedkiller on to weeds that are growing where hand weeding or spraying would be difficult without damaging nearby plants.

WEEDING IN PATHS

Using a liquid
Use a liquid weedkiller on surfaces such as paths, patios, and driveways. A dribble bar is an efficient, low-cost way of applying a liquid weedkiller.

BRIGHT IDEA

Using a shield
Protect garden plants with a sheet of cardboard when applying a weedkiller. Cover plants with cardboard boxes or plastic trash bags.

APPLYING WEEDKILLERS
● **Effective timing** Apply weedkillers when weeds are growing actively; this is usually when they are most effective.
● **Dry weather** Check the weather forecast before using weedkillers. Rain can ruin the effect of many weedkillers.
● **Nettles** When treating nettles, apply the weedkiller just before the foliage starts to die back at the end of the growing season.

AIDING ABSORPTION OF WEEDKILLERS

Some weeds absorb weedkillers more easily than others. Increase the effect of weedkiller on stubborn weeds such as goutweed and docks by crushing their foliage before application; the chemicals are more easily absorbed by bruised leaves. Use your foot or the back of a rake, but take care not to sever the foliage completely.

WEEDING BY HAND

Many weeds can be dealt with successfully using just a few hand tools. Like many other gardening jobs, the key to success when weeding by hand is timing and frequency. Remove weeds before they set seed and before they begin to compete with garden plants.

KILLING ANNUAL WEEDS

Hoeing around plants
Use a Dutch hoe to control annual weeds. During dry, sunny weather, hoe in the morning or middle of the day, and do not gather the weeds, but leave them lying on the soil; they will soon shrivel under the sun.

KNEELING PAD
● **Knee protection** Knees can become very uncomfortable during prolonged spells of hand weeding. Buy a kneeling pad from your garden center.

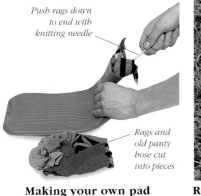

Push rags down to end with knitting needle

Rags and old panty hose cut into pieces

Making your own pad
Stuff an old hot-water bottle with rags and panty hose to make an inexpensive kneeling pad. Do not stuff the hot water bottle so full that it becomes rigid. Use just enough stuffing to create a cushion effect.

PREVENTING THE SPREAD OF WEEDS
● **When to weed** Start weeding in early spring to prevent the development and spread of weeds. Weeds can grow during mild winters and relatively warm spells, so watch for out-of-season growth, and remove it.
● **Flowering weeds** Always remove flowering weeds before they have set seed, preferably before they flower.
● **Large areas** If tackling a large expanse of weeds, start by cutting off all the flower heads and seedheads rather than removing entire weeds in a small area. This will prevent most of the seeds from escaping into the soil.

WEEDING A LAWN
● **Hand weeding** If you have a small lawn or one with only a few weeds, you will not need to use chemical weedkillers; hand weed instead.

Removing a dandelion
Use an old kitchen knife to remove a dandelion. Keep the blade as vertical as possible, and cut downward in a circle all around the weed. Rock the knife back and forth, then pull out the weed with its roots intact.

● **Pulling weed roots** Many noxious weeds can regenerate from tiny portions of roots or underground stems left in the ground. Always pull as much of the root out of the ground as possible.
● **Weed disposal** Do not put weeds that have set seed in the compost pile. Place them directly into a plastic bag for disposal elsewhere.

> ### WARNING!
> Cover the tops of stakes with upside-down flower pots or yogurt containers to protect your eyes while bending down to weed in the garden.

LOOKING AFTER A LAWN
● **Control by mowing** Regular mowing at the correct height will kill many lawn weeds. Rosette-forming weeds, such as daisies, and those that form creeping stems, such as speedwell and buttercups, will escape the blades most easily. These will require more drastic action (see p. 129).
● **Blade height** Never mow a lawn with the blades set very low. This weakens the grass considerably, making it vulnerable to invasion by unwanted weeds and moss.
● **Weeding and feeding** Apply a lawn weedkiller shortly after – or at the same time – you apply a lawn fertilizer. The fertilizer increases the rate at which the weeds absorb the chemicals that kill them. Fertilizer also stimulates the grass to grow over any bare areas left in the lawn after the weeds have died.

CLEARING NEGLECTED SITES

Without regular maintenance, a garden can quickly turn into a jungle of unwelcome weeds, particularly during the summer months. Tackle an uncultivated area by combining cultivation and chemical techniques. For heavy weed infestations, use a weedkiller.

FORKING OUT WEEDS

Removing woody weeds
Fork out large, woody weeds such as brambles. Remove the top–growth, and dig out as many of the roots as possible. Treat any subsequent growth with a brushwood killer, or dig out the remaining pieces of root.

SUPPRESSING WEEDS

Using black plastic
To protect a cleared area from new weed growth, cover it with heavy-duty black plastic. Make slits in the soil, and push the edges of the plastic into them. You may also need a few bricks if the site is exposed.

USING WEEDKILLERS
● **Contact weedkillers** Consider using a total weedkiller on a site that needs to be cleared of weeds. Use one that contains glyphosate, which will kill most weeds. It is deactivated upon contact with the soil, so you can replant the area as soon as the weeds are dead.
● **Second application** Heavily weed-infested sites will need more than one application of weedkiller. Wait until there is a good covering of foliage before reapplying.

IMPROVING THE LOOK
● **Covering up** Disguise black plastic with a layer of bark chips or garden soil.

DEALING WITH PERSISTENT WEEDS

Weeds with roots that break off into pieces underground, such as oxalis, or those with deep, creeping roots, such as bindweed, are particularly difficult to eradicate from a garden. If left unattended, however, these weeds will take over a garden in no time flat.

REMOVING BINDWEED

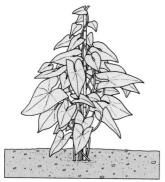

Using a stake
The twining nature of bindweed makes it difficult to treat without putting garden plants at risk. Train bindweed stems up a stake. You will then be able to apply weedkiller to the weed without damaging other garden plants.

WEEDING EFFECTIVELY
● **Disposing of roots** Never leave pieces of weed roots lying on the ground, or they may reroot. Gather them up, and either put them in the garbage, or add them to your compost pile.
● **Systemic weedkillers** For persistent weeds or for those with deep roots, choose a systemic weedkiller, which is carried from the leaves right through the plants to the roots.
● **Correct dose** Never attempt to apply a weedkiller in a more concentrated form than that recommended by the manufacturer. This may scorch the foliage, limiting the amount of weedkiller that the weed is able to absorb.

DEALING WITH OXALIS

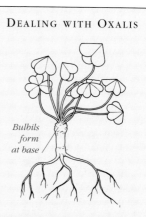

Bulbils form at base

Every oxalis has tiny bulbils around its base, each of which can form a new plant. These bulbils drop off and disperse in summer. Always dig out oxalis in spring before the bulbils spread the weed.

PRUNING PLANTS

PRUNING SERVES MANY PURPOSES. It can keep a plant's size in check, encourage flowering or fruiting, remove or deter pest and disease problems, or help to improve the overall appearance of a plant by changing its shape.

BASIC EQUIPMENT

Good-quality, well-maintained pruning tools are essential. Do not buy poor-quality tools.

● **Pruning saw** Choose a saw that has heat-treated hardpoint teeth. Use it to prune branches over 1 in (2.5 cm) in diameter.
● **Garden knife** Use a garden knife for light pruning tasks.
● **Pruners** Use pruners to prune soft stems and woody ones up to ⅜ in (1 cm) thick.
● **Loppers** Use long-handled lopper for pruning out-of-reach woody stems and branches.
● **Shears** Use hedge shears to trim hedges and some woody plants.
● **Gardening gloves** Wear sturdy gloves to protect your hands.

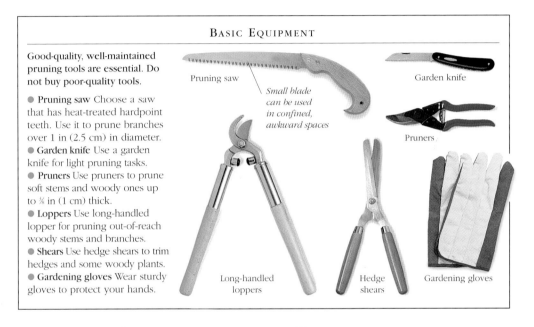

Pruning saw

Small blade can be used in confined, awkward spaces

Garden knife

Pruners

Long-handled loppers

Hedge shears

Gardening gloves

DEADHEADING AND DISBUDDING

Deadheading is the most basic pruning job of all. Regularly remove faded flowers to encourage new flowers throughout summer and possibly into autumn. Disbudding is the removal of small flower buds around the main bud so that it can develop without competition.

DEADHEADING PLANTS
● **Using hands** Deadhead soft-stemmed plants by hand. Using pruners is inefficient and time-consuming, and does not allow proper access to small flower heads.
● **Preventing disease** Remove faded flowers as soon as possible to prevent them from becoming colonized by pathogens such as *Botrytis cinerea* (see p. 106).
● **Geraniums** To encourage a second flush of flowers on herbaceous geraniums, use shears to cut back about one-quarter to one-third of the top-growth when flowering is over.

DEADHEADING ROSES

Encouraging new flowers
Use sharp pruners to remove rose blooms as soon as they start to fade. Cut back the stem to a strong shoot or to an outward-facing bud lower on the stem.

DISBUDDING DAHLIAS

Use forefinger and thumb to remove buds

Removing competition
Disbud dahlias by pinching out surplus buds with your forefinger and thumb. This will allow the remaining bud to develop into a full-sized flower.

PRUNING ROSES

Roses need regular pruning in order to produce lots of good-sized flowers year after year. A rose that is not pruned will soon lose its shape, and its flowering capacity will be diminished. Old, faded flowers and buds will also be vulnerable to attack from diseases.

LOOKING AFTER ROSES

● **Inspecting stems** Always examine rose stems carefully. Blackspot disease (see p. 121) may overwinter on the stems.

● **Avoiding disease** Prune out diseased stems. Prune cracked or injured stems, since they are vulnerable to infection.

● **Neglected roses** Sudden, excessive pruning can sometimes cause dieback and may prove fatal. Over a period of time, gradually prune any roses that have been left unpruned

● **Protecting hands** Always wear a pair of sturdy gardening gloves to protect your hands from rose thorns. It is impossible to prune properly without them.

PRUNING POOR GROWTH

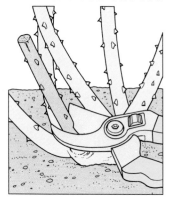

Cutting out weak growth
Use sharp pruners to prune out any diseased, damaged, dead, or weak, spindly stems. Make a diagonal cut just above an outward-facing, vigorous bud toward the base of the stem.

PRUNING STEMS

Improving air circulation
Crossing stems crowd a plant and encourage diseases such as blackspot, rust, and powdery mildew. Prune any crossing, overcrowded stems back to a sturdy, outward-facing bud.

CUTTING AT THE CORRECT ANGLE

Plants vary in their pruning requirements, and some require no routine pruning at all. Regardless of the plant, however, there are some pruning techniques that always apply. One of the most important of these is making the pruning cut at the correct angle.

ALTERNATE SHOOTS

Make angled cut above outward-facing shoot

Making a diagonal cut
Use a diagonal cut to prune stems with alternate shoots or buds. This will prevent any shoots or buds from being damaged by the pruners.

OPPOSITE SHOOTS

Making a straight cut
Use a straight cut to prune stems with opposite shoots or buds. Always use sharp pruners to make a precise, swift, and clean cutting movement.

CUTTING AND SEALING

● **Where to cut** Never cut too close to a bud, since this may damage it and cause it to produce a weak shoot. Do not prune too far away from a bud, since this leaves a "snag" of stem, which dies back and may also cause more of the stem to deteriorate.

● **Sealing wounds** Apply shellac to large pruning wounds on trees that are prone to fresh-wound diseases such as canker.

CARING FOR TOOLS

● **Blades** Keep pruners sharp. Blunt blades may crush a stem, leaving it vulnerable to infection from disease.

RENOVATING CLIMBERS

Most climbers produce vigorous growth. Sometimes this may be just what you need, but if a climber outgrows its location, it will need cutting back. Some climbers require pruning to encourage them to flower. Other, established climbers need thinning from time to time.

REMOVING OLD WOOD

Cutting back old stems
Old stems that become woody rarely flower properly. Prune old, unproductive stems back to ground level with long-handled loppers, pruners, or a saw, depending on their thickness.

PRUNING HONEYSUCKLE

Removing congestion
Many honeysuckles grow rapidly, and become dense and too heavy or extensive for their supports. Prune them by cutting away dead and damaged stems from beneath the new growth.

PRUNING CLIMBERS

● **Preserving foliage** When pruning a climber try to minimize damage to the foliage. This will prevent the plant from looking too stark after it has been pruned.
● **Checking supports** When pruning, take the opportunity to check the condition of walls, pointing, trellises, and other structures or supports. They may be in need of renovation or repair (see p. 52).
● **Looking after birds** Climbers make perfect nesting sites for a variety of birds. To keep disturbance to a minimum, try to delay major pruning work until after any fledglings have flown the nest.

PRUNING HEDGES

A well-pruned, properly maintained hedge looks attractive and can provide a functional divider or boundary within or around a garden. Proper pruning should be carried out from the very beginning if you want to keep your hedge in the best possible shape.

BRIGHT IDEA

Adding color
Brighten up a straggly or thin hedge by growing a flowering vine through it. Besides helping to mask a hedge's condition, the flowers can provide both color and scent.

SHAPING CONIFERS

Hedge cut into wedge shape

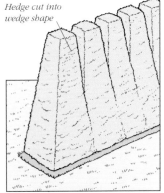

Maintaining shape
Leyland cypress and other hedging conifers need regular clipping to look good. Once a hedge has reached the desired height, cut it back into a wedge shape at least once a year.

REJUVENATING HEDGES

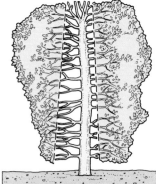

Alternating sides
Avoid cutting back all shoots severely in one season. In the first year, cut one side back hard to encourage new shoots. The next year, trim the new shoots lightly, and cut back the other side hard.

PRUNING SHRUBS

Many shrubs need regular, annual pruning in order to stimulate the production of stems that bear flower buds, and to keep them a manageable shape and size. If you are in doubt about your shrub's flowering habit, consult a book on pruning.

PRUNING DEAD WOOD

Spotting dead wood
Dead wood can be removed at any time of the year, but it is easier to spot and prune out the dead wood when the shrub is in leaf. Use sharp pruners to cut stems back into perfectly sound, healthy wood.

PRUNING OLD WOOD

Cutting out old wood
Remove up to one-fifth of a shrub's old wood, cutting back to within 2–3 in (5–8 cm) of ground level. To maintain a well-balanced, even shape, remove the stems evenly over the entire plant.

PRUNING WEAK GROWTH

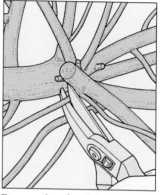

Promoting healthy growth
Prune out spindly and crossing stems. Prune back to a vigorous, outward-facing bud so that similar shoots are not encouraged. Removing unwanted stems ensures that all the nutrients go directly into the healthy growth.

WHEN TO PRUNE SHRUBS

As a general rule, if a shrub flowers after midsummer, it should be pruned in early spring. If it flowers earlier in the year, pruning should be done immediately after flowering.

EXAMPLES OF SHRUBS THAT NEED PRUNING IN SPRING
Abutilon (some),
Buddleia davidii,
Caryopteris,
Ceanothus,
Ceratostigma,
Cotinus,
Forsythia,
Fuchsia (hardy types),
Hibiscus syriacus,
Hydrangea,
Lavatera (shrubby forms),
Prunus triloba,
Spiraea douglasii,
Spiraea japonica,
Tamarix.

EXAMPLES OF SHRUBS THAT NEED PRUNING IN SUMMER
Buddleia alternifolia,
Chaenomeles,
Cotoneaster,
Deutzia,
Forsythia,
Magnolia soulangiana,
Magnolia stellata,
Philadelphus,
Syringa,
Weigela.

Fuchsia

TRADITIONAL TIP

Encouraging berries
To ensure that a *Pyracantha* is covered with berries in autumn, prune it in stages. Prune some stems in early spring, then leave them the rest of the year; the flowers they produce will turn into berries. Cut back some of the other stems immediately after flowering.

Pests & Diseases

EVERY GARDENER *encounters different garden pests and diseases, some of which can have a devastating effect. As long as you can identify them and take the appropriate action immediately, many pests and diseases need not cause too much harm or devastation to your garden plants.*

IDENTIFYING PESTS AND DISEASES

Some pests and diseases are potentially very harmful. Others may cause serious problems only if a plant is badly stressed or already under attack from something else. Use the following chart to identify the major problems and to learn how to deal with them effectively.

PESTS/DISEASE	SYMPTOMS	CONTROLS
SLUGS AND SNAILS	Both these pests feed mainly at night and after rain. Smooth-edged holes appear on foliage, stems, and petals. Both pests may tunnel into corms, bulbs, and tubers, making large holes. Silvery slime trails are often found nearby.	Use nematodes to control slugs (see p. 115). Cultivate soil to expose eggs, and remove debris. Reduce the use of organic mulches. Lure slugs to inverted citrus peels, collect the peels, and discard.
CATERPILLARS	Many garden plants are attacked by caterpillars, the larvae of butterflies and moths. Leaves, soft stems, and occasionally flowers develop holes as they are eaten. Some caterpillars spin a fine web around the leaves.	Pick off the caterpillars. Prune out damaged stems and heavily webbed areas. Spray with the biological control *Bacillus thuringiensis* or with a suitable pesticide.
GREENHOUSE WHITEFLIES	Greenhouse whiteflies are most common in greenhouses but may also be found outside in hot weather. Leaves are discolored and distorted, and may be covered with sticky excreta, which attracts black sooty mold growth.	Introduce the parasitic wasp *Encarsia formosa* (see p. 115) into greenhouses and conservatories. Alternatively, spray with insecticidal soaps, or other insecticides.
WEEVILS	Adult beetles cause notching around leaf edges. The white grubs attack many plants, particularly those in containers. They eat and tunnel into roots, tubers, and corms.	Use biological control drenches of nematodes (*Steinernema* and *Heterorhabditis* spp.). Collect and destroy adult beetles and grubs.

Slug

Snail

PESTS/DISEASE	SYMPTOMS	CONTROLS
RUST	Various fungi are responsible for rust infections. They are most severe in damp or moist weather and on soft, lush growth. Orange, yellow, or brown spots appear on leaves, mostly on the lower surface. The upper surface may have yellow blotches.	Remove infected leaves promptly. Improve air circulation around the plants. To decrease humidity, avoid wetting the foliage. Spray with a suitable fungicide.
LEAF SPOT	Various bacteria and fungi cause leaf spots. If this is caused by bacteria, spots may be irregular, with a yellow edge. Fungal spots have concentric rings and an area of tiny fungal fruiting bodies. Black, brown, or gray spots may cover the leaves.	Most leaf spots do not cause serious problems and may develop only on plants that are in poor condition. Remove badly infected leaves, and improve the plant's growing conditions. Spray with a suitable fungicide for fungal leaf spots.
POWDERY MILDEW	These mildews cause a white, powdery layer of fungal growth to appear – usually in distinct patches or spots, which then coalesce. A few mildews are pale brown and felty. Leaves, stems, and flowers may be attacked, and may wither and die.	Powdery mildew thrives in humid air. Prune to improve air circulation, and keep plants well watered and mulched. Avoid wetting leaves. Spray with a suitable fungicide.
EARWIGS	Many plants are attacked by these pests, particularly dahlias, chrysanthemums, clematis, peaches, and certain annuals. Young leaves and petals are eaten, especially during the summer. In extreme cases, a plant can be severely damaged.	Make traps with rolled-up corrugated cardboard or flower pots stuffed with straw (see p. 118); collect and destroy the pests. Alternatively, spray at dusk with an insecticide.
TOADSTOOLS	Toadstools are usually seen in lawns in the autumn, especially during mild, damp spells. Toadstools are usually short-lived and rarely survive the first frosts. They may form "fairy rings," which cause grass to become discolored.	If the grass is unharmed, simply brush off the toadstools as soon as they appear, preferably before their caps open (see p. 121). If they reappear, they may be growing on buried organic debris, such as old tree roots; dig these out.
SPIDER MITES	Several species of spider mite occur on garden and greenhouse plants. A common and troublesome species is the two-spotted, or greenhouse, spider mite. In severe cases, leaves may turn brown and die. Fine webbing may appear on affected plants.	Control spider mites with predatory mites (see p. 115). Allow adequate ventilation, and damp down frequently (see p. 83). Spray with an insecticidal soap or miticide.

PESTS/DISEASE	SYMPTOMS	CONTROLS
BOTRYTIS	Many plants are susceptible to this fungus. Fuzzy, gray patches develop on infected areas. Plant tissue becomes discolored and deteriorates, and there may be extensive dieback. White or yellow circles appear on tomato skins.	Clear out all plant debris. Remove and destroy infected tissue promptly. Avoid injury to plants, and improve air circulation around them by pruning. If necessary, spray with a suitable fungicide.
APHIDS	Aphids feed by sucking sap and may cause plant parts to become discolored and distorted. Their sticky excreta may encourage the growth of black sooty mold. Aphids can be many colors; some are covered with white, waxy wool.	Natural or introduced predators and parasites may help to reduce numbers (see p. 110). Spray with a strong stream of water from a hose to dislodge them, or with an insecticidal soap, or insecticide.
VIRUSES	Many viruses have a wide and diverse host range. Symptoms can vary. Stunting, poor growth, leaf yellowing (usually as flecks, ring-spots, streaks, or mosaic patterns), distortion, and flower-color changes are the most common symptoms.	Viruses are spread by handling or other mechanical injuries, and by pests such as aphids, thrips, and nematodes. Some are seedborne. Avoid damaging plants, and disinfect pruning tools frequently. Control virus-carrying pests, and remove infected plants promptly.
CLUBROOT	Clubroot affects many brassicas, including broccoli, brussels sprouts, cabbage, radishes, and rutabagas, as well as some ornamentals. Symptoms include distorted and swollen roots, and poorly developed, often discolored, stunted foliage.	Improve soil drainage and add lime to discourage the slime mold responsible for clubroot. Raise plants in individual pots, and plant out when they have a strong root system (see p. 120). If possible, choose resistant cultivars.
FOOT AND ROOT ROT	Bedding plants, seedlings, beans, cucumbers, tomatoes, and peas are particularly susceptible. Soil- or waterborne fungi cause discoloration of stem bases, which shrink inward. Plants grow poorly and ultimately wilt, wither, and die.	Observe strict hygiene: use sterilized commercial soil mix, clean trays and pots, and tap water. Do not overwater or crowd plants. Water seeds and seedlings with a copper-based fungicide. Remove affected plants immediately.
SCAB	These are most common on apples, pears, and Pyracantha. Gray or black, scabby patches develop on affected plants. Leaves and fruit are commonly affected, but stems may be attacked, too. Leaf puckering and fruit distortion often occur.	Avoid overhead watering. Rake up and dispose of affected leaves, and prune out infected shoots. Keep the center of plants open by pruning carefully. Spray with a suitable fungicide.

PESTS/DISEASE	SYMPTOMS	CONTROLS
CODLING MOTHS	Apples and pears may be attacked by the larvae of codling moths. Holes, often surrounded by brown, powder-like droppings, appear on ripe fruit. The codling moth larvae feed in the core of the fruit, tunneling out when mature.	Hang pheromone traps in trees from late spring to midsummer to catch male moths (see p. 119); this will reduce the number of codling moth eggs that will be fertilized by the males. Spray with a suitable pesticide.
CABBAGE ROOT FLIES	Many brassicas, including cabbage, rutabagas, cauliflower, and brussels sprouts, may be attacked by this pest. Seedlings die, and plants may wilt and become discolored. Larvae measuring up to ½ in (9 mm) long tunnel into the roots of crops.	Place collars of carpet padding, roofing felt, or cardboard around the base of each plant when it is transplanted (see p. 119). Alternatively, dust transplanted brassicas and seed rows with a suitable soil insecticide.
CARROT RUST FLIES	Carrots are the most common host to this pest, but other plants may also be attacked, including celery and parsley. Carrot rust fly larvae tunnel into roots, causing rust-brown lesions on roots and plants. Plants may develop discolored foliage.	Erect a plastic barrier around crops to keep out female flies (see p. 119), or protect a whole crop with a row cover. Avoid handling crops, since the smell of the leaves may attract adult flies. Treat seed rows with a suitable insecticide.
FLEA BEETLES	Seedlings of brassicas, leafy vegetables, radishes, stocks, nasturtiums, and wallflowers are particularly vulnerable. The tiny beetles feed on leaves, making numerous holes on the upper surfaces. Hot, dry summers encourage this pest.	Flea beetles overwinter in plant debris, so clean up debris thoroughly to avoid damage. Use sticky traps (see p. 118). Warm soil before sowing seeds, and water regularly to encourage rapid, strong growth. Use a suitable insecticide.
WIREWORMS	Many plants may be attacked, particularly potatoes and other root crops. Perennials, annuals, seedlings, and bulbous plants may also be damaged. Young plants may wilt, wither, and die as wireworms tunnel into their roots.	Recently cultivated soil, or an area recently converted from grass, is most likely to harbor these pests. Bury carrot and potato pieces as bait (see p. 120). Lift root crops as early as possible. Apply a suitable insecticide to infested soil.
PEACH LEAF CURL	Peaches, nectarines, and ornamental and edible almonds may be attacked by this fungus. Affected leaves pucker and become blistered and swollen, then turn red or purple; as spore layers develop on the surfaces, the leaves turn white.	Erect a plastic shelter over susceptible trees to prevent the air- or waterborne spores from landing (see p. 121). Pick off affected leaves. Spray with a copper fungicide in midwinter, and again two weeks later. Spray again when the leaves fall.

PREVENTING PROBLEMS

Most pest and disease problems can be avoided to a large extent with careful planting, good hygiene, the use of disease-resistant plant cultivars, and good cultivation practices. If problems do occur, immediate action is vital.

ESTABLISHING HEALTHY GARDENS

Strong, healthy plants, are generally less prone to disease and are better able to compensate for damage done by pests or diseases than weak plants. Encouraging natural predators into a garden will also help to keep the pest population under control.

MAKING A GOOD START

● **Positioning plants** Always choose the best site and location for your plants. Plants grown in a spot that suits them and that is properly maintained are unlikely to suffer serious or significant damage if attacked by pests or disease-causing organisms.

● **Spacing plants** Space plants correctly when planting. Crowded plants are prone to disease because of poor air circulation. The buildup of muggy conditions encourages a variety of diseases. Fungal spores and pests can also spread easily if plants are positioned close together.

INSPECTING PLANTS

Removing pests
Pick off pests or diseased leaves regularly. Prompt action should prevent a problem from spreading to healthy parts of a plant. Dispose of pests and diseased leaves carefully.

USING GREENHOUSES

● **Watering** Water seeds, seedlings, young plants, and container plants with tap water. Water taken from barrels often harbors soil or water-borne pathogens that attack and damage these plants.

● **Stakes** Always check that the ends of stakes are completely clean. They can contain soil that harbors fungal spores or pests.

● **Rubbish** Always clear away deteriorating or dead plant material and debris that is lying around the greenhouse; it may be infected.

● **Ventilation** Always provide good ventilation in a greenhouse or cold frame.

CULTIVATING PLANTS

● **Encouraging growth** Always use the correct amount of water and fertilizer (see p. 86) to encourage sturdy, vigorous growth. Certain nutrients, such as potassium, toughen plant growth slightly and improve a plant's resistance to attack by many pathogens.

● **Pruning plants** Pruning is a useful way of limiting certain pests and diseases. Create an open-centered crown or branch structure to reduce humidity and the onset of various diseases. Some pest and disease infestations can be eradicated simply by removing infected stems.

STERILIZING CONTAINERS

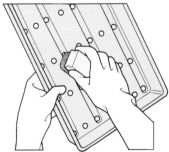

Scrubbing trays and pots
Healthy growth must be encouraged from the beginning. Before sowing seeds, use a stiff scrub brush and very hot water to clean plastic seed trays and pots. As an extra precaution, add a little kitchen disinfectant, soap, or detergent.

TRADITIONAL TIP

Using plastic containers
Use plastic trays and pots for young plants, because they are much easier to clean properly than those made of terracotta or wood. Wooden trays and clay pots are porous, so are likely to harbor pests.

PRACTICING CROP ROTATION

By rotating crops around a number of plots, you can prevent the buildup of many serious pests and pathogens. This traditional method of crop cultivation encourages healthy plants and high yields with relatively little effort. Leave one plot free for permanent crops.

USING MANURE
● **Quality soil** Whenever possible, treat vegetable plots with well-rotted manure. This results in a water- and nutrient-retentive soil that will give your crops the best possible start.

USING LIME
● **Brassicas** It is a good idea to lime the soil if you are growing brassicas, but take care if the next crop is to include potatoes: lime will encourage scab potato.

ROTATING BORDERS
● **Bedding plants** Although rotation is used mainly for vegetable crops, try rotating bedding plants in flower borders from year to year. It can have a beneficial effect.

THREE-YEAR CROP-ROTATION PLAN

Regardless of the size of your plot, you can use a system based on this three-year plan. Divide the area, and your crops, into four groups. Each year, prepare the soil as indicated, and move three of the groups to another plot, ensuring a two-year gap before these crops return to their original sites.

Plot A
Plant cauliflower, brussels sprouts, turnips, rutabagas, cabbage, radishes, kale, Chinese cabbage, broccoli, and other brassicas. Before planting, turn over the soil, and apply lime to raise the soil pH to 6.5–7.0. Incorporate blood, fish, and bone meal or another general fertilizer. Additional feeding during the growing period is beneficial.

Plot B
Plant peas, green beans, runner beans, spinach, lettuce, broad beans, Swiss chard, globe artichokes, and chicory. Two to three weeks before sowing takes place, turn over the soil, and apply blood, fish, and bone meal or another general fertilizer. Maintain a regular watering program to ensure a good set of leguminous crops such as peas and beans.

Plot C
Plant potatoes, carrots, onions, tomatoes, leeks, parsnips, beets, shallots, squash, salsify, celery, scorzonera, eggplant, and Florence fennel. Before planting, double dig the plot, and incorporate well-rotted manure into both levels of ground, adding a small amount of blood, fish, and bone meal or another general fertilizer. Some crops may need additional feeding.

Plot D
Keep a plot free for permanent crops that do not fit in the rotation plan. Leave space for some tender or half-hardy herbs. Plant rosemary, chives, parsley, mint, basil, globe artichokes, Jerusalem artichokes, rhubarb, and asparagus. In a small garden, grow some permanent crops in the flower border, ensuring adequate soil fertility for the crop.

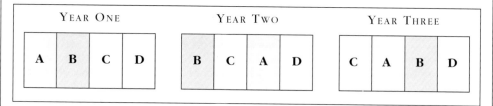

YEAR ONE	YEAR TWO	YEAR THREE
A B C D	B C A D	C A B D

ENCOURAGING USEFUL WILDLIFE

All too often, any small creature that walks, flies, or crawls in a garden is squashed, just in case it could damage the plants. The vast majority of insects, however, are completely harmless to plants. Many are actually beneficial and should be encouraged and protected.

BENEFICIAL GARDEN CREATURES

Many insects – in either their adult or their juvenile stage, or sometimes both – are active predators. They help to reduce the number of plant pests by eating them. In some cases, this may mean pesticides are unnecessary.

Centipede
Centipedes feed on many different soil pests. Do not confuse them with harmful millipedes.

Ladybug
Both the adult beetles and their larvae feed on pests, aphids in particular.

Lacewing
Lacewings lay their eggs on leaves. When they hatch, the larvae eat vast quantities of aphids.

Garden spider
Spiders feed on a range of insects, including many pests, which they ensnare or catch.

Hoverfly
Hoverflies and their larvae, which look like caterpillars, feed on aphids. The flies also pollinate flowers.

ENCOURAGING ALLIES
● **Garden allies** There are many beneficial garden creatures. These include assassin bugs, frogs, toads, snakes, bees, earthworms, ground beetles, praying mantises, many birds, parasitic wasps and ants.
● **Providing shelter** Although you should aim to have a clean, tidy garden to prevent as many pest and disease outbreaks as possible, try to leave a few dead leaves and stems as shelter for beneficial garden creatures.
● **Using chemicals** Use chemical sprays (see p. 117) only if they are absolutely necessary. Select the spray carefully, and choose one that is as specific as possible in order to reduce the risk to harmless insects.

ATTRACTING BIRDS

Some birds can cause damage to gardens, but this can be kept to a minimum by using nets or other barriers (see p. 113). Many birds are useful predators of garden pests, such as slugs, caterpillars, and aphids, and should be actively attracted into the garden.

FEEDING BIRDS
● **Providing food** Hang suitable food directly from tree branches. Nuts and fat will help to keep many bird species alive during a cold winter. Do not feed them with spicy or salty food.
● **Providing water** Always make sure that garden birds have a source of water so that they can drink and bathe throughout the year. Replace water regularly in winter so that it does not freeze.
● **Lurking cats** Make sure you place bird food and water out of the reach of lurking cats.

SUPPLYING FEEDERS

Using a bird feeder
Erect a bird feeder so that you can supply suitable food in a safe place. Use it to hang suet, peanut feeders and halved coconuts.

TENDING CLIMBERS

Protecting birds
Climbers are ideal nesting sites. Remember this when cutting back climbers, and try to avoid pruning during the nesting season.

CREATING A WILDLIFE POND

A pond never fails to add interest to a garden, but if constructed to encourage and attract wildlife it can be a special feature all year long. Birds, toads, frogs, and a wide range of other small animals and beneficial insects will visit to feed and drink.

ATTRACTING WILDLIFE TO A POND

Shallow, sloping sides allow animals to leave easily

Deep water provides safe hiding and overwintering sites

Plants around pond edge provide shelter, hiding, and mating places

Marginal plants provide sites for creatures that prefer moist environments

Floating plants create shade and help to prevent water from becoming too warm

Stones and rocks provide spots for sunbathing and drinking

The ideal wildlife pond
A well-constructed wildlife pond is beautiful to look at and can include a wide range of native plants. It provides food, water, and an attractive environment for a vast array of animals throughout the year.

PLANTING TO ATTRACT INSECTS

Insects not only add interest to a garden, but many species also help to keep down pest populations and pollinate flowers. Any garden will attract some insects, but – to make sure you encourage the ones you want – provide as varied a collection of plant life as possible.

ATTRACTING INSECTS

Growing varieties
Grow a wide range of plants to create food sources for insects. *Helianthus, Nicotiana, Stachys, Gazania*, and fennel – and others with open, daisylike blooms - are particularly useful.

PLANTING FOR INSECTS
● **Single flowers** Always try to include some single-flowered varieties in your planting. These plants are far more attractive to bees and other pollinating insects than double-flowered plants.
● **Weeds** Include a rough area to accommodate a few weeds. These provide a useful source of insects early in the year, which will attract many predatory insects. Cut back the weeds in midspring so that the predators move on to other plants, where they will help to control pests.

SUITABLE PLANTS

Include as wide a variety of plants as possible in your garden. Daisylike flowers are particularly accessible and attractive to insects.

Alyssum, Anchusa azurea, Anemone x *hybrida, Arabis, Campanula, Erigeron, Eryngium* spp., *Geranium* spp., *Geum* spp., *Gypsophila paniculata, Liatris spicata, Papaver* spp., *Polemonium caeruleum, Rudbeckia, Salvia* x *superba, Scabiosa* spp., *Veronica longifolia.*

GROWING COMPANION PLANTS

Companion planting involves growing a combination of plants that benefit one or more of the plants in the particular area. Not all gardeners believe in companion planting, and attempts to prove its success are often inconclusive. It is, however, worth a try.

GROWING CROPS

● **Onions and carrots** Plant a combination of onions and carrots to minimize attacks by both onion flies and carrot rust flies. For best results, plant four rows of onions for every row of carrots.

● **Cabbage and beans** To reduce the number of cabbage aphids and cabbage root flies, plant one row of a compact form of cabbage with one row of dwarf beans.

● **Marigolds and cabbage** Try planting French marigolds between rows of cabbage plants. The marigolds may help to deter attacks from cabbage whiteflies.

● **Mixing crops** Avoid planting a large area with a single crop. This acts like an advertising sign, and it will attract plenty of hungry pests.

GREEN TIP

Planting marigolds
Marigolds are thought to attract hoverflies, control pests, and deter whitefly and nematodes. Whether they do all of this or not is debatable, but it is worth experimenting. Plant them with crops such as tomatoes, either in a growbag or in open ground.

PLANTING PEPPERS

● **Peppers** These plants are prone to aphids. Grow them with basil, which seems to grow well with peppers, and okra. All these plants need warmth and shelter.

Deterring fungi
Try planting *Capsicum* peppers among plants that are prone to *Fusarium* foot or root rots or wilts. The secretion from the peppers' roots is believed to deter attack from these fungi.

PROTECTING POTATOES

● **Companion plants** *Tagetes* (marigolds), *Lamium,* savory, and nasturtiums may all help to protect potatoes from pests. Peas are also thought to be beneficial when grown with potatoes.

● **Nematodes** Try growing French marigolds in soil that is infested with nematodes which attack potatoes in particular. The secretion from the marigold roots is said to kill these destructive pests.

GROWING ZUCCHINI

● **Mutual benefit** Try growing zucchini with peas, beans, and corn. The legumes turn the nitrogen in the soil into a usable form, the zucchini shades the soil, and the corn provides support.

HELPING ROSES

● **Roses** To prevent roses from being attacked by aphids, try planting them with alliums and catmint. Parsley, thyme, and *Limnanthes douglasii* may also be beneficial to roses.

Combining plants
There is some evidence that foxgloves, rhododendrons, and azaleas thrive when grown together. Foxgloves help to keep the shrubs healthy and seem to grow particularly well themselves.

DISGUISING CROPS

● **Visibility** Large areas of a crop are easily visible to pests. Grow small areas, and disguise the crop by interplanting with unrelated vegetables.

Hiding vegetables
Grow ornamental plants and vegetables together. This makes the crop less obvious to those pests that see their host plants instead of smelling them.

CONTROLLING ANIMALS

MANY ANIMALS ARE LIKELY to come into a garden, including birds and other wildlife, as well as domestic animals such as cats and dogs. These are often harmless but may need to be deterred if they cause any damage.

CONTROLLING BIRDS

Most birds are welcomed by gardeners, but some, such as finches, eat fruit tree buds and the buds of ornamental shrubs and trees during late autumn and winter. Others, such as blackbirds and thrushes, eat ripening fruits, while starlings may pull up seedlings.

PROTECTING SQUASH

Using panty hose
Use an old pair of panty hose to protect ripening squash from birds and other pests. Pull a leg section over each squash, and tie at each end.

MAKING A SNAKE

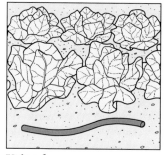

Using hose
Use an old hose to deter large pests such as birds and cats. Lay it in a bed, and bend the hose in a couple of places so that it resembles a snake.

DETERRING BIRDS
● **Humming tape** Keep birds away from crops by using thin strips of commercial buzzing or humming tape stretched between posts. As the wind blows, the vibrating tape produces a sound that deters many birds. The tape from the inside of a broken music cassette is a useful alternative.
● **Netting** Drape netting over crops, but check regularly to ensure that no birds or other animals are trapped in it.
● **Fake cats** Make cutout cats, using marbles for eyes. Hang these in vegetable plots.

CONTROLLING MOLES

Moles create unsightly mounds of loose soil in flower beds and on lawns. Their underground activity loosens the soil. This can cause plants to suffer from drought stress, because their roots can absorb water only from firm soil.

USING SMELLS
● **Smoke** Consider using commercial mole smokes that are placed inside, or at the entrance to, a mole tunnel. Although these are often effective, the mole may return once the smoke has dispersed.
● **Strong smells** Put household items such as strong-smelling scents, mothballs, and orange peels inside a mole tunnel.
● **Plant smells** Try planting caper spurge, (*Euphorbia lathyrus*) the smell of which seems to be intensely disliked by moles.

MAKING VIBRATIONS

Planting bottles
Dig several holes, and push an empty bottle into each one. As the wind blows across the top of each bottle, it will produce a noise that drives away moles.

CREATING SOUNDS
● **Windmills** Push plastic toy windmills into the ground at regular intervals. The noise they make as they spin in the wind can often deter any nearby moles.
● **Using ultrasound** Try using electronic devices that emit ultrasonic waves. These seem to work in some cases.

USING PROFESSIONALS
● **Last resort** If all else fails, employ the services of a reputable exterminator to deal with the problem for you.

CONTROLLING RABBITS AND MICE

Both rabbits and mice can cause considerable damage in gardens and greenhouses. Rabbits particularly enjoy vegetables, fruit, and tender young shoot growth, while mice are particularly fond of fruit, vegetables, and seeds – especially when other food is in short supply.

PROTECTING CROPS AND TREES FROM RABBITS

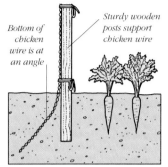

Bottom of chicken wire is at an angle

Sturdy wooden posts support chicken wire

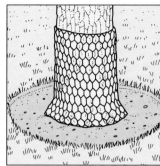

Making a rabbit fence
Make a rabbit-proof barrier with galvanized chicken wire that is at least 3 ft (90 cm) high. Bury about 1 ft (30 cm) below the soil. Angle the bottom 6 in (15 cm) outward so that rabbits cannot tunnel underneath it.

Making a tree guard
Rabbits may gnaw at tree bark, particularly on young trees. To prevent this, wrap a collar of chicken wire around a trunk. Check the wire at least once a year to make sure that it is not restricting trunk expansion.

CURBING MICE
● **Conventional traps** Use mousetraps in greenhouses, plastic tunnels, and cloches if mice are a serious problem. This is also the most effective way of controlling mice that are raiding seeds stored inside a shed or garage.
● **Humane traps** These trap mice, but do not kill them, which means that you can dispose of the mice humanely. If released several miles from your garden, they are unlikely to trouble you again.
● **Feline solution** If you do not mind dead mice being brought into the house from time to time, a cat may help to control this pest.

CONTROLLING CATS AND DOGS

Domestic animals can prove to be some of the worst pests in the garden. If at all possible, try to deter them from going into the garden in the first place. If this fails, there are a number of solutions to some of the problems that cats and dogs can cause.

DETERRING CATS

Lay bottle on ground among plants

Positioning bottles
Cats seem to strongly dislike the reflections from clear plastic bottles half-filled with water. To keep cats away from areas that they use as a litter box, place these bottles among plants. This can look unsightly but may force cats to look for another litter area.

USING OTHER METHODS
● **Moist soil** Keep soil moist to deter cats. Water regularly, and use a moisture-retentive mulch whenever possible.
● **Chicken wire** Buried chicken wire may prevent a cat from digging up soil where seeds have been recently sown. Lay the wire on the ground surface, and cover it lightly with soil.
● **Buried prickles** Buried prickly stems, such as holly, are often enough to deter a cat as soon as it begins to scratch up the soil.
● **Electronic devices** Use these to deter cats and dogs; they emit a high-frequency sound that humans cannot hear, but cats and dogs dislike it.

BRIGHT IDEA

Keeping dogs out
Stop a neighbor's dog from crawling under or through a fence into your garden by planting a prickly hedge. Shrubs such as *Pyracantha* work well. Plant them so that they will grow to form an impenetrable barrier.

USING PEST CONTROLS

WHENEVER GARDEN PESTS ARE A PROBLEM, there is usually a cultural or chemical remedy. In many cases, it is a combination of the two methods that proves to be the most effective solution in the long run.

BIOLOGICAL CONTROLS

The use of biological controls has become increasingly popular over recent years, and the range of predators and parasites available to gardeners has increased dramatically. Many biological controls are most effective when used in a greenhouse or conservatory.

IN THE GARDEN

● **Helping out** Try to remove some pests by hand to help predators or parasites. Be sure to leave enough pests so that the population of the biological control agent can build up sufficiently.
● **Chemicals** Before using chemicals to control pests, check that they will not harm any biological control agents.
● **Caterpillars** Use a biological control for caterpillars. Mix *Bacillus thuringiensis* with water, and spray it on caterpillar-infested plants. Eating the sprayed foliage poisons the pests.

CONTROLLING SLUGS AND VINE WEEVILS

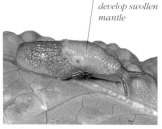

Infected slugs develop swollen mantle

Infecting slugs
Use a nematode parasite to control slugs. Infected slugs develop a swollen mantle, stop feeding, and die within a few days. The soil must be moist and warm for this to work.

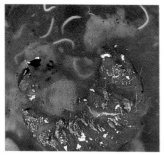

Eliminating vine weevils
Control vine weevil grubs with nematodes, tiny, white worms that kill and then feed on the remains of the grub's body. This method is most effective on plants grown in containers.

GREENHOUSE CONTROLS

Biological controls are generally most successful in the controlled environment of a greenhouse or conservatory. Make sure that you introduce enough predators or parasites to deal with the pests.

Parasites are supplied as eggs inside a plastic tube

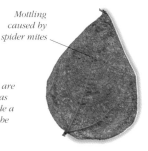

Mottling caused by spider mites

Controlling whiteflies
Use the wasp *Encarsia formosa*, which parasitizes young whiteflies. A wasp develops inside the whitefly, then kills it.

Controlling spider mite
The predatory mite *Phytoseiulus persimilis* moves rapidly and eats all stages of the spider mite, including the eggs.

IN THE GREENHOUSE

● **Suitable pests** Try using biological controls for aphids, slugs, vine weevils, thrips, caterpillars, mealybugs, and scale insects.
● **Temperature** Always make sure that the temperature in a greenhouse is suitable before introducing biological controls.
● **Timing** Introduce biological controls when pests are present, but do not wait until the infestation is too heavy; the biological controls may not be able to multiply rapidly enough to keep up.
● **Ventilation** Ventilate a greenhouse when necessary. Predators and parasites will not escape – they usually stay where the pest population is.

ORGANIC CONTROLS

Organic controls are derived mostly from plants. Although they can be effective, the range of problems they control is limited, and none are systemic (carried to the roots). Many organic remedies are not selective and kill a variety of insects, including beneficial ones.

USING DERRIS
● **Uses** Derris is derived from *Derris* and *Lonchocarpus* roots. It controls flea beetles, thrips, caterpillars, raspberry beetles, sawflies, and spider mites.

Applying powder
For effective control, apply derris powder regularly and thoroughly, following the manufacturer's instructions. Derris is not selective, so target only the pests you wish to control.

USING PYRETHRUM
● **Uses** Pyrethrum is derived from the flowers of *Chrysanthemum cinerariifolium*. Use it to treat caterpillars, whiteflies, ants, and aphids.

Spraying liquid
Pyrethrum is a nonselective but quick-acting pesticide, so aim at target pests only. Spray leaves on both surfaces to ensure that most of the pests are killed. Pyrethrum is harmless to mammals.

APPLYING CONTROLS
● **Nonpersistent controls** Many organic treatments remain active for no more than a day, so you may therefore need to apply them more frequently than their chemical counterparts.
● **Spraying** Always use a good-quality sprayer to apply a control, and be sure to wash it out thoroughly between applications. Never keep leftover solution for future use.
● **Protecting bees** Never allow spray to drift onto open flowers, especially blossoms, or you may harm visiting bees.
● **Harvesting crops** It is usually safe to eat most crop plants fairly soon after an organic control has been applied, but always check the product label carefully for preparation details.

GREEN TIP

Making a barrier
To lay their eggs, vine weevils must crawl or climb to their destination, since they cannot fly. To prevent weevils from laying eggs in soil mix, apply a circle of nonsetting glue around pots. Remove any debris that accumulates on the glue.

USING OTHER ORGANIC CONTROLS

There are several different types of organic treatment available to gardeners, but availability may change, since, like chemical controls, they are constantly subject to legislation. Because some organic treatments are not selective, find out all you can about each one to determine which products are suitable for your purposes.

● **Insecticidal soaps** Use these for effective control of aphids, spider mites, thrips, leafhoppers, scale insects, mealybugs, and whiteflies. Insecticidal soaps are made from fatty acids produced by animal or plant sources. The soaps are not selective in their action, however, and last only approximately one day.

● **Copper-based sprays** Copper-based fungicides are suitable for use on edible crops. They control a range of plant diseases, including potato blights, celery leaf spot, apple canker, bacterial canker, and leaf spots on fruits.
● **Sulfur** Use sulfur to control diseases such as storage rots and powdery mildew on ornamental plants and fruits.

SAFETY TIPS
● **Storage** Keep all organic concentrates out of reach of children and pets.
● **Checking the label** Read the manufacturer's instructions, and follow them very carefully.
● **When to use** Spray on a calm day, in the evening.

CHEMICAL CONTROLS

There are many different chemicals available to gardeners for use against a large number of pests and diseases on a wide range of plants. Provided that they are used safely, carefully, and never indiscriminately, chemical controls are a useful aid to trouble-free gardening.

USING CHEMICAL CONTROLS SAFELY

- **Combining methods** Use chemicals only if they are absolutely necessary. Whenever possible, combine chemical controls with cultivation methods.
- **Accurate choice** Choose the chemical that is most appropriate for a particular problem, and follow the instructions carefully. Not all products are suitable for every type of plant.
- **Checking the label** Always observe the stated precautions and restrictions.
- **Protecting hands** Always use gloves when handling or mixing chemical concentrates.

- **Avoiding contamination** Never eat, drink, or smoke when working with pesticides. Always wash your hands thoroughly after using them.
- **Using chemicals safely** Avoid contact with the skin, and wash off any splashes immediately. Do not inhale any dusts or sprays.
- **Treated areas** Keep children and animals away from the area being treated. Most chemicals are considered safe once the foliage in the treated area is dry.
- **Conditions for use** Do not spray or treat with pesticides on windy, gusty, or very hot days.

- **Bee protection** If possible, spray at dusk to minimize risk to pollinating insects, such as bees.
- **Containers** After use, always thoroughly wash out containers used to apply chemicals.
- **Labelling items clearly** Always label every piece of equipment used for applying pesticides. Never pour chemicals into other containers.
- **Storage** Store pesticides in their original containers, and make sure they are tightly closed. Keep all pesticides in a safe place well out of the reach of animals and children.

AVOIDING DAMAGE

- **Following instructions** All pesticides carry detailed instructions. Always apply the product at the precise rate and frequency stated. If used incorrectly, pesticides can damage both the plant and the environment.

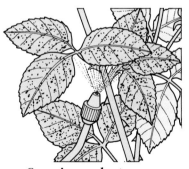

Covering a plant
Many pests and diseases, such as rose rust, lurk on the undersides of leaves. To ensure efficient coverage and control of the pest or pathogen, use a curved nozzle so that you can spray the undersides of the leaves as well as the upper surfaces.

APPLYING CHEMICALS

- **Suitability** If you are uncertain about whether a particular chemical will cause an adverse reaction in a plant, test it first on a small area before treating the whole plant.
- **Size of spray** Choose a fine-droplet spray for controlling insects, since they are most likely to be killed by small droplets. Large droplets are more suitable for weed control.
- **Ready-mixed chemicals** If you have only a minor problem or a small garden, buy ready-to-use commercial pesticides and fungicides in a spray bottle.
- **Minimizing stress** Do not apply chemicals to young plants or plants under stress; these can be easily damaged.
- **Shiny leaves** If you need to treat a plant that has shiny leaves, choose a product that contains a wetting agent. Without this, the chemicals will not adhere to the leaf surfaces and will not be effective.

DISCARDING CHEMICALS

- **Leftover solution** Always dispose of old left-over chemicals. Apply any excess to a suitable plant, or dispose of it properly. Never pour unwanted chemicals down the toilet or sink, or into bodies of water.

RESISTANCE TO CHEMICALS

More and more pests and pathogens are becoming resistant to chemicals – spider mite and greenhouse whitefly, for example. Some thrips and aphids are also now resistant to common pesticides.

- **Changing products** Reduce the likelihood of resistance by using pesticides only when really necessary, and by changing the product from time to time. Some fungi are resistant to specific fungicides. Choose an alternative product.

CONTROLLING SPECIFIC PROBLEMS

ALTHOUGH PESTS AND DISEASES CAN BE CONTROLLED by currently available pesticides, some are often most easily kept at bay by cultivation or organic methods. You can use these as an alternative to, or in conjunction with, pesticides.

SLUGS, SNAILS, AND EARWIGS

Slugs and snails can strip plants of their leaves. They feed mostly at night and in wet weather, attacking seedlings, annuals, shrubs, herbaceous perennials, climbers, bulbs, vegetables, and fruits. Earwigs are particularly fond of chrysanthemum, dahlia, and clematis leaves and petals.

SLUGS AND SNAILS

Making a barrier
Slugs and snails dislike crawling over rough surfaces. Use this to your advantage: Create a barrier around susceptible plants with coarsely crushed eggshells.

EARWIGS

Creating a hiding place
Make a shelter in which earwigs will collect by using rolled-up, corrugated cardboard. Tie a roll onto a stake near earwig-prone plants. Crush the earwigs.

METHODS OF CONTROL
- **Snail search** Hunt for slugs and snails after rain, and with a flashlight at night. Collect and dispose of the pests.
- **Beer traps** Pour a little beer into a small container, and sink it so that the edge protrudes just above the soil. Slugs and snails will drink the beer, fall in, and drown – but, unfortunately, so will other species that are not pests.
- **Flower pot traps** Trap earwigs by placing an inverted flower pot filled with hay on a stake near susceptible plants.

FLEA BEETLES

Although small, these black, metallic blue, or striped jumping beetles are capable of causing a lot of damage, since they can make hundreds of small holes in plant leaves. Young plants are particularly prone to attack and are likely to be seriously damaged or killed.

METHODS OF CONTROL
- **Sticky card** Try using a yellow card coated with non-setting glue for catching flea beetles. These and other flying or jumping pests are attracted by the color yellow and will fly or jump onto the card.
- **Clearing debris** Flea beetle grubs may cause slight damage by nibbling on roots of seedlings. Clear away plant debris to remove the grubs' usual overwintering sites.
- **Using chemicals** If an infestation is severe, dust the soil surface, as well as plant leaves, with an insecticide.

TRAPPING FLEA BEETLES ON INFECTED PLANTS

1 Coat the surface of a piece of board measuring about 6 x 3 in (15 x 7.5 cm) with heavy grease or nonsetting glue. Take care not to disturb the foliage of infected plants.

2 Run the sticky side of the board over the plants, about 1–2 in (2.5–5 cm) above them. Many of the flea beetles will jump or fly up and stick to the grease or glue.

CABBAGE ROOT FLIES AND CODLING MOTHS

These pests are not related to one another, but the damage that both cause can be limited by anticipating and interrupting their reproductive cycles, and by setting traps. Cabbage root flies devastate brassica crops, while codling moths lay their eggs on apples.

CABBAGE ROOT FLIES

Surrounding stems
To prevent female cabbage root flies from laying eggs close to host plants, cut out circles of carpet padding, felt, or cardboard. Make slits in the circles, and place the circles around the base of young brassica plants.

CODLING MOTHS

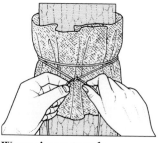

Wrapping a trunk
Scrape off loose bark on an apple-tree trunk in midsummer, and wrap a small area of each trunk in burlap. As the moth caterpillars crawl up the trunk to pupate, they will hide in the burlap; remove and discard it.

METHODS OF CONTROL

● **Moth traps** In late spring, try hanging pheromone traps in apple trees. These triangular, plastic boxes contain sticky paper, and in the middle of each is a capsule containing pheromone, which a female moth excretes to attract a mate. The male moths are attracted by the smell and become trapped on the sticky paper. The female's eggs remain unfertilized.
● **Last resort** If all else fails, protect transplanted cabbages and seedlings with a suitable contact insecticide, or start over again and replant.

CARROT RUST FLIES AND POLLEN BEETLES

Carrot rust flies can kill young carrots and other susceptible crops, including parsley, celery, and parsnips. Although pollen beetles do not cause much direct damage, they are present in large numbers on flowers and can be very irritating when cut flowers are brought indoors.

CARROT RUST FLIES
● **Resistant plants** Select relatively resistant carrot cultivars to grow. Contact a local vegetable expert for specific cultivars.

Obstructing flies
Protect young carrot plants by making a plastic barrier 24 in (60 cm) high. The carrot rust fly is a low-flying pest and will not be able to reach the crop.

METHODS OF CONTROL
● **Timing** To avoid much of the damage caused by carrot rust flies, sow carrots after late spring, or harvest the crop before midsummer.
● **Killing larvae** When sowing carrot seed, treat the row with a soil insecticide to kill off any fly larvae in the soil that have not yet hatched.
● **Avoiding smells** Avoid bruising the carrot crop, or excessive thinning, since the smell of carrots attracts carrot rust flies. Use pelleted carrot seed, which is easier to sow thinly and reduces or eliminates the need for thinning the crop.
● **Row cover** Lay row covers over carrot crops. Make sure that there are no gaps through which the flies can enter.

BRIGHT IDEA

Removing pollen beetles
Shake any cut flowers infested with pollen beetles, and leave them overnight in a dark shed or garage with a single light source. Most of the beetles will fly toward the light, leaving the flowers beetle-free.

WIREWORMS

Wireworms are the larvae of click beetles. Although they are common, especially in recently cultivated soil, wireworms are mainly a vegetable pest. They bore into potato tubers and other root crops, and sometimes attack perennials, annuals, and bulbs as well.

METHODS OF CONTROL

- **Exposing pests** If you are developing a new garden or plot that was previously grass, turn the soil over regularly. This will expose both the eggs and hatched wireworms to predators.
- **Planting wheat** In the first year or two of cultivating new ground, try growing a row of wheat between crops. The wireworms will be attracted to the wheat, which you can then dig up and discard.
- **Chemical control** As a last resort, use insecticide as an effective wireworm control.

MAKING WIREWORM TRAPS

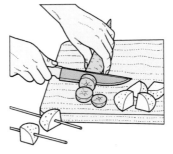

1 Make wireworm traps by cutting unwanted potatoes and carrots into chunks. Spear each piece with a wooden skewer, which will act as a marker for each trap.

2 Bury the chunks among crops to entice the wireworms away from the vegetables. When the traps are infested, remove them, and dispose of the wireworms.

CLUBROOT

Clubroot is a vegetable grower's nightmare. The fungus attacks several members of the cabbage family. It can also infect stocks and wallflowers. The symptoms of this disease are distortion and swelling of the roots, and affected plants fail to develop properly, if at all.

AVOIDING CLUBROOT INFECTION

- **Growing from seed** Raise your plants from seed. Clubroot is often introduced into gardens via soil adhering to roots of infested plants.

- **Strong roots** Help your plants to resist attack by establishing strong roots before planting out. This can work for kale, cabbage, and brussels sprouts.

1 Check seed catalogs, and choose disease-resistant cultivars whenever possible. Sow the seed in a tray. When the seedlings are about 1½ in (4 cm) tall, transfer each one to a pot that is at least 2 in (5 cm) in diameter.

2 Water the pots regularly, and grow the plants for about six weeks, until the roots fill the pot. Plant them in open ground, and water well. The plants should be strong and healthy enough to cope with any club root.

METHODS OF CONTROL

- **Adding lime** The slime mold responsible for clubroot thrives in heavy, acidic soils. Improve drainage and add lime to decrease the mold's chances of thriving.
- **Limiting spread** Do not move soil from areas infected with clubroot to other areas. Clean all tools and boots thoroughly after use.
- **Regular weeding** Keep the vegetable plot free of weeds, which can harbor infection.
- **Checking roots** Inspect the roots of all vulnerable plants very carefully before planting out. Discard any vegetables with roots that appear to be swollen or distorted.
- **Disposing of plants** Do not compost infected plants. Dispose of them, with the household trash.

PEACH LEAF CURL AND BLACKSPOT

Peach leaf curl is caused by a fungus that attacks ornamental and edible nectarines, peaches, and almonds. An unrelated fungus causes rose blackspot, and affects only roses. These leaf infections cause leaves to fall early from a plant, progressively weakening it.

PEACH LEAF CURL

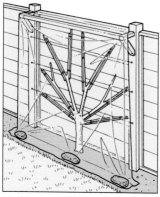

Making a shelter
The fungal spores of peach leaf curl are carried in rain and on air currents. Protect plants by erecting an open-sided shelter with narrow strips of wood and clear plastic. Put in place by late winter, and remove in midspring.

BLACKSPOT

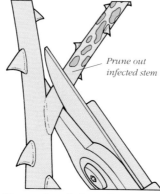

Prune out infected stem

Removing infected stems
Blackspot fungus is able to overwinter on fallen leaves and rose stems. When pruning in early spring, cut out any stems bearing the tiny, purple-black lesions that are typical of this disfiguring fungal disease.

METHODS OF CONTROL
● **Using fungicide** Spray trees infected by peach leaf curl with a copper-based fungicide such as Bordeaux mixture; apply in midwinter and again two weeks later. This mixture will kill the majority of the overwintering spores and will protect the new leaves as they open in spring.
● **Early treatment** Straight after pruning roses in spring, spray the whole of each plant with a suitable fungicide.
● **Fallen leaves** Rake up and dispose of fallen leaves infected with black spot; the fungus may overwinter on them. Do not add them to the compost pile or leave them lying around the garden. Discarding them is the safest option.

LAWN PROBLEMS

A lawn may occasionally suffer from unsightly brown or yellow patches, which can be caused by drought, fungal diseases, or pests. Sometimes a lawn is disfigured by heaps of fine soil – molehills. Dealing with moles can be difficult, but there are remedies (see p. 113).

CONTROLLING PROBLEMS
● **Lawn maintenance** Follow a regular schedule of lawn maintenance (see p. 128–129). A well-fed and properly watered lawn – which is also aerated, spiked, and scarified – will be less vulnerable to pests, diseases, and weeds.
● **Late feeding** Do not feed a lawn with a high-nitrogen fertilizer very late in the year, since this will encourage the development of *Fusarium* patch (snow mold).
● **Nitrogen deficiency** Feed a lawn throughout the season to avoid nitrogen deficiency, which can lead to the onset of red thread disease.

REMOVING TOADSTOOLS

Sweeping toadstools
Most lawn toadstools are short-lived and have little detrimental effect. Use a stiff broom to break the fungi before the caps open to release their spores. Collect and dispose of the fungi.

ANIMAL URINE

Large brown patches on a lawn may be caused by dog, fox, or cat urine. Prompt action can alleviate the problem considerably. If you catch an animal in the act, wash down the area immediately with plenty of water. This will noticeably reduce the scorching effect on the grass. If you reseed an area, make sure you remove all the urine-soaked soil first; otherwise, the grass seed will not germinate. Prevent animals from urinating on small areas of lawn by using plastic netting.

LAWNS

A GREEN, GRASSY CARPET *can be the perfect setting and foil for the colors of an ornamental garden. If a lawn is seeded or sodded properly, maintaining it will not be difficult. Regular mowing and watering are required in the summer, but other routine tasks need to be done only occasionally.*

SELECTING THE RIGHT SURFACE

Choosing the right type of lawn is essential to its future success. Standard lawn grass mixtures (see below) are not always ideal in certain situations. There are grasses to meet all kinds of needs, so take the time to research the various possibilities, and choose carefully.

LAWN ALTERNATIVES
● **Moist areas** *Cotula squalida* has soft, fernlike, bronzy green foliage and forms a closely knit carpet. It prefers a moist site and light shade, although it will tolerate direct sun. Moneywort *(Lysimachia nummularia)* also thrives in moist areas.
● **Sunny banks** *Acaena novae-zelandiae* is a semievergreen subshrub that forms a dense, 1–2 in (2.5–5 cm) carpet of soft, feathery foliage. It is especially useful where mowing is difficult. *Dichondra repens* is another good choice, as are many junipers and *Sedum*.

CREATING A NONGRASS LAWN

Chamomile lawn
Chamomile makes a good alternative to grass, but it requires weeding by hand. The fine leaves are strongly aromatic when crushed underfoot. Chamomile grows best in an open, sunny site.

Thyme lawn
Thyme has tiny, dark green, aromatic foliage and produces purple-pink flowers in summer. It is best suited to a well-drained, sunny site and works well on uneven or stony ground.

CHOOSING A SEED TYPE

Use a standard seed mixture for most situations, except those mentioned below. You can buy mixtures that grow rapidly or that do not need much mowing because they grow slowly.

● **Family lawns** Mixtures with a high proportion of rye grasses are best for play areas.

● **Shady sites** Choose a special shady lawn seed mixture for growing under trees, or if your yard is not very sunny.
● **Fine lawns** To create a formal, high-quality lawn with even color and texture, choose a special seed mixture that contains a high proportion of fine-leaved bent and fescue grasses.

THE PROPOSED SITE
● **Measuring** Always measure the area to be sown before buying grass seed, and remember to subtract areas such as island beds and paths.
● **Eradicating weeds** Eliminate perennial weeds that have deep taproots or underground rhizomes before sowing seed. Spray the weeds with a suitable weedkiller (see p. 124).

LAWN EQUIPMENT

The equipment you need to maintain your lawn depends on both its size and your budget. Most of the necessary items are readily available.

● **Cutting and trimming** Lawn mowers are essential items for cutting. The most common are rotary and reel types. A rotary mower is always powered, and performs well on long, uneven grass. A reel mower may be manual or powered, and gives a neat cut on a good-quality lawn. A half-moon edger is useful for neatening edges and for cutting and shaping sod. Long-handled edging shears allow you to neaten the edges of an established lawn quickly and easily, and without danger of straining your back.

● **Maintenance** A garden fork can be used to prepare the ground before a lawn is seeded or sodded. A fork also comes in handy for aerating small, compacted areas in autumn. A spring-tined rake is useful for raking up leaves and small twigs. It is also ideal for removing moss once it has been killed, and for raking an established lawn to remove dead grass, leaves, small twigs, and other debris.

● **Sowing seed** Small items such as stakes, string, and plastic are useful for helping to shape your lawn.

● **Watering** Unless you have a tiny yard, a garden hose is essential. An oscillating sprinkler, which delivers water evenly over a rectangular area, or a rotating sprinkler, which covers a circular area, makes watering your lawn an almost effortless task.

WARNING!
To be safe, install a circuit breaker if you are using electrical tools in the yard. Do not use electric mowers on wet grass.

Rotating sprinkler

Oscillating sprinkler

Garden hose

Spring-tined rake

Long-handled edging shears

Half-moon edger

Garden fork

Stake

Plastic

String

Powered reel lawn mower

Powered rotary lawn mower

CREATING A LAWN

Whether you decide to seed a lawn or lay sod, creating a lawn does not take too long. It is the preparation that consumes the most time and is the most important factor contributing to the ultimate success of your lawn.

SEEDING A LAWN

Sowing seed may not produce the instant results that you can achieve with sod, but it is much more economical. Unless you have access to a wide range of sod types, sowing seed also allows you the greatest choice. Select the most appropriate seed mixture for your yard.

STRAIGHT EDGES

Using a plastic sheet
Lay down a piece of heavy-duty plastic, and use the edge to make a straight line. Sow the grass seed over the area. The ground under the plastic sheet will remain unseeded.

SMOOTH CURVES

Using stakes and string
Mark a curve using two stakes and some string. Tie the string to one stake, and drive this into the ground. Tie another stake to the free end of the string, pull it taut, and draw a curve into the soil.

AVOIDING PROBLEMS
● **Weeds** Kill off all old grass and weeds before you start to sow any seed. Choose a non-selective weedkiller such as glyphosate. This is inactivated upon contact with the soil, so once the weeds are dead, you can start to work safely.
● **Sowing thinly** Sowing grass seed very sparsely adds work in the long run. Thin grass is readily invaded by weedy grasses, broadleaved weeds, and moss.
● **Sowing densely** This can lead to problems, since the poor air circulation caused by dense sowing encourages a variety of fungal diseases.

SOWING GRASS SEED
● **Before sowing** Thorough preparation is essential. Remove all large stones and other debris. Then apply a complete or balanced fertilizer to the whole area to encourage strong, healthy growth.
● **Using a mask** Grass seed can be very dusty. To avoid breathing this dust, wear a dust mask when sowing the seed.
● **Where to start** Start sowing at the far end of the designated area so that you do not need to walk on the newly sown seed.
● **Raking** After sowing, lightly rake a thin layer of soil over the seed. This improves germination and helps to protect the seed from birds.

BRIGHT IDEA

Keeping birds off
To protect a small, newly sown area from birds, push stakes into the ground, and put flower pots on top of them. Drape lightweight fruit netting over these, and weigh the edges down with stones.

SEED DISTRIBUTION

To help you distribute grass seed evenly, use a plastic flower pot with several holes in the bottom as a shaker. Once you know how much area a pot full of grass seed covers, this method will help you sow at a consistent rate.

LAYING SOD

Making a lawn from sod can be one of the most instantly gratifying garden jobs. Once you have prepared the site, the next step is easy, and the results are immediate. Always buy good-quality sod from a reputable supplier; cheap sod may be infested with weeds, pests, and diseases.

STORING SOD
● **Rolls** Sod is often delivered in rolls. Order it for delivery on the day you need it; sod should not be left rolled up for more than a day or two.

Unrolling sod
If you cannot use the sod right away, you must unroll it. If you do not, the grass will deteriorate rapidly. Once the sod is unrolled, water it, and keep it moist until you are ready to lay it.

GOOD LAYING PRACTICE
● **Best time** Sod can be laid most of the year, but late summer, early autumn, or early spring are the best times. Avoid very wet, dry, or cold weather.

Staggering rows
Lay the first row alongside a straight edge. To lay the next row, kneel on a board to protect the sod. Stagger the seams to give an even finish, and brush top-dressing into any gaps.

TRADITIONAL TIP

Boxing sod
If you are using sod lifted from another area of your yard, it may be uneven. To trim these pieces so they are the same depth, place each piece upside down in a box of the correct depth, then scrape off excess soil with any suitable sharp implement. Re-lay the sod as soon as possible.

SHAPING SOD

The edges of a newly laid lawn are formed by the ends of the sod pieces, which will need to be shaped. It is easier to do this after laying the sod than beforehand. The same technique can be used for reshaping the lawn once it is established.

DEALING WITH EDGES
● **Sharp spade** Use a sharp spade to shape sod if you do not have a half-moon edger.
● **Straight edge** Use two pegs and some string to mark off a straight edge. Drive the pegs into the ground, then mark off the line by stretching the string taut between the two pegs. Cut just inside the line.
● **Watering** Do not water a new lawn until you have finished shaping the edges. Watering before cutting will make it hard to make a sharp cut, and will increase the amount of damage done as you stand on the sod.

MARKING AND CUTTING A CURVE

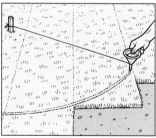

1 Drive a short piece of wood into the ground, and tie a piece of string to it. Pull the string tight, then attach a funnel to the string. Fill the funnel with sand, and use the funnel to mark off an accurate and even curve on the sod.

2 When you have finished marking the curve on the sod, use a half-moon edger to cut alongside it. To make a sharp, accurate cut, stand directly above the edger and cut with a straight, downward motion.

PLANTING IN A LAWN

Aн expanse of pure green is ideal in some situations, but you may decide to break up and enliven the area. Whether you choose to plant bulbs, shrubs, or trees, or to introduce an island bed (see p. 12), the effect can be dramatic.

PLANTING BULBS

Many bulbs are suitable for growing in lawns, especially those that flower in the spring. Once they are established, most bulbs naturalize well and multiply each year. Planting bulbs in a lawn is easier if you cut the grass as short as possible beforehand.

PLANTING SMALL BULBS

Cutting turf
Make a cut in the turf, and peel back the flaps. Turn the soil over lightly, and add fertilizer. Set the bulbs in place, replace the turf, then tamp it down by hand or with the back of a rake.

PLANTING LARGE BULBS

Scattering bulbs
To create a random, informal display, scatter bulbs over the planting area. While planting the bulbs, make sure they are not touching one another to prevent the spread of diseases.

BULBS IN GRASS

● **Choosing** Choose bulbs with relatively small foliage. Dwarf cultivars of *Narcissus* work well. Small foliage is especially important if you are planting in an area you need to mow.
● **Preparation** Before planting bulbs, cut the grass short to make the job easier.
● **Planting hole** When using a bulb planter, make sure that the base of the bulb is firmly in contact with the soil.
● **Feeding** Feed naturalized bulbs once a year to ensure that they continue to grow and flower well (see p. 87).

NATURALIZING BULBS

Drifts of naturalized bulbs in a lawn can look stunning, but try to keep the extent of a drift in proportion to the size of the lawn. If you are planting a small area, it may be best to use dwarf bulb varieties. Always consider what the drift will look like once flowering is over.

CARING FOR BULBS IN GRASS
● **Soil** Make sure that the soil is not too dry for the type of bulb you choose. The soil underneath trees and large shrubs is often very dry.
● **Flowering** When bulbs become overcrowded, they may flower poorly. Prevent this by dividing and replanting clumps regularly (see p. 156).
● **Foliage** Leave *Narcissus* foliage intact for at least six weeks after flowering; if it is tied up or cut back any sooner, flowering will be affected the following year.

● **Feeding** If bulbs in grass need feeding, use a high-phosphorus fertilizer to encourage flowering (see p. 85). Do not use a nitrogen-rich fertilizer; if you do, the grass will grow at the expense of the growth of the bulbs.

SHAPING DRIFTS
● **Drifts** Plant bulbs in naturally shaped, uneven drifts with irregular edges. If planting more than one area, make each one a slightly different shape and size.

SUITABLE BULBS

● **Economical choice** Daffodils and other narcissi are often naturalized. Purchased in large quantities, they are reasonably priced and can produce a great show over a number of years.
● **Snowdrops (*Galanthus*)** These naturalize well and quickly increase in number.
● ***Crocus*** Select a complete mixture of colors, or restrict your choice to just one or two. Choose crocuses that reach the same height.

PLANTING A WILDFLOWER MEADOW

When surrounded by grass, wildflowers can transform an uninteresting or unattractive patch of land into a flower-rich area that attracts insects and other wildlife into the yard. Choose fine grasses, such as bents and fescues, that will not overwhelm the other plants.

SOWING SEED

Add seed to sand in bucket

Sowing evenly
To ensure that the seeds are evenly distributed, mix grass seed, wildflower seed, and some fine sand together in a bucket before sowing. Do not fertilize the soil beforehand.

USING AN EXISTING SITE
● **Soil** Wildflowers thrive in poor soil. If your lawn is not growing well, consider turning it into a wildflower meadow.

Planting holes
Use a trowel or bulb planter to make holes in existing grass. Plant up with pot-grown wildflowers. For the most natural effect, plant several of a single type in each group.

BUYING SEED
● **Conservation** Buy wildflower seed from a reputable source. Seeds of wild origin may carry diseases or pests; make sure that you buy commercially cultivated wildflower seeds.

MAINTENANCE
● **Cutting a meadow** Never cut the grass until the flowers have set seed; otherwise, you may seriously limit the meadow's life span.
● **Infertile soil** Never feed a wildflower area, since these flowers thrive in soil that is poor and infertile. Feeding invariably causes excessive growth of grass and weeds at the expense of the wildflowers.

ADDING INTEREST

Take a good look at your lawn before you decide how to make it more interesting. A tree could create a visual break, for example, but what effect would it have on the rest of your yard? If your grass is not thriving, it may be best to abandon the idea of a lawn altogether.

PLANTING A TREE

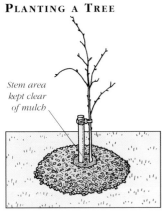

Stem area kept clear of mulch

Digging a hole
When planting a tree in a lawn, make the hole three or four times the diameter of the tree's root ball to minimize competition from grass. Lay a mulch 2–3 in (5–7 cm) deep around the tree.

LAWN ALTERNATIVES
● **Maintenance** Areas of lawn that are difficult to maintain are perfect for shrubs, bulbs, or single trees. A thriving planted area looks much better, and is easier to maintain, than grass that grows poorly.
● **Island bed** Break up a large expanse of grass by creating an island bed. Plant this up with herbaceous plants or shrubs and bulbs so that it looks good throughout the year.
● **Damp areas** Grass in very damp areas is quickly invaded by moss and other weeds. A site like this is ideal for planting up with moisture-loving plants, or for converting into a bog garden (see p. 133).

BRIGHT IDEA

Plants help to keep soil on slope in place

Planting a slope
The angle of a slope may make it extremely difficult to mow, especially if the slope is extensive. Instead of putting in grass, try planting the slope with groundcover plants and climbers.

LAWN MAINTENANCE

I F YOU WANT A LAWN TO BE PROUD OF, you need to do a certain amount of routine maintenance. The results you achieve are almost entirely dependent on the amount of time and effort you put into caring for your lawn.

MOWING A LAWN

Regular mowing is essential if a lawn is to look good. Mowing must be done to the correct height for the time of year. If left too long, a lawn will become yellow and uneven when cut; cutting too short can scalp a lawn. Both of these extremes encourage weak grass.

ESTABLISHING AND MAINTAINING A NEAT EDGE

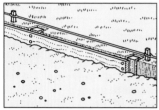

Buried edging
Use a narrow strip of lumber, corrugated metal, or plastic lawn edging to create a buried edge. Set it so that most of it is buried in the soil but the top is slightly higher than the grass roots.

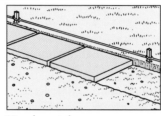

Mowing strip
A mowing strip made from bricks or narrow paving slabs prevents grass from spreading into adjacent flower beds. Instead of using edging shears, simply mow over the edges.

CUTTING GRASS
● **Dry weather** Avoid mowing in dry weather. If you do mow, raise the blades so that the grass is not cut very short.
● **Wet weather** Do not mow if the ground is very wet. This will encourage soil compaction, and the wet clippings may clog the mower.
● **Lawn edging** Always set edging lower than the grass. It must be level with, or only slightly higher than, the roots of the grass. If set too high, it could damage your mower.

TRIMMING EDGES

Even if your lawn is growing well, it will still look untidy if the edges are left uncut, or if they are uneven. Once lawn edges start to collapse, it is better to recut them than to try to neaten them up. Even on neat lawns, it is worth doing this once or twice a year.

STRAIGHT EDGES

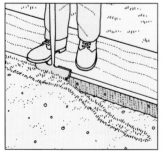

Using a board
Use a board to guide you when cutting a lawn edge with a half-moon edger. This will ensure that you make a straight edge and will prevent you from crushing the edge when you step on it.

SUITABLE TOOLS
● **Tools** Use edging shears to trim or cut lawn edges regularly. Once or twice a year, use a half-moon edger to neaten the edges. This tool cuts cleanly through soil and through any grass that has escaped into the borders.
● **Adjustable heads** Some lawn trimmers have an adjustable head that allows you to use them for edging as well as for cutting. Check for this feature before you buy.
● **Cutting technique** Cut down through the roots, and keep the edger in a vertical position. Compost any trimmings.

TRADITIONAL TIP

Frozen grass
Do not walk on frozen or frost-covered grass. This causes damage that makes the grass susceptible to diseases such as *Fusarium* patch.

FEEDING A LAWN

Your lawn will need feeding if it is to grow dense and lush. When grass is mowed regularly, it responds by growing more, which uses a lot of energy. There are different methods of feeding; choose the one that best suits your lawn and your budget.

APPLICATION RATES

Estimating quantity
Use four flower pots to mark off a test area measuring 1 sq yd (1 sq m). Weigh out the quantity of fertilizer recommended for this area, and apply it using another flower pot. Use this as a guide for feeding the rest of the lawn.

APPLYING FERTILIZERS
● **Selecting fertilizers** Choose the right fertilizer for the time of year. Some formulations are more suitable for spring application; others are more appropriate for autumn.
● **Late feeding** Avoid feeding late in the year, since this can promote new growth, which is vulnerable to winter damage and fungal attack.
● **Avoiding scorch** Use a liquid lawn fertilizer if the weather is very dry, or if a dry spell is forecast. This minimizes the likelihood of scorch.
● **Excess fertilizer** Avoid over-application or double-dosing the lawn; this can scorch grass.

BRIGHT IDEA

Feed the birds
If you have starlings feeding on grubs in your lawn, you should not need to apply insecticides, unless the grub infestation is particularly severe. The hungry birds will do the work for you.

WEEDING A LAWN

No matter how well you plant your lawn and subsequently maintain it, some weeds are bound to appear. For small areas, hand weeding may be the answer (see p. 98), but in most cases a chemical weedkiller is necessary to rid the lawn of weeds.

USING A DRIBBLE BAR
● **Special attachment** Apply a selective weedkiller using a dribble bar. Keep one watering can just for weedkillers.

Applying weedkiller
Use a dribble bar for accurate application with the lowest risk of contaminating plants. More than one application may be necessary for stubborn weeds.

IMPROVING DRAINAGE
● **Aeration** Prevent moss from growing on damp, compacted soil by aerating the lawn regularly (see p. 131).

Eliminating moss
Apply moss killer, and wait for the specified time before raking any dead moss out. If it is not dead, you will spread the spores and make the problem worse.

USING WEEDKILLER
● **When to apply** To avoid accidental contamination of garden plants, choose suitable weather and time of day for applying lawn weedkillers (see p. 94).
● **Saving time** Do two jobs at once by using a combined fertilizer and weedkiller.
● **Strength** Select a weedkiller with two or more active ingredients to increase the chances of killing all weeds.

WEEDKILLER SAFETY
● **Reading instructions** Most lawn weedkillers are safe for pets, wildlife, and humans. If applying a liquid weedkiller, allow time for the treated area to dry before use. Check the label for details (see p. 94).

LAWN PROBLEMS

T HE WEAR AND TEAR ON A LAWN can be considerable, especially if the lawn is subjected to heavy use. Both the weather and the type of soil you have in your yard can affect the sorts of problems your lawn may develop.

REPAIRING A DAMAGED EDGE

N eat edges are just as important as the lawn itself. However well maintained a lawn is, the overall effect will be spoiled if the edges are left untrimmed or damaged. Edges that have been damaged in only one or two small areas can be repaired very easily.

LIFTING AND TURNING TURF

1 To repair a damaged edge, use a half-moon edger to cut an accurate square of turf around the damage (see right). Carefully lift the turf, and turn it around so that the damaged area faces the lawn.

2 Re-lay the turf, checking the level, and reseed the damaged area with suitable grass seed mixed with a little topsoil. Water well. Away from the edge, the damaged area will be able to recover quickly.

CUTTING TURF
● **Accuracy** Always cut a section of turf into an accurate, regular square or oblong shape so that it fits in place when rotated 180 degrees.

PROTECTING EDGES
● **Mowing strips** Consider installing a mowing strip or brick edge. Both of these will protect edges (see p. 128).
● **Using containers** Give frequently damaged areas alongside a path a rest by placing a stable container of flowers on the path by the damaged area.

REPAIRING A DAMAGED PATCH

L ocalized soil conditions or frequent heavy use by children may cause parts of an otherwise healthy, vigorous lawn to deteriorate. The resulting patches can spoil the appearance of the entire lawn. If ignored, the problem may become worse, so always take prompt action.

LAWN REPAIRS
● **Timing** The best time to do lawn repairs is when grass seed or sod is most likely to establish quickly and thoroughly. Spring and late summer or early autumn are generally the best times of year for this task.
● **Starting again** If damage to a lawn is extensive, or if it recurs frequently, this could suggest a fundamental problem. It may be best to replant the whole area, but be sure to prepare it thoroughly first.

REPLACING DAMAGED TURF

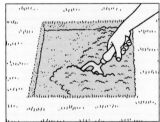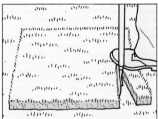

1 Use a half-moon edger to cut around the damaged area, and remove the turf with a spade. Lightly turn over the exposed soil, and incorporate a liquid or granular fertilizer. Firm the surface before resodding.

2 Try to use grass of the same type and quality as the original in order to achieve a good match. Place the new sod in the hole, and use a half-moon edger to cut it to size. Firm the sod in, and water.

HEAVY-USE AREAS

Some parts of a lawn are more likely than others to be subjected to heavy use – around a barbecue, a children's play area, or strips used as shortcuts, for instance. These areas will probably need more attention than other areas that get less use.

IMPROVING DRAINAGE

● **Annual maintenance** Poor drainage is often the cause of poor grass growth. Improve drainage by aerating and top-dressing once a year in autumn. This improves root growth and rain penetration.

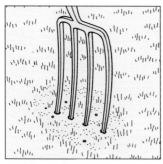

Spiking a lawn
Aerate compacted areas using a garden fork. Drive the fork into the lawn to a depth of at least 4 in (10 cm). Repeat this action every 6 in (15 cm) or so, easing the fork backward and forward each time to enlarge the holes.

LAWN MAINTENANCE

● **Top-dressing** After spiking a lawn (see left), use a brush to work a sandy top-dressing mixture into all the holes. Doing this will create long-lasting drainage channels.
● **Aerating large areas** If you need to aerate a large area, consider renting a power aerator machine. This tool will remove cores of soil every time it is driven into the turf, and is especially useful for aerating heavy soil.
● **Mowing height** Never cut grass very short in a heavily used area. A regular schedule of feeding, watering, and general maintenance (see p. 128–129) will encourage replacement grass to grow quickly, densely, and vigorously.
● **Making a path** An area that is subjected to heavy use may benefit from the installation of a path. Use stepping-stones to create a pathway (see below).

(see p. 128–129)

PLAY AREAS

To help protect the grass under a swing or other play equipment, secure sturdy netting to the ground with U-shaped staples. If this does not give enough protection, reseed the area with a specially formulated mixture of tough grasses (see p. 122), after incorporating ground-up tires in the soil (see p. 14). Or, change the surface completely: Use 2–3 in (5–7 cm) of finely chipped bark in areas that are prone to damage.

(see p. 122), (see p. 14).

HOMEMADE PAVING

Making your own paving slabs allows you to design exactly the shape and size that you want, and for a fraction of the cost of manufactured slabs. If you want colored slabs, buy concrete dye to mix in with the cement mixture. To make an irregular surface on your slabs, lay a crisscross of small twigs in the bottom of the mold, and pour the mix carefully so that you do not dislodge them.

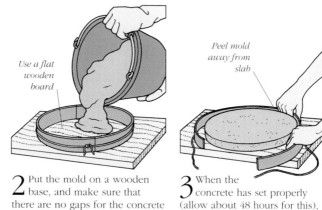

Use a flat wooden board

Peel mold away from slab

1 Use semirigid, smooth plastic or metal to form the sides of the paving slab mold. Allow for expansion during setting by tying the side pieces together with string or plastic tape.

2 Put the mold on a wooden base, and make sure that there are no gaps for the concrete mix to seep out. Carefully fill the mold with concrete. Wipe up any spillage with a damp cloth.

3 When the concrete has set properly (allow about 48 hours for this), remove the mold. Protect the slab from frost until the concrete is completely dry.

WATER FEATURES

*I*NTRODUCING *WATER INTO A GARDEN* instantly adds life. *The sight or sound of water helps to give a feeling of calm and relaxation, whatever the size or style of the garden. The water will soon attract all kinds of wildlife, too (see p. 111). If you do not have room for a pond, add a small water feature instead.*

BASIC EQUIPMENT

● **Creating ponds** To convert an old half barrel into a miniature pond, use a wire brush, scraper, paintbrush, and wood preservative. Wear rubber gloves to protect your hands. Heavy-duty plastic can be used to line a bog garden. Use a garden hose to fill a large pond.

● **Siting and maintaining plants** When positioning planted-up containers, soft twine is useful for lowering down the plants. Gravel can be used for weighing the plants down and keeping them in place. Lining a container with burlap trimmed with scissors helps to retain the soil around the plant's roots. You may need a sharp knife to trim water plants. An old colander is an effective piece of equipment for removing unwanted algae and other weeds from the surface of the pond.

● **Protecting your pond** Plastic netting is useful for catching fallen leaves, which can cause the buildup of toxic gases. A log will help to protect your pond from ice damage.

Wire brush

Paintbrush

Colander

Rubber gloves

Gravel

Scissors

Twine

Sharp knife

Wide gauge

Log

Garden hose

Narrow gauge

Plastic netting

Scraper

Wood preservative

Burlap

Heavy-duty plastic

WARNING!
Always install electrical equipment properly; use a professional, if necessary. Be sure that it is inspected and serviced regularly.

INTRODUCING WATER

BEFORE CHOOSING A WATER FEATURE, take the time to look at the variety of features offered in catalogs and at garden centers. Consider the style, shape, and size, and think about how the feature will fit in with the rest of your garden.

POND SAFETY

ALWAYS consider the potential danger of water in a garden used by children. If you feel a pond is unsuitable, there are many features you can buy or make yourself that do not require deep water. Existing features can be made safe by filling them with smooth pebbles.

MAKING WATER SAFE

● **Natural barrier** Block access to a pond by creating a miniature rock garden or a wide planting strip around it.
● **Pond covering** Place heavy-duty mesh across the surface to keep young children out.
● **Shallow end** Make a shallow end to a pond, and line it with large stones to help children climb out if they fall in.
● **Water pots** Using a selection of pots and a pump is the safest way of introducing water to a garden (see p. 134). However, do not allow water to accumulate to any depth.

RAISED POND

Creating a barrier
A raised pond is less dangerous than a pond at ground level. A child would have to climb in, rather than fall in, which is how accidents usually occur.

BUBBLE FOUNTAIN

Trickling water
A bubble fountain is an attractive and safe alternative to a pond. Water is pumped up through the center of an object, then trickles down over pebbles.

MAKING A BOG GARDEN

SOME of the most interesting plants can be grown around the edges of a pond in boggy or marginal areas. You may even prefer to drain the central area of water and have a larger area purely for marginal plants. It is possible to make a bog garden even if you do not have a pond.

DIGGING AND PREPARING A SITE

1 Dig out the designated area, and line it with a sheet of heavy-duty plastic. Use a fork to make a few holes in the plastic to allow excess water to drain away.

2 Fill the hollow with garden soil, and firm gently. Water thoroughly, adding the water in stages so that it soaks right through. Leave overnight to settle before planting up.

PLANNING A BOG

● **Size** A large bog garden does not dry up as quickly as a very small one, so is easier to keep looking good.
● **Different depths** Slope the sides of a bog garden, or cut shelves into it to provide varying depths of soil. The wider the range of conditions, the more plants you will be able to grow successfully.
● **Attracting wildlife** Make a small depression in the bog garden, and line it with a tray or basin to make a mini-pool to provide water for wildlife.

USING CONTAINERS

Water in the garden does not have to be restricted to ponds or pools. Features such as freestanding ponds, bubble fountains, and spouts provide the sight and sound of running water, and all are suitable for small areas – or even a conservatory.

SUITABLE CONTAINERS
● **Durability** All water containers must be frostproof, since they are especially vulnerable to extensive damage from frost.
● **Avoiding toxins** Do not use containers that are coated with flaking paint, which could harm plants or fish.
● **Unique feature** Try a combination of pots piled on top of each other. Use a pond pump to circulate the water from one pot to another.

ELECTRICAL SAFETY
● **Cables** Make sure that any electrical cabling is buried underground in a conduit to protect it from damage.

TERRACOTTA POTS

Bubbling water
Used singly or in groups, pots make an attractive water feature. A bubbling spout of water coming from each one provides both movement and the relaxing sound of moving water. Pots such as these can be used in even the smallest garden.

SUITABLE PLANTS

Single dwarf waterlilies, such as *Nymphaea alba* 'Pygmaea', or water hyacinths (*Eichhornia crassipes*) work well in a small pond or in a container. Many normal water plants can be used, but because of their potential size, they will need to be divided and cut back regularly.

Nymphaea alba 'Pygmaea'

MAKING A BARREL POND

A half-barrel miniature pond is particularly suitable for a small or overcrowded garden. It is also portable, which allows you to take it with you if you move. In addition, you can move it out of a central spot into a secluded area when the plants begin to die back in winter.

PREPARING THE WOOD

Coat inside of barrel with sealant

Sealing the surface
Use a scraper and wire brush to scrape off all loose or rotted wood on the inside. Make sure that the wood is completely dry before applying plenty of sealant (see right) with a paintbrush. Allow this to dry thoroughly before applying a second coat.

BEFORE PLANTING UP
● **Sealant** Make sure that the sealant you use is not toxic to plants and animals.
● **Suitable weather** Do not attempt to apply sealant in frosty or extremely cold weather; the sealant may not work effectively.
● **Drying** Allow the sealant to dry thoroughly out of direct sunlight or frost. Wait to fill the barrel with water until the sealant is completely dry.
● **Metal bands** Treat any rust, and repaint the metal bands.
● **Allow to stand** Make sure that the barrel is watertight by allowing it to stand full of water for several hours. Discard this water, and refill before planting up.

SITING A HALF BARREL

Standing or burying
You can stand a barrel pond on almost any surface in the yard, such as a gravel area, or a paved patio or terrace. Alternatively, you can partially bury a barrel in soil in a suitable spot in the garden, or sink it to just beneath the level of its rim.

WATER PLANTS

IT IS PLANTS THAT BRING A POND TO LIFE, and the combination of plants and water that brings wildlife to a pond. There are plenty of water plants to choose from; hardy plants are easier to maintain than those requiring special attention.

PLANTING DEPTHS

Different water plants have different needs and preferences. Of these needs, planting depth is the most important. If planted at an unsuitable depth, even a vigorous plant will fail to flourish. If you are building a pond, incorporate shelves to create different depths.

SITING WATER PLANTS

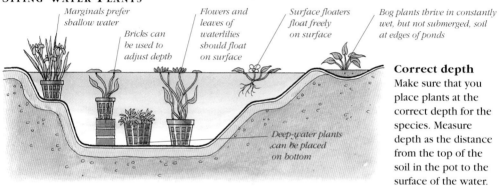

Marginals prefer shallow water

Bricks can be used to adjust depth

Flowers and leaves of waterlilies should float on surface

Surface floaters float freely on surface

Bog plants thrive in constantly wet, but not submerged, soil at edges of ponds

Deep-water plants can be placed on bottom

Correct depth
Make sure that you place plants at the correct depth for the species. Measure depth as the distance from the top of the soil in the pot to the surface of the water.

ADJUSTING DEPTH
● **Stacking bricks** Use bricks to place a plant at exactly the right depth. If necessary, you can remove some of the bricks as the plant grows.

SURFACE FLOATERS
● **Deterring algae** Use surface floaters to provide shade, which deters algae. Some surface floaters grow rapidly, so they may require thinning.

MARGINAL PLANTS
● **Wildlife shelter** Include marginal plants in your planting design. Not only do they look good, they also provide shelter for wildlife.

OXYGENATING PLANTS

Oxygenating plants are essential for a healthy pond. The oxygen released from their leaves helps to deter algae, especially during the summer. Some oxygenators need to be planted; others should be left to float on the surface.

● **Planting oxygenators** Some oxygenators are planted as bunches of unrooted cuttings. Prepare a small container (see p. 136), then insert several bunches together.
● **Keeping wet** Keep oxygenating plants moist until they are ready to plant. Even while being planted, they should not be exposed to the air any longer than absolutely necessary.

SUITABLE PLANTS
Callitriche spp., *Ceratophyllum demersum, Elodea canadensis, Fontinalis antipyretica, Hottonia palustris, Lagarosiphon major, Potamogeton crispus.*

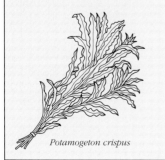

Potamogeton crispus

TIME-SAVING TIP

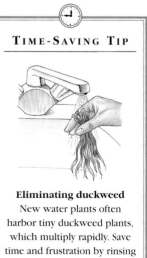

Eliminating duckweed
New water plants often harbor tiny duckweed plants, which multiply rapidly. Save time and frustration by rinsing all new water plants.

PLANTING UP

Like any new planting, a newly planted pond takes time to become established, but it will soon take shape. For best results, choose plants for as many depths as possible, and include a few surface floaters. In addition, select plants with striking foliage.

BASKET LININGS
● **Burlap** Use basket linings to help keep soil around the roots of a plant without interfering with the flow of water. Burlap is traditionally used for this purpose, but coconut-fiber hanging basket liners also work well.

PLANTING CONDITIONS
● **Keeping moist** Water plants are easily damaged by dry conditions, so make every attempt to minimize this risk by keeping them in water until you are ready to plant up. Always plant in the shade, never in direct sunlight.

GRAVEL
● **Preventing disturbance** A 1-in (2.5-cm) thick layer of gravel on the soil surface helps to keep the soil and plant in place. It also prevents disturbance by fish or other pond creatures, and helps to weigh the pot down.

PLANTING A WATER PLANT IN A BASKET

Trim excess burlap

Position plant in center

Add gravel to just beneath rim of basket

1 Choose a basket large enough to hold the root system of the plant when the plant is fully grown. Line the basket with burlap, and fill it halfway with aquatic soil to hold the burlap in place.

2 Place the plant in the center of the basket. Add more soil as necessary, and firm gently. Top up the soil to within about 1 in (2.5 cm) of the basket rim. Water the plant gently; do not flood the basket.

3 Gently top-dress the soil with a layer of horticultural gravel or tiny stones. Take great care not to bury any small leaves as you do this, or to damage the vulnerable young shoots and stems.

SUITABLE MATERIALS
● **Soil** Use aquatic soil, not garden soil. Aquatic soil contains the correct amount of nutrients for healthy growth.
● **Gravel** Use horticultural or special aquatic gravel. Avoid builder's gravel, which may contain several contaminants.
● **Alternative containers** Try using plastic crates, which you can buy in most supermarkets at a fraction of the cost of special pond baskets.
● **Taking notes** Always keep a record of the water plants you use and where you plant them. This information will come in handy if you ever need to replace the plants.

ADDING HANDLES

Thread string through holes in basket

Lowering a water plant
Position a planted basket easily and safely by attaching string handles to opposite sides of the basket's rim. Allow enough string to lower the basket to the correct depth, whether this is on a shelf or in the middle of a large pond.

ANCHORING A PLANT

Young plants, especially those with small root systems, are easily dislodged. Use several large stones, or an extra-deep layer of gravel, to help anchor a plant and keep its roots beneath the soil. The extra weight also helps to keep the container in place.

POND MAINTENANCE

A LTHOUGH A POND or water feature requires a lot less maintenance than many other areas of a garden, it may deteriorate over time if left unattended. A little routine maintenance should keep everything in order.

REMOVING WEEDS

Weeds can build up in water very quickly, especially if a pond has not yet reached a good, natural balance. Unwelcome water weeds can be present in the soil of new plants (see p. 135), while other weeds may be introduced by visiting birds and other wildlife.

BLANKET WEED

Using a stick
Blanket weed is formed from a very dense, matlike growth of algae. Left to grow unchecked, this weed will soon clog the water. Use a stick to remove it, turning the stick slowly in one direction to gather up the weed in large quantities.

DEALING WITH WEEDS
● **Natural balance** A new pond invariably turns bright green with algae soon after it is planted up. However, do not be tempted to clear it out and refill with fresh water, since this usually makes it worse. Be patient; the situation should improve once a natural balance is established.
● **Seasonal growth** Algal blooms and duckweed infestations are usually seasonal; depending on the temperatures, most die down in autumn or winter. Keep a close eye out for any reappearance in spring, and remove them promptly.

DUCKWEED

Using a colander
Duckweed floats on the surface of the water and can be scooped off a small pond with a large sieve or colander. Use a slow skimming or scooping motion to gather it up. Remove as much of the weed as you possibly can; duckweed multiplies rapidly.

DISPOSAL OF DUCKWEED

Burying duckweed
Duckweed is a natural survivor and spreads very easily. Once you have removed it, never leave it lying around. Dispose of it safely by burying it in a deep hole, or by putting it in the compost pile or in a garbage can.

PREVENTING WEEDS
● **Surface floaters** Use surface floaters such as waterlilies. Algae thrives in the sun, and the large leaves of these plants help to provide shade.
● **Fish** Overstocking with fish can cause a sudden and dramatic increase in algal growth, due largely to the nitrogenous material in fish excreta. Combat this with oxygenating plants (see p. 135).

LARGE PONDS
● **Removing duckweed** Hold a board vertically, and pull it slowly across the surface of the water to collect the duckweed. Remove with a colander or sieve.

GREEN TIP

Using straw
To help keep a pond clear of unwanted algae, stuff a leg of panty hose with straw. Tie both ends securely, and attach a weight to the bundle before submerging it.

WINTER CARE

Autumn is the time of year when a water feature or a pond will need the most maintenance. While many plants die back over winter, it is essential that the remaining plants, water, and living creatures are protected from the effects of plummeting temperatures.

LOW TEMPERATURES

● **Feeding fish** Fish do not eat much in the winter, since their metabolism slows down. Do not allow fish food to accumulate in the water.

● **Plywood cover** If severe weather is forecast, cover a small pond or water feature with a piece of plywood. Make sure that the water plants are not deprived of light for too long, however.

● **Heating the water** If you have a pump, consider replacing it with a water heater during the late autumn and winter months. Be sure to put the heater in place before the really cold weather arrives.

PROTECTING PLANTS

● **Using buckets** Protect tender plants by removing them from the water and placing them in a bucket of water. Leave the bucket in a sheltered, frost-free location until spring.

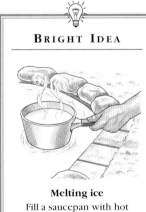

BRIGHT IDEA

Melting ice
Fill a saucepan with hot water, and rest it on the ice. Hold it there until it melts a hole in the ice, so that any potentially toxic gases can escape.

DIVIDING AND TRIMMING

● **Container plants** Divide any crowded water plants in early autumn. Treat them like herbaceous perennials, discarding any weak or damaged sections before replanting the rest (see p. 60).

Trimming leaves
In late autumn, trim back deteriorating and trailing foliage on all water plants, including marginal plants. Be sure not to let any leaves fall into the water; gather them up, and add them to the compost pile.

DEALING WITH ICE

● **Removing ice** Never smash up any ice on a pond, since the vibrations this would cause could seriously harm any fish or other wildlife.

● **Creating air space** If water freezes over, melt a hole in the ice. Carefully bail out water to lower the level by 1 in (2.5 cm). If the water freezes over again, any toxic gases will accumulate in the gap between the ice and the water.

● **Open water** Install a small submersible electric pump in the area of the pond to be left open. This will keep ice from forming while the water is aerated by the pump, regardless of the ambient temperature.

FALLEN LEAVES

● **Toxic gases** Prevent leaves from falling into the water. If the water freezes over, leaves can cause the buildup of methane and other toxic gases that are harmful to fish and other pond wildlife.

Catching falling leaves
Use rigid plastic netting to prevent leaves from falling into the water. To make collecting many of leaves easier, lay a curtain over the netting. When the curtain is covered with leaves, remove it, and shake it out.

AVOIDING ICE DAMAGE

Floating a log
As water freezes and expands, it can cause substantial damage to a pond or water container. To prevent this, float a log or plastic ball on the water. The floating object will absorb some of the pressure, thus alleviating pressure on the pond or container.

POND REPAIR

However carefully you install your pond, it may start to leak at some stage, and repairs will be necessary to maintain the water level. The method you use will depend entirely on the material from which your pond is made.

EMPTYING A POND

You will need to drain your pond before making any repairs. Most ponds can be drained either with an electric pump or by siphoning off the water. Small ponds and individual water features can be emptied by bailing out the water with a bucket.

SMALL POND

Removing contents
You may have to remove some or all of the pond's contents before making any repairs. Put plants, fish, and any other aquatic life into plastic buckets. Handle everything as carefully and as gently as possible.

CONCRETE PONDS
● **New lining** If a concrete or rigid-lined pond is leaking badly, you will probably need to reline it. Empty the pond, then simply lay a rubber liner over the old shell. Refill the pond with water.
●**Tiny cracks** Clean and dry the surface thoroughly, then paint the whole area with a commercial pond sealant.
● **Large cracks** To prolong the effectiveness of a repair, undercut the crack (see p. 166) so that it is wider at the base than it is at the surface.
● **Ice** In very cold areas, you may need to empty a concrete pond entirely to prevent damage from freezing water.

LARGE POND

Making a temporary pond
Provide a home for the contents of a large pond by making a temporary pond. Dig a hole, and line it with heavy-duty plastic. Fill it with water from your pond, and gradually add the plants and any pond animals.

REPAIRING CONCRETE

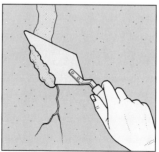

Filling a large crack
Concrete ponds are the most difficult to repair once they have sprung a leak. First, chisel out the crack with a chisel. Then fill it with waterproof cement, which should prevent further leakage. Follow this with a coat of pond sealant.

CHECKING PLANTS
● **Unhealthy plants** When removing plants from a pond, take the opportunity to dispose of any that show signs of disease or pest infestations.

TEMPORARY STORAGE
● **Providing shade** Be sure to store pond plants and creatures in the shade. Without the usual depth of water to protect them, they will be particularly susceptible to damage from high temperatures.
● **Providing protection** Place wire mesh over temporary containers to prevent cats and other animals from preying on any fish or frogs.

MENDING A POND LINER

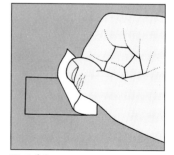

Patching a tear
Dry and clean the damaged area. Place double-sided adhesive sealing tape over the tear, and wait until it becomes sticky. Cut out a patch from a spare piece of liner, and press it firmly onto the adhesive, making sure that all edges are stuck down flat.

PROPAGATING PLANTS

PROPAGATING YOUR OWN PLANTS *is immensely satisfying and exciting. Growing plants from seed is the most common method of propagation, but it is not the only one. Other methods include layering, dividing, and taking cuttings. Whether you collect propagating material in your own garden or from a friend, you can quickly build up your collection of plants without having to spend a lot of money.*

EQUIPMENT FOR SOWING SEEDS OUTDOORS

You can achieve excellent results with minimal equipment by sowing seeds directly into the ground. This makes direct sowing extremely economical, even if you buy the seeds.

● **Surface preparation** The soil must be prepared properly before sowing. Use a rake to create a fine, level seedbed.
● **Warming the soil** Use black plastic or floating row covers to warm up the soil. Hold the plastic or row covers in place with bricks or large stones.
● **Marking** Use stakes and twine to mark off rows, which are particularly useful for sowing vegetable seeds.
A hand fork and trowel are useful for marking off straight lines for sowing annuals, and are also essential for moving or thinning seedlings and young plants. Use white sandbox or other fine sand in a plastic bottle to mark off areas when creating a mixed border of hardy annuals. Do not use builder's sand, which can harm the seedlings. Mark each area with a label.
● **Watering** Use a watering can to water seeds; the spray from a hose may be too strong.

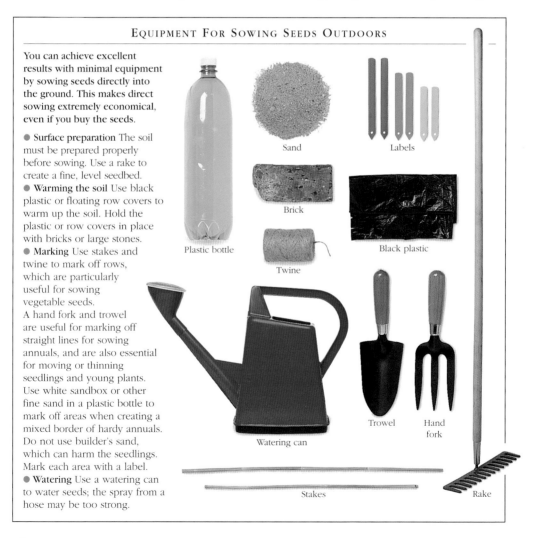

Plastic bottle

Sand

Brick

Labels

Black plastic

Twine

Watering can

Trowel

Hand fork

Stakes

Rake

EQUIPMENT FOR SOWING SEEDS INDOORS

Although you need slightly more equipment for sowing seeds indoors than outdoors, much of it need not be specially purchased. A propagator, preferably one that is heated, is a useful item but not essential.

● **Sowing** Seed trays are available in either full or half sizes and are usually made from semirigid plastic. Invest in a selection of small plastic pots, and reuse any that come with plants you buy. Use a screen to remove the large lumps and partly decomposed twigs often found in soil mix. A light dusting of screened soil mix can also be used to cover fine seeds. A plant mister is useful for moistening the surface of soil mix with minimal disturbance to the seeds or seedlings.

● **Storing seed** Film canisters and envelopes make excellent containers for storing any seeds that you have collected, and for leftover seeds from any opened packets (see p. 147). Use paper towels and newspaper to dry seeds before storage.

● **Aftercare** Use plastic wrap to cover seed trays while the seeds germinate, to prevent the soil mix from drying out. Plastic wrap also protects the tiny seedlings from cold drafts, which can damage them.

● **Transplanting** A plastic dibber and fork are invaluable for transplanting seedlings.

Seed trays

Plastic pot

Plastic wrap

Paper towels

Screen

Film canisters

Envelopes

Plant mister

Newspaper

Dibber

Fork

SEED-STARTING MIXES

Most seeds can be sown in any potting or seed-starting mix. The most important feature of these mixes is that they have an open texture and a suitable nutrient content. For healthy seedling growth, provide a relatively low level of nutrients; otherwise, the roots will be scorched and will die back.

Peat-free mix

Soil-based mix

All-purpose potting mix

SOWING SEEDS OUTDOORS

S OME SEEDS CAN BE SOWN directly into the ground, without the need for trays, soil mix, or a propagator. This works particularly well for seedlings that resent root disturbance. Check each seed packet for individual seed requirements.

SOWING VEGETABLE BEDS

M any vegetables can be raised successfully from seeds sown into the ground where they are to mature. To ensure success, prepare the soil by adding organic matter (see p. 38) and fertilizer (see p. 76) well before sowing. Keep all seeds and young plants well watered.

STRAIGHT ROWS

Mark stake to indicate correct sowing depth

Making rows
Push a stake into the ground at each end of the proposed row. Tie string tightly between the two stakes to indicate the position of the row. Use another stake to mark a straight line along the string.

GOOD SOIL CONTACT

Sowing seeds
Sprinkle seeds into a row, and cover them with soil by running the back of a rake down the middle of the row. Use the back of the rake to tamp down the soil gently so that the seeds are in close contact with the soil.

EARLY SOWINGS

Warming up the soil
Early sowings are possible if you warm up the soil first. A few days to a week before sowing, cover the prepared seedbed with a sheet of black plastic or floating row cover. Weigh down the edges with bricks or stones.

SOIL COMPACTION

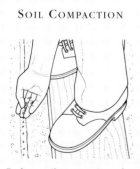

Reduce soil compaction when you sow seeds in a vegetable plot by standing on a board. If you do this whenever you work in the plot (use a brick and board bridge, if necessary), you will need to redig only every five years or so.

SUCCESSFUL SOWING

● **Seed stations** For most direct-sown vegetable seeds, sow two seeds at each station to allow for poor germination. Thin if more than one seed germinates in any one spot.
● **Intersowing** To save space, try sowing two different crops in a single row. Sow a slow-growing crop, such as parsnips or carrots, at well-spaced intervals, and a fast-growing crop, such as lettuce or radishes, in between.
● **Capturing heat** If you are using a floating row cover or black plastic, try to position it over the soil during the warmest part of the day.

AVOIDING DISEASE

● **Soil condition** Sowing under cold, damp conditions may cause the seeds to rot. If the soil is very wet or frozen, delay sowing until conditions are more suitable.
● **Preventing disease** Water rows with a copper-based fungicide to reduce the risk of damping off (a fungal disease). Guard against slugs and snails (see p. 118).
● **Crop rotation** Rotate all vegetable crops to minimize the risk of disease. Some crops, such as beans and peas, are especially prone to foot- and root-rotting diseases that build up in the soil (see p. 106).

SOWING FLOWER BEDS

Propagating by seed produces a wealth of new plants with very little effort. A bright, colorful summer border is easy to achieve with direct sowing, and the only cost is that of a few packets of seeds. It is an ideal way to raise many annuals – and wildflowers, too.

MARKING OFF INDIVIDUAL AREAS FOR SOWING

1 Rake the soil level before marking individual areas to be sown. To mark off sowing areas, fill a plastic bottle with fine sand, and pour it out to mark off each separate area.

2 Rather than scattering the seeds, mark off straight rows for them within each area. You will then be able to distinguish between the seedlings and young weeds.

3 Cover the seeds with soil. Mark each area with a weather-resistant label. Push the labels firmly into the soil to prevent them from being dislodged by wind or animals.

SELF-SEEDING PLANTS

Shake plant over soil to scatter seeds

Scattering seed
Create new patches of flowers by lifting plants that have set seed. Shake the seedheads where you want new plants to grow.

SEEDS AND SEEDLINGS
● **Using colors** For an elegant effect, restrict yourself to a few colors when sowing a hardy annual border. Use a wider range of shades for an eye-catching display.
● **Good value** Save partially used seed packets from one year to the next (see p. 147).
● **Second choice** Transplant any seedlings you have thinned out from the main display into containers or into another patch of ground. They may be seconds, but most flowers will still look good if they are well watered and fed.

HARD-COATED SEEDS
● **Successful germination**
Help seeds with hard coats to germinate by soaking them overnight in water. To encourage water absorption, file very hard seeds with a nail file before soaking them.

TIME-SAVING TIP

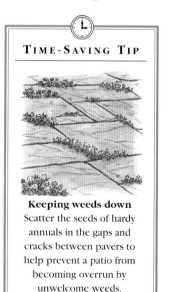

Keeping weeds down
Scatter the seeds of hardy annuals in the gaps and cracks between pavers to help prevent a patio from becoming overrun by unwelcome weeds.

SEEDS FOR DIRECT SOWING

Amaranthus caudatus, Brachycome iberidifolia, Calendula officinalis, Centaurea cyanus, Clarkia elegans, Consolida ajacis, Convolvulus tricolor, Dimorphotheca aurantiaca, Echium lycopsis, Eschscholzia californica, Gilia lutea, Godetia grandiflora, Gypsophila elegans, Iberis umbellata, Linaria maroccana, Lobularia maritima, Lychnis viscaria, Malcolmia maritima, Nemophila menziesii, Nigella damascena, Papaver rhoeas, Reseda odorata.

SOWING SEEDS INDOORS

SOWING SEEDS IN TRAYS OR POTS, either in a greenhouse or on a windowsill, gives you control over the growth of the seedlings. The extra warmth is especially suitable for seeds that do not germinate reliably outdoors.

SOWING IN TRAYS

Trays are ideal containers for sowing seeds; they already have drainage holes and are the correct depth for the early development of seedlings. If you want to grow only a small number of any one type of seedling, choose trays that are divided into strips or cells.

SOWING SEEDS IN PLASTIC TRAYS

Place soil mix lumps on bottom of tray

1 Large lumps of soil mix inhibit seed germination. If you do not have a screen, remove large lumps from the soil mix by hand, and place them in the bottom of the tray.

Hold seed tray level

2 Use the bottom of an empty seed tray to level the soil mix. Holding the tray level, press it down firmly into the soil mix to create an ideal surface for sowing.

Cup your hand slightly

3 Dry your hands thoroughly, and place a small amount of seed in the palm of one hand. Gently tap your palm with the other hand to distribute the seeds evenly.

TRADITIONAL TIP

Sowing fine seeds
Sowing fine seeds evenly can be difficult. To make it easier, fold a piece of cardboard or paper in half. Tip the seeds into the fold, and gently tap the cardboard with your finger to scatter the seeds over the soil mix.

SOWING SMALL SEEDS

Gently shake screen over seeds

Covering small seeds
Small seeds should not be covered with too much soil mix. To avoid dislodging the seeds when covering them, use a screen to shake a fine layer of soil mix over them.

SUCCESSFUL SOWING
● **Sticky hands** To stop seeds from sticking to your hands, sow seeds in a cool room, or run cold water over your wrist before you begin sowing.
● **Watering** Water the soil mix before you sow seeds, to prevent them from being washed into a heap.
● **Tiny seeds** Settle tiny seeds into the soil mix with a fine mist from a plant mister.
● **Light** If your seeds require light for germination, cover the tray with a sheet of glass or plastic wrap to prevent the soil mix from drying out.
● **Heat control** Too much or too little heat can hinder germination. Invest in a propagating thermometer.

SOWING IN POTS

Some seeds, particularly large ones, are best sown in individual pots, since they need room to develop. This also minimizes root disturbance when the seedlings are transplanted. Using separate pots is ideal if you are sowing only a small quantity of each seed.

PLANTING IN POTS

Seeds sown thinly in each pot

Filling gaps
Use thinly sown seedlings in pots as temporary gap fillers to provide spots of color in flower beds. You can plant out entire pots and then remove them once the beds fill out.

SOWING SWEET PEAS

Put one sweet pea seed into each tube

Avoiding root disturbance
Roll newspaper strips into 1½ in- (3 cm-) diameter tubes. Fill each one with soil mix, and moisten before sowing the seeds. Plant out each tube; the roots will grow through the newspaper.

SEEDLING CONTAINERS

Use empty household pots as seedling containers. Yogurt and dessert containers make good pots, and margarine tubs can be used as seed trays. Make sure that you clean all containers thoroughly, and remember to make drainage holes in the bottom.

LOOKING AFTER SEEDLINGS

The correct conditions and proper care are essential for growth once seeds have been sown. Always consult each seed packet for details on temperature and light requirements. When the seeds have germinated, the seedlings usually require a lower temperature.

CARING FOR SEEDLINGS
● **Using fungicide** Prevent fungal diseases from developing by drenching the soil mix with a copper-based fungicide before sowing seeds. Repeat once the seedlings have emerged.
● **Best conditions** Provide plenty of natural light, increase air circulation, and lower the temperature.
● **Sun scorch** Do not put developing seedlings in direct sunlight, since this may cause too great a rise in temperature.
● **Reflecting light** If light levels are low, place trays or pots of seedlings on aluminum foil. Put foil behind the seedlings, too, to ensure that they receive plenty of reflected light.

USING PLASTIC WRAP
● **Versatility** Cover seedlings with a sheet of plastic wrap to conserve moisture, keep out drafts, and keep the temperature constant.

Remove plastic wrap gently

Preventing condensation
Remove the plastic wrap from time to time to prevent the buildup of condensation. Allow any water droplets to run back into the tray or pot before replacing the plastic.

PROVIDING LIGHT
● **Lighting** Light is essential for the development of sturdy seedlings. Seedlings that do not receive enough light soon become pale and leggy.

Turn pots and trays regularly

Turning toward the light
Seedlings grown by a window or exposed to a one-sided light source will grow toward the light. Prevent them from becoming lopsided and bent by turning the container regularly.

IDEAL GERMINATION CONDITIONS

Some seeds are capable of germinating under almost any conditions, but most have fairly specific requirements. Temperature is a major factor. Check the recommended temperature for sowing, and make sure that you provide it throughout the germination period.

PROVIDING HEAT IN A GREENHOUSE

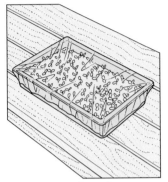

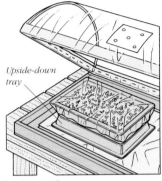

Upside-down tray

Propagating mat

Greenhouse bench
Seeds and seedlings that do not require much heat can be placed in a frame or on a greenhouse bench. Cover them with plastic wrap to help reduce temperature fluctuations and exposure to damaging drafts.

Indirect heat
Some seeds and seedlings can be damaged by high temperatures, but still require extra warmth. Place them on an upside-down tray in a propagator so that they are not in direct contact with the heated propagating mat.

Direct heat
Seeds that require high temperatures for germination can be placed directly on a heated propagating mat in a propagator. This makes it possible for them to benefit from the highest temperatures.

PROPAGATORS

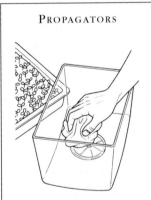

● **Condensation** Wipe the inner surface of the lid regularly to remove condensation, which can reduce the amount of light reaching the seedlings if it is allowed to build up.
● **Algae** Wiping the lid of the propagator will also prevent the buildup of algae, which not only looks unsightly, but also prevents light from reaching the seedlings.

USING A PROPAGATOR
● **Uneven heat** The heating element in the propagator may supply heat unevenly. Find the warmest and coolest areas, and use them for the appropriate plants.
● **Water supply** Always keep the capillary matting at the bottom of a propagator moist. This ensures a constant supply of water for the seedlings.
● **Cleaning** After each use, clean out the propagator thoroughly to limit the risk of disease buildup. Take care not to wet the electrical apparatus.
● **Safety** If you are worried about the safety of your propagator, have it checked by a qualified electrician.
● **Bottle propagator** To make a basic propagator, cut off the bottom of a clear plastic bottle, remove the screw top, and place the top half of the bottle over a pot of seedlings.

MONEY-SAVING TIP

Ready-made propagator
Use the warmth of a linen closet to propagate seeds that do not need light. Check the temperature on each shelf with a thermometer to determine the best place for each tray. Cover the trays with plastic wrap, and check them daily. Remove each tray as soon as the first seedlings emerge.

COLLECTING AND STORING SEEDS

Collecting seeds from your own plants is great fun and can be a very inexpensive and exciting way to fill your beds and borders with color. Swap your seeds with friends and neighbors, too. Remember that home-saved seeds may not grow true to type.

CATCHING SEEDS

● **Paper bag** Most garden plants reliably set seed. Tie a paper bag loosely around ripe seedheads to catch the seeds as they are released.

On a dry day, shake seeds onto folded paper

Collecting seedheads
Cut ripe seedheads off plants, and shake them to release the seeds inside. Store these in an envelope or paper bag. Mark each one clearly with the plant name and date of collection.

STORING SEEDS

● **Suitable containers** Seeds are best stored in an airtight container. They must be completely free of moist plant material; otherwise, they may rot or start to germinate.

Use folded paper to pour out seeds

Excluding light
Black film canisters are good for storing seeds. Be sure that the seeds are thoroughly clean and dry before putting them in the canisters, and remember to label each canister clearly.

COLLECTING SEEDS FROM VEGETABLES AND FRUITS

● **Plant variations** Many vegetable varieties will not produce plants identical to the parent plant, so be prepared for variations.

Remove seeds from fleshy fruits with thumb

Scooping out seeds
Choose ripe, healthy-looking vegetables or fruits. Cut each one in half, and carefully scoop out the seeds. Examine them carefully, and discard any that do not look perfect.

STORING PODS

● **Seed pods** Seeds in pods should not be stored in airtight conditions. To dry naturally, the pods require air circulation. Once the seeds are ripe, they can be removed.

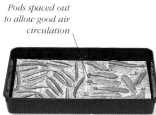

Pods spaced out to allow good air circulation

Drying seed pods
Store pods on newspaper in a seed tray until they are quite dry. Do not apply artificial heat. When the pods are completely dry, carefully remove the seeds, and store them in paper bags.

● **Diseases** Some viral diseases are seed-borne. Minimize the risk of producing unhealthy plants by collecting only from healthy-looking plants.

Leave seeds to dry on paper towel

Drying seeds
Dry home-saved seeds by spreading them out on a clean paper towel. Put this into a clean, dry seed tray, and allow the seeds to dry thoroughly. Store them in a cool, dry place.

CYCLAMEN SEEDS

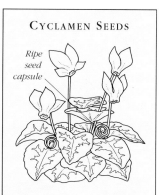

Ripe seed capsule

● **Seed capsules** Collect seeds from hardy cyclamen as soon as the capsules begin to split open. Tie a paper bag loosely around the capsules to ensure that no seeds are lost.
● **Soaking seeds** To improve germination, remove the seeds from each capsule and soak them overnight. Sow them as soon as possible.

THINNING SEEDLINGS

Once seedlings have emerged, they usually require thinning or transplanting. Although this is quite a delicate job, it gives you the chance to select the best seedlings, which you can then provide with a fresh supply of nutrients.

THINNING IN OPEN GROUND

Seedlings raised in open ground are usually thinned as soon as they are large enough to handle. A few seeds – mainly vegetables – are sown thinly and then transplanted. Thinning is best done twice, providing two chances to choose the most vigorous seedlings.

THINNING SEEDLINGS

Weak seedlings
Carefully remove any weak or diseased seedlings. Be careful not to disturb the roots of the remaining seedlings.

TRANSPLANTING PLANTS

Moisture loss
Use a hand fork to lift young plants. Immediately put them into a plastic bag to reduce moisture loss from the leaves.

MOVING SEEDLINGS

● **Before lifting** To reduce root damage, water the soil thoroughly before lifting plants for transplanting.
● **Cool temperatures** Thin or transplant seedlings and young plants during the coolest part of the day – preferably at dusk. This reduces both moisture loss and stress on the plants. The plants will also have sufficient time to recover before temperatures rise again.
● **Watering** To settle the soil around the roots, water well after thinning or transplanting.

THINNING IN POTS AND TRAYS

Seedlings raised indoors will need thinning or transplanting, too. The controlled conditions make the timing less critical, but you should still minimize stress to the seedlings by working out of direct sunlight. Water the seedlings well, both before and after transplanting them.

TRANSPLANTING AND WATERING SEEDLINGS

Remove seedling with widger

Water is absorbed by soil

1 Ease the roots of the seedling out of the soil mix, then support it by gently holding it by the seed leaves. Do not hold the seedling by the stem or the true leaves.

2 Make a hole with a dibber, and carefully lower a seedling into the hole. Press the soil mix firmly around the seedling so the roots are in close contact with the mix.

3 To prevent the soil mix from being washed away from the base of the seedlings, water them by placing the pot in water until the soil surface appears moist.

CARING FOR YOUNG PLANTS

Seedlings and young plants need special care and attention. Their stems and foliage are relatively soft, which makes them especially vulnerable. Young plants need to be weaned gradually so that they have time to adjust to their new conditions in the garden.

MAINTAINING PLANTS

● **Avoiding extremes** Young plants can suffer in extreme conditions. Do not subject them to very bright sunlight or very dark conditions. Avoid extremes in temperature, too.

● **Watering** A regular and adequate water supply is essential, since young root systems are easily damaged by erratic moisture levels.

● **Disease** Reduce the risk of fungal diseases by watering with a copper-based fungicide after transplanting or thinning.

● **Scorching** Soft foliage is easily scorched, especially if it is exposed to sunlight when wet. Keep moisture off the leaf surfaces, particularly in bright light and when temperatures are low.

PROTECTING YOUNG PLANTS FROM DAMAGE

● **Plant care** Protect plants from pests and diseases (see p. 104) and adverse weather conditions (see p. 82–83).

Making a mini-cloche
Put half a clear plastic bottle over seedlings or young plants to make a mini-cloche. Harden off the plants gradually by making holes in the bottle.

● **Pest barriers** Prevent pests from ever reaching young plants with a strategically placed barrier. Some barriers can also insulate large areas of plants from the cold.

Floating row covers
Perforated plastic and fabric covers allow light and air to penetrate. They also protect against cold and pests. Weigh down or tuck in the edges.

MAKING A PLASTIC TUNNEL

Plastic tunnels are usually used to protect low-growing plants from extreme weather conditions (see p. 82–83). Make a tunnel to cover a small area of your vegetable patch. For each supporting hoop, you need 6.5 ft (2 m) of ½ in (12 mm) diameter flexible pipe and two 18 in (45 cm) lengths of dowel to fit inside the pipe. You will also need clear plastic, narrow strips of wood, and thumbtacks.

1 Mark off the tunnel base with narrow strips of wood. Push a piece of dowel into each end of the pipe. Make hoops by pushing the dowels into the ground just inside the strips.

2 Place the hoops about 5 ft (1.5 m) apart along the length of the strips, and cover them with plastic. Wrap the plastic edges under the strips; hold down with thumbtacks.

3 Secure the plastic at the ends of the tunnel with bricks or large stones. Seal the tunnel for maximum warmth, and open it up to provide ventilation when the weather gets warm.

LAYERING PLANTS

PROPAGATING PLANTS BY LAYERING is not difficult. Plant stems are encouraged to produce roots, usually by bending them down to ground level and covering them with soil. Making a cut in the stems helps to stimulate the rooting process.

BASIC EQUIPMENT

Layering does not require much equipment. Some plants self-layer, needing little more than a covering of soil where the stem touches the soil.

● **Rooting hormone** Hormone rooting powder stimulates the natural rooting process. Treating the cut stem area produces the best results. A good-quality soil mix or rooting medium also encourages rapid rooting. This can be used in a sunken plastic pot, or it can be incorporated into the soil around the plant you are layering.

● **Other items** Stakes, twine, a sharp knife, and some metal pegs are useful for many types of layering techniques.

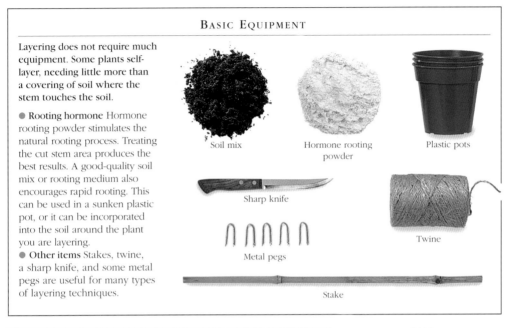

Soil mix

Hormone rooting powder

Plastic pots

Sharp knife

Metal pegs

Twine

Stake

SUITABLE PLANTS FOR LAYERING

Many commonly grown trees, shrubs, and climbers are propagated by layering. Those described as self-layering will root unaided when in contact with garden soil. Pot them up when they are well rooted.

Actinidia, Akebia, Andromeda, Aucuba, Carpenteria, Cassiope, Celastrus (S), *Chaenomeles, Chionanthus, Cissus, Corylopsis, Ercilla, Erica, Fothergilla, Hedera* (S), *Humulus, Hydrangea petiolaris* (S), *Kalmia, Laurus, Lonicera, Magnolia, Mandevilla, Osmanthus, Parthenocissus* (S), *Passiflora* (most), *Periploca* (S), *Pileostegia,*

Rhododendron, Rosa, Rubus, Scindapsus, Skimmia, Stachyurus, Strongylodon, Syringa, Trachelospermum (S), *Vaccinium corymbosum, Vitis amurensis, Vitis coignetiae, Wisteria.*

(S) – plants that are self-layering

Magnolia

BRIGHT IDEA

Foliar feeding
Invigorate a developing young plant by spraying the leaves with a foliar feed of water-soluble fertilizer. This method of feeding also helps to stimulate root growth, ensuring a well-developed and strong root system.

LAYERING TECHNIQUES

There are a number of layering techniques, all suited to different plants and to different purposes. Simple layering, as shown below using a clematis, is the most straightforward method. Propagating clematis in this way is best suited to the large-flowered hybrids.

CUTTING, ROOTING, AND SECURING A CLEMATIS

1 Sometime between autumn and spring, choose a vigorous, flexible stem that you can bend down to the ground. Make a diagonal cut on the lower side of the stem, preferably just below a node joint. Cut about halfway into the stem to form a "tongue."

2 Sink a pot of moist soil mix beneath the plant, close to the stem you are layering. Dip the cut stem, into hormone rooting powder, and shake off any excess. Hold the cut open with a piece of wood to ensure the powder gets right inside it.

3 Bury the cut area into the pot of soil mix. Hold it in place with a metal peg or a small piece of wire. Water the cut area well, and continue to water over the next few months. After six months, check for roots by pulling gently on the end of the stem.

IMPROVING THE SOIL

● **Soil condition** If rooting directly into the soil, improve the soil's texture and fertility by incorporating compost. If the soil is heavy, dig in some sand as well; good drainage is essential for healthy roots.

Use twine to tie shoot to stake

Avoiding moisture loss
Mound moist soil mix over the pegged area to prevent the soil from drying out and to encourage root development. Tie the shoot carefully to a stake to minimize any disturbance to the developing roots from wind.

STEMS AND SHOOTS

● **Healthy stems** Always choose healthy, flexible stems for layering. These are easy to bend down and most likely to produce good-quality plants.
● **Shoots** Prune the plant hard in the appropriate season to encourage shoots for layering.

OTHER METHODS

● **Serpentine layering** This method is suitable for climbing plants such as *Clematis, Celastrus, Campsis,* and *Schisandra.* Make a cut in a long, young stem close to each node. Peg the stem down with the buds exposed, to produce several plants along one stem.
● **Air layering** Shrubs such as *Hamamelis, Kalmia, Magnolia,* and *Rhododendron* respond well to air layering. Make a cut in the stem, and wrap it in moist sphagnum moss tied into position with plastic. New roots will grow into the moss.

MONEY-SAVING TIP

Mound layering
Instead of buying new heather plants, revitalize old, straggly heathers by mound layering. To do this, place a mound of rooting medium in the center of the plant, and firm it around the shoots. Moisten the medium. New roots will form in the rooting medium in about six months.

TAKING CUTTINGS

TAKING CUTTINGS IS AN ECONOMICAL WAY of increasing your stock. Remember, though, that cuttings have to survive until new roots have grown, so they need the best possible conditions and care throughout the rooting process.

BASIC EQUIPMENT

You probably already own most of what you need to raise cuttings. These items are all you need to produce plants from those in your garden, and from friends and neighbors, too.

- **Tools** Use a sharp knife or pruners to take cuttings.
- **Rooting mediums** A good-quality soil mix or rooting medium is suitable for rooting many cuttings. Some will root in garden soil, but this is not suitable for cuttings raised in pots. Hormone rooting powder helps to stimulate root formation. Choose a brand that contains a fungicide to deter fungal attack.
- **Identification tags** Labels are essential, since cuttings can look remarkably similar until they start to develop.
- **Containers** Plastic and terracotta pots are both suitable. Glass jars and yogurt pots can also be used (see p. 145).
- **Other items** Chicken wire (for securing softwood cuttings), rubber bands (for creating a mini-cloche), and plastic bags are also useful items.

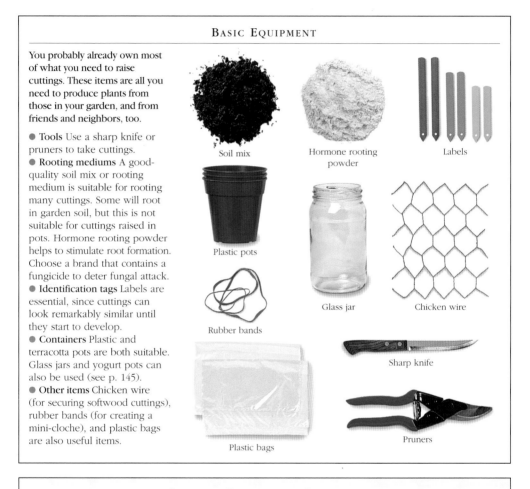

Soil mix

Hormone rooting powder

Labels

Plastic pots

Glass jar

Chicken wire

Rubber bands

Sharp knife

Plastic bags

Pruners

SUITABLE PLANTS FOR CUTTINGS

SOFTWOOD CUTTINGS
Abelia, Abutilon, Betula, Bignonia, Caryopteris, Catalpa, Ceratostigma, Clematis, Cotinus coggygria, Enkianthus, Eucryphia lucida, Forsythia, Fuchsia, Hydrangea, Koelreuteria paniculata, Kolkwitzia, Liquidambar styraciflua, Lonicera, Metasequoia glyptostroboides, Parthenocissus, Perovskia, *Philadelphus, Potentilla, Prunus, Solanum, Tropaeolum, Ulmus, Wisteria.*

SEMIRIPE CUTTINGS
Abutilon, Andromeda, Aucuba*, Berberis*, Camellia, Carpenteria*, Caryopteris, Ceanothus*, Chamaecyparis*, Clematis, Cotoneaster x cupressocyparis*, Cupressus*, Cytisus*, Daphne, Deutzia, Elaeagnus*, Enkianthus, *Eucryphia lucida, Fallopia, Garrya*, Ilex, Juniperus*, Lavandula, Ligustrum lucidum, Magnolia grandiflora*, Mahonia, Olearia*, Parthenocissus, Philadelphus, Photinia*, Pieris*, Prunus lusitanica, Rhododendron*, Skimmia*, Solanum, Thuja*, Tsuga*, Viburnum, Weigela.*

* = take cutting with a heel

SOFTWOOD CUTTINGS

Take softwood cuttings in spring, when the new shoot growth should root readily. Softwood cuttings require extreme care; although they root easily, they can also wilt and deteriorate quickly. Choose the strongest, healthiest, nonflowering sideshoots.

TAKING A CUTTING

Removing lower leaves
Choose a shoot with three to five pairs of leaves. Use a sharp knife to take a 3-5 in (7-12 cm) cutting, making a straight cut just below a leaf node. Pinch off the lowest pair of leaves.

STANDING IN WATER

Place several cuttings in jar

Securing cuttings
To hold cuttings in place, bend a piece of chicken wire over a jar of water, and secure it with a rubber band. Softwood cuttings can also be rooted successfully in a rooting medium.

COLLECTING CUTTINGS

Preventing moisture loss
Young shoots lose moisture rapidly. To avoid this, leave cuttings in a plastic bag until you are ready to prepare them.

SEMIRIPE CUTTINGS

Take semiripe cuttings from stems of the current year's growth during mid- to late summer or in early autumn. Some cuttings, particularly evergreens, root best if taken with a "heel" of old wood at the base. Always choose a healthy-looking, vigorous shoot.

TIPS FOR SUCCESS

● **Woody stem base** Choose cuttings where the stem base is slightly woody but the tip is still soft. If in doubt, take several batches of cuttings at two-week intervals.
● **Cutting leaves** Reduce moisture loss from large-leaved shrub cuttings by cutting the leaves in half before inserting the cuttings in soil mix.
● **Rooting** Apply hormone rooting powder to stimulate growth of new roots and to deter fungal infections. Shake off any excess; too much can damage the cutting base.
● **Labeling** Put pots of cuttings into a propagator or a cold frame. Label them with date and plant name.

SEVERAL CUTTINGS

Slice away strip of bark 1–1½ in (2.5–4 cm) in length

Making a heel
Trim a healthy stem into several cuttings, each about 4-6 in (10-15 cm) long. Sever each one just below a node. Remove sideshoots and the lowest pair of leaves. Stimulate root formation by removing a sliver of bark from one side of the base.

USING A PLASTIC BAG

Secure bag with rubber band

Making a mini-cloche
If you do not have a propagator, use a clear plastic bag as a mini-cloche instead. This will retain both moisture and warmth. Before removing the bag completely, harden off the cuttings gradually by cutting the corners of the bag.

HARDWOOD CUTTINGS

Hardwood cuttings are taken from fully ripened or hardened stem growth that is produced during the current season. Suitable stems can be selected from midautumn to early winter. Wait until the leaves have fallen before taking cuttings from deciduous plants.

TAKING CUTTINGS

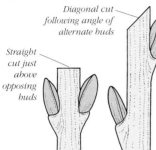

Diagonal cut following angle of alternate buds

Straight cut just above opposing buds

Different cuts
Take cuttings large enough to trim to about 6 in (15 cm). Cut off any soft wood at the tip of each cutting. Make a straight cut above opposing buds and a diagonal cut above alternate buds.

PLANTING CUTTINGS

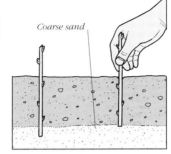

Coarse sand

Sandy trench
Insert cuttings 5-6 in (12-15 cm) deep into a well-prepared bed or trench with a 1-2 in (2.5-5 cm) layer of coarse sand at the bottom. Plant the cuttings against the side of the trench.

ADDITIONAL TIPS
● **Suitable shrubs** *Forsythia, Salix, Spiraea, Tamarix,* and *Philadelphus* root easily from hardwood cuttings.
● **Soft fruits** Many soft fruits can be increased with hardwood cuttings. For gooseberries and red currants, prepare cuttings that are at least 15 in (81 cm) long. Remove the lower buds, leaving only the top three or four. Leave all the buds on black currant cuttings.
● **Roses** Take rose cuttings from shoots that have flowered.
● **Saving space** If you need to root only a few cuttings, insert them at the back of a border.

ROOT CUTTINGS

Root cuttings should be taken when the plant is dormant. Lift a young plant, and tease the root system apart to expose the roots, then loosen the surrounding soil. Alternatively, cut out part of the root system of larger plants, leaving the rest of the roots in the ground.

SUCCESSFUL CUTTINGS
● **Suitable plants** *Acanthus, Aesculus parviflora, Anemone* x *hybrida, Aralia, Campanula, Clerodendrum, Echinops, Erodium, Gypsophila, Papaver orientale, Phlox, Primula denticulata, Pulsatilla vulgaris, Rhus, Trollius,* and *Verbascum.*
● **Watering** Water cuttings after inserting. This may prove sufficient until the cuttings have rooted; excess moisture may lead to rotting.
● **Nematodes** Avoid attack by nematodes by taking root cuttings; the pests do not enter the roots.
● **Keeping moist** Keep root cuttings in a plastic bag until you prepare them for insertion. This will prevent them from drying out quickly.

MAKING AND INSERTING ROOT CUTTINGS
● **Minimum size** Choose roots from a healthy plant. The roots should be at least ¼ in (5 mm) in diameter and close to the base of the stem.

Cutting technique
Cut off any lateral roots. Make a straight cut at the end where the root has been removed from the plant. Make a diagonal cut at the other end. Repeat this process along the length of the root.

● **Ideal length** The ideal length of the roots depends on the plant. After trimming, each root cutting should be 2–6 in (5–15 cm) long.

Space cuttings about 2 in (5 cm) apart

Inserting in soil mix
Firm soil mix into a tray, and insert the cuttings with the diagonal cut facing downward. Add soil mix so that the tips of the cuttings are just showing. Cover with ⅛ in (3 mm) of sand.

DIVISION

MANY HERBACEOUS PLANTS respond well to division, especially those that produce lots of basal shoots and those with a wide-spreading root system. The best time for dividing most plants is between late autumn and early spring.

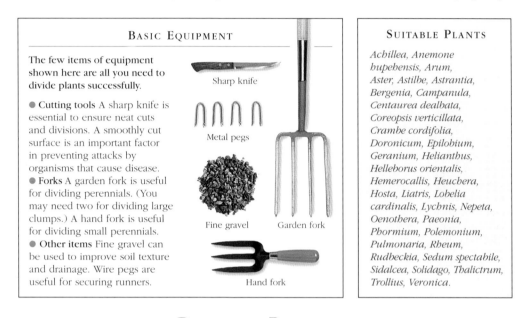

BASIC EQUIPMENT

The few items of equipment shown here are all you need to divide plants successfully.

Sharp knife

Metal pegs

Fine gravel   *Garden fork*

Hand fork

● **Cutting tools** A sharp knife is essential to ensure neat cuts and divisions. A smoothly cut surface is an important factor in preventing attacks by organisms that cause disease.
● **Forks** A garden fork is useful for dividing perennials. (You may need two for dividing large clumps.) A hand fork is useful for dividing small perennials.
● **Other items** Fine gravel can be used to improve soil texture and drainage. Wire pegs are useful for securing runners.

SUITABLE PLANTS

Achillea, Anemone hupehensis, Arum, Aster, Astilbe, Astrantia, Bergenia, Campanula, Centaurea dealbata, Coreopsis verticillata, Crambe cordifolia, Doronicum, Epilobium, Geranium, Helianthus, Helleborus orientalis, Hemerocallis, Heuchera, Hosta, Liatris, Lobelia cardinalis, Lychnis, Nepeta, Oenothera, Paeonia, Phormium, Polemonium, Pulmonaria, Rheum, Rudbeckia, Sedum spectabile, Sidalcea, Solidago, Thalictrum, Trollius, Veronica.

DIVIDING RHIZOMES

Division of plants provides the opportunity to rejuvenate old clumps of rhizomes and bulbs, and to create new clumps at the same time. Tough plants may require two large forks back-to-back to divide them, but many can be divided by hand or with a knife.

LIFTING, TRIMMING, AND PLANTING IRIS RHIZOMES

Cut out and discard old rhizomes

1 Use a large fork to lift the clump. To reduce the risk of root damage, drive the fork into the ground at an angle and well away from the rhizomes. Shake off excess soil, and split up the clump.

2 Detach any new, healthy rhizomes from the clump, and trim their ends with a sharp knife. Dust the cut surfaces with a sulfur-based fungicide. Discard old or diseased rhizomes.

3 Make a diagonal cut on each leaf to about 6 in (15 cm) to minimize root disturbance from wind rock. Replant, leaving just the tops above soil level. Be sure the foliage is upright.

CARING FOR BULBS

Bulbs require some attention if they are to perform well over a long period. Clumps become overcrowded after a few years and need to be divided. It is best to lift clumps during dormancy, and to replant the bulbs in irregular groups immediately after division.

BULB MAINTENANCE

● **Marking clumps** When clumps begin to flower unreliably, it is a sign that they need to be divided. Mark these clumps with a stake when the foliage starts to die back so that they can be identified easily when dormant.

● **Foliar feeding** Bulbs that need dividing are often considerably undersized. Help to boost their growth by giving them a foliar feed immediately after replanting. Continue to feed regularly during the growing season.

● **Offset bulbs** Do not discard offset bulbs. Plant them in a separate site or nursery bed until they are fully grown.

DIVIDING OVERCROWDED BULBS

Lifting a clump
Lift a clump using a hand fork. A garden fork may be necessary for big or deep clumps. Try to avoid piercing any bulbs, and discard any that are damaged. Prepare a fresh planting hole, and incorporate fertilizer into it.

Remove offsets from parent bulb, along with loose outer layers of bulb tunic

Removing offsets
Carefully remove offsets from the parent bulbs; discard bulbs that appear unhealthy. Replant bulbs that are full-size or nearly full-size immediately, at the correct depth (see p. 57), and in a suitable site for the bulb type.

SCALING BULBS

Bulb scaling is a method of propagation for any bulbs with scales. It is most frequently used for lilies and *Fritillaria*, and it is carried out in late summer or early autumn. Look for scales with bulbils (miniature bulbs), which form at the base of the scales.

PROPAGATING WITH LILY SCALES AND BULBILS

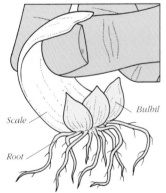

Scale
Bulbil
Root

1 Remove any soil and damaged or diseased scales from around the bulb. Gently pull off any healthy scales that have bulbils at the bases. Be careful not to separate the scales from the bulbils.

Shake scales in sulfur to deter fungal infections

2 Shake the scales in a bag containing sulfur. Remove the scales, and tap gently. Put them in a bag of peat and perlite. Seal, and keep in the dark at 70°F (21°C) for three months.

3 Plant the scales in individual pots of sandy potting mix. The tops of the scales should be just beneath the surface of the mix. Keep in a cold greenhouse or well-shaded cold frame.

DIVIDING PLANTS

Most plants will reproduce readily in their natural habitat, and propagation often takes advantage of this process. Propagation by division produces sizable plants very quickly. Correct timing and proper aftercare of new plants are the key to guaranteed success.

DIVISION SUCCESS

● **Timing** Choose the time of day carefully for this task. Divisions are likely to fail if they become dehydrated. Try to divide plants during the coolest part of the day – if possible, early in the evening.
● **Cool spot** Replant any divisions as soon as possible to minimize moisture loss. Keep the new plants in a cool spot out of direct sunlight.
● **Healthy material** Use only healthy stock as propagating material. When dividing plants, take the opportunity to discard weak or old sections.
● **Weeds** Before replanting divisions, remove any weeds that are growing among the crown and roots.

USING RUNNERS

Dividing strawberry plants
Strawberry plants produce runners that make propagation very easy. Space the runners out around the plant, and peg them down. When they are rooted and showing signs of strong growth, sever the runners from the plants, and replant.

USING OFFSETS

Dividing *Sempervivum*
These plants produce many small plants in clusters. Carefully remove these from the parent plant. Some may have already grown small root systems, but even those that have not will readily root when potted up in sandy potting mix.

DIVIDING RASPBERRY PLANTS

Raspberry canes naturally form suckers. If these are healthy and disease-free, they can be used to replace old stock or to add to the existing crop. In late autumn, you can lift any suckers that have developed around vigorous, healthy plants.

1 Select suckers from a well-established plant. Use a fork to lift suckers, taking care not to damage the roots. Sever each sucker with pruners or a sharp knife. Be sure that each sucker has a good root system.

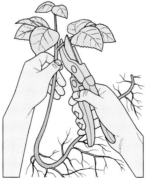

2 Remove the remaining leaves, and replant the rooted suckers in a well-prepared site. Choose a new site to limit the risk of soil-borne pests and diseases. Water the suckers well.

DIVIDING PERENNIALS

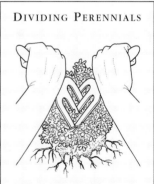

● **Clumps** Perennials respond particularly well to propagation by division. Once a clump has become well established, there are few herbaceous plants that will not benefit from this propagation method.
● **Timing** Division is usually carried out while the plant is dormant in autumn or early spring. Spring division is usually most successful in heavy soils (see p. 60).

GENERAL MAINTENANCE

PLANTS ARE NOT THE ONLY FEATURES in a garden that benefit from care and attention. Tools, structures, and buildings should be kept in good condition. The materials from which they are made determine the type and frequency of maintenance required. Use the chart below to assess the pros and cons of each material.

GARDEN MATERIALS

MATERIAL	PROS	CONS
HARDWOODS Hardwoods – such as beech, mahogany, and teak – are used in the construction of most garden structures and furniture.	Hardwoods are strong and long-lasting, and are not easily damaged. They retain their finish with relatively little maintenance, and are not prone to rotting.	Hardwoods are available mainly from specialized suppliers, and items made from them can be costly. Be sure the wood comes from a sustainable source.
SOFTWOODS Softwoods – such as cedar, fir, pine, and spruce – are used principally to make garden furniture, arches, pergolas, gates, and fences. They can be stained or painted.	Production of softwoods is widespread and, as a result, they are cheaper and easier to obtain than hardwoods, and come in a wide variety of sizes. Their light density and weight make them easy to work with.	Softwoods have a shorter lifespan and are more prone to damage than hardwoods. Regular treatment with a preservative is essential if these woods are to last, particularly if kept outside over winter.
PLASTIC Injection-molded plastic is a popular construction material for garden furniture, as well as for windowboxes, pots, and other plant containers.	Plastic does not rot, warp, or corrode; it is not affected by cold or damp weather; and it requires little maintenance. One of a gardener's less expensive options, it is also lightweight.	The colors in which plastic is available can seem too bright and artificial for a small or traditional garden. The color of some plastics will fade after prolonged exposure to the sun.
CAST IRON Cast iron was used in the last century to make garden furniture and ornaments.	Cast iron is very heavy, making it ideal for containers in which stability is required. It is easy to paint with a brush or spray gun.	Cast iron must be painted regularly to prevent rust. Its weight makes it difficult to move, and it may break on impact.
ALUMINUM This alloy is used for structures such as frames and greenhouses.	Aluminum can be painted with enamel for consistent color. It is lightweight and easy to move.	Weathered aluminum surfaces can become covered with a white and powdery corrosion.
STEEL Steel is used for items such as children's play equipment.	Steel is strong and sturdy, and is not easily damaged, so it requires minimal maintenance.	Paint on galvanized steel surfaces may chip and peel off over time.

BASIC EQUIPMENT

Maintaining garden features may require a range of tools. Consider the nature of the particular task before deciding whether to purchase or hire expensive equipment.

● **Removing deposits** Use a stiff wire brush for demanding cleaning jobs, such as removing rust, paint, algae, and other deposits from hard surfaces.
● **Cleaning surfaces** Use a stiff bristle brush to clean surfaces that may be stained or rusty.
● **Painting** Select paintbrushes in a range of sizes to apply wood treatments and stains, paints, and other liquids.
● **Filling small areas** Remove rotten wood or crumbling mortar with a chisel, then fill the hole with wood filler or putty. Apply these with a putty knife for a smooth finish.
● **Filling large areas** Fill in and smooth large areas of concrete or mortar with a trowel.
● **Replacing nails** Remove old nails with a claw hammer. Replace with galvanized nails.
● **Hammering** Pound fence posts and paving stones into place using a club hammer.
● **Handling** Wear sturdy gloves when moving rough or sharp materials and objects.

Stiff wire brush

Stiff bristle brush

Small paintbrush

Large paintbrush

Putty knife

Chisel

Bricklayer's trowel

Hammer

Club hammer

Galvanized nails

Sturdy gloves

ADHESIVES, PRESERVATIVES, AND SEALANTS

Liquid treatments can often be customized to your needs by mixing with paints and other materials.

● **Protection** Apply wood preservative regularly to extend the life of a wooden structure.
● **Color** Select a wood filler that matches the wood in color.
● **Strength** PVA adhesive is a sealant and bonding agent. It can be mixed with materials to strengthen them.
● **Repairs** Sealants are available for repairing particular features or structures, including roofs and ponds.

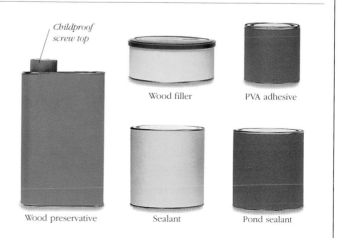

Childproof screw top

Wood filler

PVA adhesive

Wood preservative

Sealant

Pond sealant

WOODEN STRUCTURES

Wood complements almost any garden. Soft- and hardwoods are available in a range of colors, weights, sizes, and prices. They can be stained, treated, or painted to alter their color and blend in with their environment.

REPAIRING SHEDS

A shed can last for many years. It should not need a great deal of maintenance, but routine jobs, such as treating the wood and painting it occasionally, will extend a shed's life considerably. Repairing or replacing the roof and replacing glass may also be necessary.

REPAIRING ROOFS
● **Reroofing** Do this in warm weather, when felt is unlikely to crack. If you must climb onto the roof, kneel on a board to spread your weight.
● **Roofing felt** Select a thick grade of roofing felt. Make sure that it is sufficiently flexible for easy handling.
● **Old nails** Remove old nails from the roof with a claw hammer before replacing felt. If any break, hammer them in before securing the new felt with rustproof, galvanized nails.
● **Wood** Strip off the roofing felt, and make sure the wood underneath is sound.

REPLACING DAMAGED ROOFING FELT

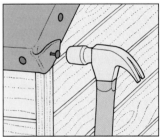

Eliminating air pockets
Place the first sheet of felt so that it extends over the eaves by about 1 in (2.5 cm) and the ends overlap the fascia boards by about 1 in (2.5 cm). Press down with a strip of wood to smooth out air pockets in the felt.

Securing a corner
Where the eaves and fascia boards meet, tuck the felt into a triangle, and fold it toward the fascia board, securing it in place with galvanized nails. Tuck the corner in to ensure that it does not collect rainwater.

REPAIRING WOOD SIDING

Wood siding has a tendency to splinter, crack, and rot. If a small area is affected, it is a relatively simple process to replace the wood. Once it has been replaced, be sure to protect it from moisture by filling gaps with putty, then treating the wood with wood preservative.

1 Lift the siding with a crowbar, and drive wedges under the damaged area. Insert a thin piece of wood to protect the wood below, then cut out the damaged area with a saw.

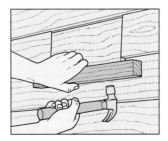

2 Measure and cut a replacement section, then hammer it in, protecting the new board from the hammer with a block of wood. Nail the board in with galvanized nails.

USING WOOD
● **Cut ends** Treat freshly cut ends before using the wood.
● **Drying** After treating wood, allow it to dry before use.
● **Damaged boards** If more than one area of a board is damaged, replace the whole board.
● **Siding** Use pressure-treated wood to extend the life of siding. This wood resists insects and fungi, and is ideal for damp locations.
● **Wood putty** For filling gaps, select wood putty that matches the color of the wood.

MAINTAINING GUTTERS

It is essential that gutters and downspouts on greenhouses, conservatories, and sheds are kept in good condition. Pipes are liable to become blocked and may leak or overflow, causing serious damage to the structure, which will take time and money to repair.

PREVENTING PROBLEMS

● **Rust** Scrape off rust as soon as it appears, and apply an antirust solution. Allow this to dry before painting the area with oil-based paint.
● **Plastic gutters** Replacing a damaged section of plastic guttering is more effective in the long run than repairing it. However, minor damage can be repaired with a sealant or PVA adhesive. Waterproof tape is also useful for short periods.
● **Chicken wire** If inspecting or repairing gutters, take the opportunity to attach narrow-gauge chicken wire along the length of the gutters to prevent them from becoming blocked with debris.

REPAIRING PLASTIC AND METAL GUTTERS

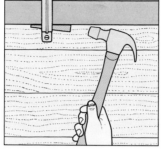

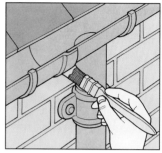

Repairing a sagging gutter
Loose or sagging plastic gutters will not drain properly, and this may cause their contents to overflow. As a temporary measure, hammer in a wooden wedge between each bracket and the gutter to hold each section in place until you can replace it.

Sealing a crack
If metal gutters crack and develop leaks, scrape off any rust, then paint the affected area with a sealing compound. Protect from rain until the sealant has dried. If the gutter is damaged at several points, replace the entire section.

INSULATING AND SECURING SHEDS

To serve its purpose effectively, a shed must be dry and watertight. It should also be a safe, secure, and comfortable place in which to work and store tools and equipment. With a little effort, an unwelcoming, damp shed can be transformed into a warm, dry workplace.

INSTALLING INSULATION

Using polystyrene
Nail polystyrene panels between the supporting struts of the roof and walls on the inside of a shed. Use short nails to avoid damaging the outer surface of the siding or the roofing felt. Cover the polystyrene with a layer of hardboard.

MAINTAINING SHEDS

● **Wood preservative** If the wood on your shed needs to be treated with preservative, do this in the summer months. In warm weather, the shed door and windows can be left open to diffuse any noxious fumes.
● **Curtains** Hang a curtain over a shed door for added insulation against drafts.
● **Drafts** Install foam strips around the door and window frames to keep out drafts.
● **Heating** If working in a shed during cold and wet winter months, use a kerosene heater to keep it warm and dry. Be sure the heater is well maintained and operated so that it does not pose a fire or health hazard.

LOCKING SHEDS

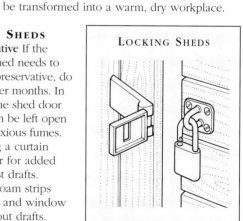

Many locks on sheds are easily broken. Install a strong locking bar with screws drilled through the back of the door. Fasten with a good-quality padlock. Block out windows with blinds if the shed is used for storing valuable tools.

PREVENTING WOOD FROM ROTTING

Garden structures and furniture are continually exposed to the adverse effects of the weather. Seasonal changes and damp conditions encourage rotting. If wood comes in contact with soil or any other moist material, the damage can be extensive.

PRESERVING WOOD

Wear gloves to protect hands

Cleaning and applying

Prevent the wood from rotting by applying a coat of suitable wood preservative. Clean off all loose material and debris, and be sure that it is thoroughly dry before applying the preservative.

DISCOURAGING ROT

● **Using preservative** Place the legs of wooden furniture in saucers of wood preservative for several hours to ensure that the solution is absorbed.
● **Positioning furniture** Place garden furniture on a flat, even surface that does not collect rainwater. Avoid putting wooden furniture on grass.
● **Treating corners** Wood is likely to rot in the corners of structures. Prevent this by regularly treating these areas with wood preservative.
● **Removing debris** The accumulation of debris on or around wood encourages decay. Remove fallen leaves and encroaching undergrowth.

FUNGAL ROT

Fungal rot – dry and wet – is not difficult to identify but, apart from treatable patches of wet rot, should be dealt with by a professional.

● **Dry rot** The first signs of dry rot are white, fibrous growths that become dusty red. Wood surfaces split into cubes and are covered by gray mold; if probed with a knife, the wood will crumble. Plaster bulges and cracks.
● **Wet rot** This affects only areas where moisture has penetrated. It produces narrow, brown strips of fungus, and causes wood to crack, and paint to flake.

TREATING ROTTED WOOD

It is best to prevent wood from rotting, but occasional treatment of damaged areas will still be necessary. Before making any repairs, make sure that the wood is as dry as possible; bring wooden furniture under cover for a few weeks before repairing it.

REMOVING DAMAGED WOOD AND FILLING HOLES

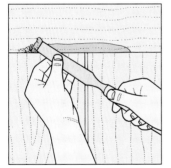

1 Remove damaged wood with a chisel or sturdy kitchen knife. Cut back to the sound wood, removing any discolored or decayed areas. If in doubt, keep cutting; just be sure you do not diminish the overall strength of the structure.

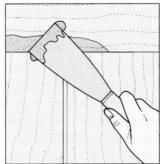

2 If possible, select a wood filler that dries to the same color as the structure being repaired. Fill the hole with the filler, firmly pressing it in to expel any air bubbles. To deter moisture accumulation, angle the surface. When this is dry, apply a preservative.

DRYING WOOD

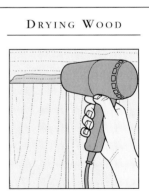

Treating a small area
Frequently, a small patch of wood on a large structure needs to be repaired. Instead of waiting for the entire structure to dry out naturally, try drying the damaged area quickly with a hair dryer.

MAINTAINING FENCES

Fences must remain outside regardless of the weather. The location of some sections may expose them permanently to cold and damp conditions. Dense planting of climbers and shrubs also encourages the buildup of moist air. Ultimately, deterioration is inevitable.

REPAIRING FENCES

● **Crushed stone** Drive crushed stone firmly into place using the base of a concrete spur or a spare wooden post.
● **Concrete** If you have only a few posts to replace and little time to spare, use a quick-setting concrete mix.
● **Winter protection** In cold and wet weather, create a screen to protect fence posts from frost and to prevent water from accumulating on the surface of any concrete.
● **Decayed wood** Do not repair a fence post that shows signs of deterioration; its strength as a support has probably been reduced, and the whole post should always be replaced.
● **Corrosion** Check metal bolts and nails for corrosion, which may reduce their strength.
● **Treatment** Regularly treat fences with wood preservative.

REPLACING A SECTION

Adjusting size and fit
Fence sections are available in standard sizes, making their replacement relatively easy. However, if a new section is too thin, insert a board or a small strip of pressure-treated wood between the fence post and the edge of the section. Nail the section in position with galvanized nails.

REPOSITIONING AND MENDING POSTS

● **Loose foundations** Repair a loose post promptly to avoid damage to the fence. Avoid disturbing nearby plants.

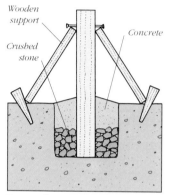

Wooden support
Crushed stone
Concrete

Restoring a wooden post
Dig a hole 8 x 8 in (20 x 20 cm) around the post. Reposition the post, using a level, if necessary, and hold it in place with wooden supports. Pour crushed stone around the base, force it down, then set in concrete.

● **Concrete** Rotted wood can make a fence unstable. Replace the base with concrete, which is impervious to moisture.

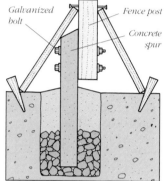

Galvanized bolt
Fence post
Concrete spur

Replacing a section
Replace a post section with a concrete spur and, if necessary, a new post. Attach the post to the spur above the soil with galvanized bolts. Hold with temporary supports, and pack with crushed stone and concrete.

PROTECTING AND MAINTAINING FENCES

● **Avoiding damp** Fit a concrete or timber board along the base of a fence to protect it from rising damp. Try to keep gravel and soil away from the board.
● **Matching color** A new section may appear out of place on an old, weathered fence. After replacing a section, treat the entire fence with a colored wood preservative to give it a uniform look.
● **Wide sections** Plane the edges of a new section if it is a little too wide to fit into the frame of a fence.
● **Plants** To keep damage to nearby plants to a minimum, repair and maintain fences in the autumn or winter.

Damaged post
Timber   Stone

Removing a post
If a damaged post is difficult to remove, lever it out with a length of sturdy timber and a large stone or pile of bricks. Tie the timber firmly to the damaged post, balancing it over the stone. Push down repeatedly on the timber with your foot until the post is free.

CONCRETE AND BRICKWORK

S TONE, CONCRETE, AND BRICKS ARE RESILIENT, long-lasting materials. However, some weather conditions, such as cold or heavy frost, may cause these normally sturdy substances to chip and break, making maintenance and repairs necessary.

PREPARING CONCRETE AND MORTAR

MIXING CEMENT
● **Small amounts** Mix the components together by hand if you need only a small amount of concrete. This saves on preparation time and money, enabling you to measure the required quantities of sand and stone accurately.
● **Large amounts** If a large amount of concrete is needed, it is worth renting a cement mixer, which will make the process relatively quick and simple.

MAKING CONCRETE
● **Mixing** Measure out the sand and stone according to the instructions on the packet. Mix the components together on a flat surface, smooth the top of the mixture, make a depression in the center, and pour in the cement. Combine, and add water, if necessary.
● **Consistency** Slap the surface of the mixture with the back of a trowel. If water trickles out, add more sand and stone.

MAKING MORTAR
● **Ready-mixed mortar** Although this is expensive, ready-mixed mortar is more time- and cost-effective for small jobs than buying separate components.
● **Preparation** Dampen the surface of a mixing board, and pour the mortar powder onto it. Flatten the top of the dry mixture, and make a depression in the center. Add water slowly, mixing thoroughly to produce a moist, even consistency.

MAINTAINING WALLS

The external and dividing walls of a garden, as well as those on which sheds and greenhouses are built, should serve a purpose and look attractive. A weathered wall can look good, but an excessive buildup of algae and other deposits can spoil its appearance.

REMOVING DEPOSITS
● **Efflorescence** A white, salty deposit, called efflorescence, may appear on the surface of new bricks. Remove these deposits to prevent ugly marks.

Brushing off deposits
Scrub with a dry wire brush to remove efflorescence. Repeat this process several times. Do not wash deposits off with water, because extra moisture will make the problem worse.

DEALING WITH DEPOSITS
● **Prevention** Use sealants and treatments on brickwork to keep walls dry and prevent deposits from collecting.
● **Gutters** Check gutters for debris to ensure that they do not overflow and encourage the buildup of algae on walls.
● **Cleaning agents** When removing deposits with a brush, be sure not to use cleaning agents or soaps that can encourage efflorescence.
● **Recurring deposits** If algal deposits recur, remove with a commercial algicidal product.
● **Pressure washing** Walls that are difficult to clean should be pressure-washed. Do this in warm weather, when water will evaporate rapidly, and make sure nearby doors and windows are shut firmly.

BRIGHT IDEA

Restoring bricks
Renovate discolored, stained, or marked brickwork using an old brick of a matching color. Keep the old brick wet (place a bucket of water nearby), and rub the brick vigorously over the damaged areas.

REPAIRING BRICKWORK

Over time, the mortar in a brick wall may crack, allowing moisture to penetrate through to the interior walls of a structure. Extremes of weather can cause the mortar to become loose, crumble, and begin to fall away. Accurate and immediate repair is essential.

WEATHERPROOFING

● **Loose mortar** Remove all loose mortar from a wall to a depth of 1 in (2.5 cm) before attempting to replace with fresh mortar.
● **Power drill** Remove large amounts of loose mortar with a power drill. Protective goggles are essential.
● **Depth** If in doubt, chip away between the bricks until all loose mortar has been removed, but make sure that you do not damage the surrounding brickwork.
● **PVA adhesive** Increase the strength of the new mortar by adding PVA adhesive. This will also increase the bonding ability of the mixture.
● **Cleaning** Remove all excess mortar from the brickwork immediately. Use a wet brush or stiff cloth.

CHOOSING A FINISH

● **Matching mortars** Try to match the finish of new mortar with that of the old. This will help to disguise repairs made to the brickwork.

Using a garden hose
Use a piece of an old garden hose to create an even, concave surface after applying the mortar to the brickwork. Bend the hose into a slight curve to make it easy to handle.

REPOINTING BRICKS

● **Preparation** Chip away any loose mortar with a screwdriver or a slim chisel and a club hammer. Wear goggles to protect your eyes.

Removing loose mortar
Use a soft brush to wipe away sandy deposits after removing loose mortar. Wipe the affected area with a sponge soaked in water before repointing. This will help the new mortar adhere better to the bricks.

ANGLING MORTAR

● **Trowel** To achieve angled pointing, use a trowel to project the mortar over the top of a brick and recess into the base of the brick above.

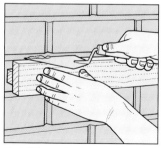

Catching excess
Nail a block of wood to each end of a board, then hold it level with the edge of the mortar. Drag a trowel across the board, in line with the bricks. Excess mortar will fall onto the wood.

APPLYING MORTAR

● **Equipment** Repoint a wall using a good-quality bricklayer's trowel. Be sure it is small enough to maneuver and it gives a smooth finish.

Renovating brickwork
Begin by replacing the mortar in the vertical joints. When a section is completed, move on to the horizontal joints. Wet the wall again if it starts to dry out. Press the mortar in firmly, and trim away excess mortar.

TIME-SAVING TIP

Harmonizing colors
The color of new mortar may change considerably when it dries. To avoid color clashes on a wall, mix a small quantity of the new mortar and allow it to dry, then scoop it onto a trowel, and compare it with the old.

REPAIRING CRACKS IN CONCRETE

Concrete paths and steps may develop cracks and even break up, particularly if they have been subjected to heavy use. Cold, wet, and frosty weather, foot traffic, heavy wheelbarrows, and other factors will eventually take their toll on these essential garden features.

MAINTAINING CONCRETE

● **Hairline cracks** Do not immediately fill a thin crack. Wait for a month or two to be sure it does not increase in size before making necessary repairs.

● **Foundation** Large cracks can be caused by a weakness in the foundation on which a step or path is laid. Remove the area, and lay it again on a new, strong foundation.

● **Drying** Cover a repaired area with a plastic sheet to protect the concrete filler from rain. Allow it to dry gradually.

● **Insulating** If freezing weather conditions are forecast, cover a newly filled surface with newspaper, cloth, or other insulating material.

PREPARING AND FILLING CRACKS IN CONCRETE

● **Enlarging areas** Repair any crack or hole that is more than ½ in (1.5 cm) in depth. Enlarge the area to ensure that the filler is packed firmly.

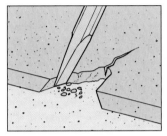

1 Use a chisel to chip away material in the affected area. To ensure that the filler will be held firmly in place, angle the chisel to make the hole larger at the base than at the surface.

● **Preparation** Remove debris that may have accumulated in the affected area, since it will prevent the filler from adhering to the concrete.

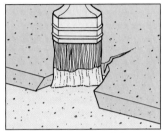

2 Brush away any debris, then apply PVA adhesive to the sides of the crack or hole. Plug the hole with concrete filler, making it level with the surrounding area.

REPAIRING CONCRETE EDGES

The edges of a concrete path or steps are subject to potentially damaging wear and tear. Air pockets beneath the surface, formed when the concrete is first laid, can cause the material to decay and crumble. For this reason, edges require frequent maintenance.

REPAIRING EDGES

Using wooden edging
Hammer blocks of wood into the ground with a mallet to create a temporary wooden edge. Make sure that the top of the wood is level with the concrete. Fill the space with fresh cement.

MAINTAINING EDGES

● **Loose material** Remove any loose or crumbling material from around a broken edge, leaving a stable rim. If in doubt, remove more material than is necessary.

● **Crushed stone** If any of the base stone is exposed during repairs, pack it down firmly with a wooden post or concrete spur. Pack a new layer of crushed stone into any weak areas.

● **Protective covering** If small children or pets are likely to use a freshly repaired area, cover the new edge with a sheet of plastic and a layer of chicken wire until the concrete has dried.

SAFETY MEASURES

It is essential that eyes, skin, and lungs are fully covered and protected when making any repairs to concrete or stone paths, steps, or walls.

● **Goggles** Wear goggles when working with concrete and stone; small fragments of debris can injure the eyes. Be sure they are clean so that you can see clearly.

● **Gloves** Wear rubber gloves to protect your hands from the caustic effects of cement.

● **Face mask** Cement dust is harmful to the lungs. To prevent lung damage wear a face mask when mixing the components together.

REPLACING PAVING SLABS

Patio paving slabs can be exposed to a great deal of stress, especially during periods of warm weather. Eventually, they will need to be repaired as cracks appear or mortar crumbles. However, the repairs should not be extensive or costly if they are done promptly.

INSTALLING SLABS

● **Individual slabs** Replace any slabs that have shattered or cracked. Use the opportunity to make sure that the crushed stone below is firm and level.

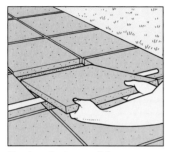

Easing into position
To prevent the surrounding slabs from being damaged, lay a broom handle or piece of pipe across the gap to be filled. Use this as a support to ease the new paving stone into place.

WORKING WITH SLABS

● **Safety** The edges of paving slabs can be very sharp, particularly if cut using a chisel. Wear goggles when cutting, and use thick gloves when handling sharp slabs.
● **Cutting surface** Place a slab on a solid, flat surface to ensure an accurate cut.
● **Level surface** When a new slab is in place, use a level to make sure that the surface is completely level before replacing the mortar.
● **Uneven slabs** To realign an uneven slab, place a block of wood on the surface to prevent damage to the slab, and lightly strike it with a club hammer until level.
● **Cleaning** When the mortar is dry, wash the entire paved surface with a commercial cleaning agent.

FILLING JOINTS

● **Positioning** Before filling in a joint with mortar, allow the replacement paving stone to settle on the crushed stone for a minimum of two days.

Using a wooden jigger
Fill the joints using a wooden jigger. Align the narrow central opening to the joint, and push the mortar through. Used correctly, a jigger prevents excess mortar from spilling onto the slabs.

PLACING AND CLEANING

● **Spacing** If existing slabs are separated by mortar, use a wooden spacer of the same width as the mortar to position a new slab. Remove the spacer when laying mortar in the joint.
● **Cleaning** Clean up excess mortar with water and a stiff brush or broom as promptly as possible. Mortar sets quickly and can be difficult to remove once it is dry.
● **Planting up** If a paving slab is badly damaged and you are unable to find a suitable replacement, consider removing the damaged slab and replacing it with plants (see p. 20).
● **Stains** Paving slabs can be marked by oil, rust, and moss. Use a commercial cleaning agent to remove the stains.

CUTTING A PAVING SLAB

Paving slabs are available in a wide range of sizes. However, the shape of a patio or terrace may require a slab to be cut to size. Rent an angle grinder if you have a number of slabs to alter.

Work along score mark

Chisel

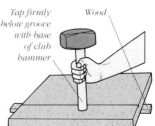

Tap firmly below groove with base of club hammer

Wood

1 Score both sides of the slab with a chisel. Work along the line with a club hammer and chisel to make a groove ⅛ in (3 mm) deep. If the slab has to fit tightly, cut it to size, less ¼ in (6 mm) all around to allow for uneven edges.

2 Rest the paving slab on a firm surface. Place a section of wood under the groove. Tap the surface of the slab with the base of a club hammer, to one side of the score mark. Repeat until the slab breaks. Protect your eyes from flying debris.

REPAIRING BRICK PATHS

Individual bricks are not easily broken in a path or patio, but occasionally one will crack or shatter. A damaged brick should be replaced as soon as possible. Once the brick is cracked, moisture may penetrate and freeze in cold weather, making the problem worse.

DESIGNING WITH BRICKS

● **Color** Try to match the color of a new brick with its surroundings. Although it will stand out when new, the brick will weather with age.
● **Used bricks** Buy second-hand bricks for an instant weathered effect. Make sure that the bricks are frostproof before you purchase them.
● **Combinations** If you cannot locate new bricks that match the old, use the originals to replace broken sections, and place the new bricks in less conspicuous spots.
● **Contrast** Place different bricks among the originals to create contrast between the old and new bricks, and raise some above the others to form a pattern.

REPLACING BRICKS

● **Removing** Chip away any surrounding mortar, then use a bricklayer's trowel to pry out the broken brick, taking care not to damage adjacent paving.

Inserting a new brick
Place a piece of wood on top of the new brick to avoid damaging the surface, then tamp with a club hammer. Fill in any gaps between the bricks with sand.

BRIGHT IDEA

Storing bricks
If bricks become damp, they will not adhere to mortar. Store them in a dry place, or cover with a heavy plastic. Stack bricks on a board that has been placed on a level, firm surface. To prevent the pile from collapsing, place the bricks in a pyramid shape so that the outer layer leans inward.

RECONSTRUCTING CONCRETE STEPS

If the main body of a set of steps begins to fall down, the entire set should be replaced because the steps may be unsafe and collapse without warning. However, it is normally the fronts of the steps, and occasionally the sides, that are most likely to incur damage.

MAINTAINING AND RESTORING CONCRETE STEPS

● **Preparation** Remove the damaged area. Brush off all dust and other loose material, then apply PVA adhesive to the newly prepared surface.
● **Concrete** To form a good replacement edge, be sure to use a dry mixture of concrete made up of one part cement to five parts ballast.
● **Prevention** Avoid further damage to a set of steps by occasionally varying your path, especially if carrying a heavy load or pushing a heavy wheelbarrow. Simple measures, such as steering the wheel away from the center of a step, will help.

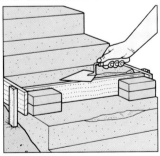

Using a wooden form
A new step edge must be straight. Hold boards in place with bricks and stakes hammered into the ground. Firmly pack the concrete mixture into this form, and smooth over with a trowel.

COMPLETING REPAIRS

● **Form** Check that boards used to make a form are not warped or marked with knots.
● **Setting** Leave the supporting boards in place for a minimum of four weeks after carrying out a repair. This gives the concrete time to set completely.
● **Protecting** To protect newly repaired areas on concrete steps from rain or frost, cover them with a plastic sheet.
● **Aging** Dust the surface of wet concrete with sifted sand to give the edge an aged look. When the concrete is set, brush off any excess sand.

GARDEN FURNITURE

I F LEFT OUTSIDE THROUGHOUT THE YEAR, garden furniture will rapidly start to show signs of aging. If possible, shelter these items in wet or windy weather. Or, cover bulky furniture with plastic to avoid using valuable storage space.

MAINTAINING FURNITURE

The kind of maintenance your garden furniture requires depends upon the material from which the item is made, and how it has been treated in the past. The appearance of old garden furniture can be greatly improved or altered with a coat of paint or a stain.

CARING FOR WOOD

● **Softwood** To prolong the life of softwood, be sure to apply a coat of wood preservative every year.
● **Hardwood** Treat hardwood with an annual application of teak oil. Although hardwood has a long life expectancy and is not prone to rotting, it will benefit from treatment.
● **Preparation** Before treating or painting wood, rub the surface down to remove any loose material, and allow the wood to dry thoroughly.

PAINTING AND STAINING WOODEN FURNITURE

● **Color** Wooden furniture can be painted or stained using a colored wood preservative, or a coat of paint followed by a coat of wood preservative.

Pour paint into measured quantity of preservative

Creating a color
Create your own color by mixing latex paint with clear wood preservative. Line a container with foil, pour in the two components, and stir thoroughly.

CARING FOR PLASTIC

● **Cleaning** Wash down plastic garden furniture regularly to keep it clean and comfortable, and to minimize any scratching on the surface.
● **Painting** Restore a stained or discolored item using paint made for plastic furniture. Ask for advice at a hardware store or paint store.

LOOKING AFTER METAL

● **Light metal** If purchasing furniture made of light metal, ensure that it is strong and stable. Dents in metal are difficult to remove successfully.
● **Weatherproofing** If a metal item is to remain in the garden throughout the winter, protect all the exposed surfaces with an application of heavy oil. Wipe off the residue before using the furniture again.

MONEY-SAVING TIP

Renovating sagging cane
If the seat of a cane or wicker chair has begun to sag, it may be possible to reverse the process. In warm weather, scrub the seat with plenty of soapy water, then rinse with clean water. Leave the chair outside to dry. The seat should shrink slightly, reducing the sagging.

OILING FURNITURE

● **Dealing with rust** Choose an aerosol product that inhibits rust. If it has an extension tube, it can also be used as a lubricant for springs, hinges, and rivets. Wipe off the oil before use.
● **Using paint** If rust does appear, rub it off with a wire brush. Treat the area with antirust paint, and allow it to dry before painting with the color of your choice.

GARDEN TOOLS

G ARDEN TOOLS ARE VALUABLE PIECES OF EQUIPMENT, and are well worth keeping in good condition by maintaining them on a regular basis. Regular care will ensure that your tools continue to perform efficiently.

MAINTAINING TOOLS

R outine maintenance needs to be done only once a year if tools are handled with care, cleaned, and oiled if necessary, and repaired promptly and correctly. Regular care ensures that damage and deterioration of valuable equipment are kept to a minimum.

CLEANING A FORK

Scrape away lumps of soil

Making digging easier
When working in soil that is heavy and sticky, periodically remove soil from the tines of a fork. At the same time, remove any stones that are jammed between the tines that may cause the metal to bend.

REMOVING SOIL

● **Dried soil** An old, but sturdy kitchen knife makes an excellent tool for manually removing lumps of soil that have dried on garden tools.
● **Clay soil** To remove stubborn lumps of clay from a fork or spade, push the tool into a compost pile or a bucket of fine, oily gravel. Much of the adhering clay will come off and mix with the compost or gravel.
● **Tires** Clean the tires of a wheelbarrow regularly. A heavy coating of mud may conceal sharp stones that could cause punctures when the wheelbarrow is used again.

LOOKING AFTER BLADES

Thoroughly wipe blades with oil

Oiling blades
Cutting blades must be clean and dry before oiling. Put plenty of oil on a clean rag, and use this to wipe over the blades and other metal parts. This should be done at least several times a year, and preferably after each use.

LOOKING AFTER WOOD

● **Drying** Before putting tools away, stand them upright to dry, preferably in the sun. If the tools are still damp, store them vertically to prevent water from accumulating and rotting the wood.
● **Removing splinters** To remove scratches or splintered areas on wooden handles, rub down the whole handle with fine-grade sandpaper, following the grain of the wood.
● **Applying oil** When storing equipment for a long period of time, rub linseed oil on the handles or shafts of wooden tools. Allow the oil to penetrate, and remove any excess with a dry rag.

COVERING UNCOMFORTABLE TOOL HANDLES

Wrap electrical insulating tape around handle

Taping around wood
Wrap a layer of insulating tape around wooden tool handles that have become rough or splintered. Make sure that the wood is completely dry so that the tape can adhere properly. The tape should last for several months and can be easily replaced.

Foam pipe insulation

Making a foam handle
Small sections of foam, such as pipe-insulating material, can form a soft covering for an uncomfortable handle. Hold the foam in place with insulating tape at each end. Make sure that the foam is not too bulky for a comfortable grip.

PREPARING TOOLS FOR STORAGE

During much of the winter, many tools will be required only occasionally, unless digging and soil preparation need to be done during this time. Before putting equipment away in an appropriate place, ensure that it is clean, dry, and ready to be stored for a long period.

CHECKING EQUIPMENT

● **Dried debris** Rub dried garden debris off metal blades using a clean cloth soaked in denatured alcohol.
● **Fuel tanks** Cold weather may cause gasoline to freeze. Before storing gasoline-driven equipment, make sure all fuel tanks are empty.
● **Cords** Check the cords of electrically driven equipment for signs of wear and tear. Replace cord if necessary.
● **Clean blades** To keep blades and tines in good condition, scrub them with a wire brush and warm water. Allow to dry, then file the cutting edges if they have deteriorated.

PREVENTING RUST

Oily sand

Cleaning and oiling
Mix with a bucketful of sharp sand. To clean and oil large tools before storage, plunge them into the sand several times. Use oily sand to clean nonelectrical equipment, such as forks, spades, and other tools with metal heads.

SHARPENING BLADES

Maintaining cutting tools
Cutting tools, such as pruners and shears, need regular sharpening if they are to continue to cut well. Run the blades regularly through a sharpener, or take the equipment to a professional for servicing.

STORING TOOLS

When the gardening season comes to an end, tools should be placed in a suitable place for storage. Before storing the tools, be sure that the area is dry to avoid problems such as rust, wood rot, and frost damage. If in doubt, check the condition of the tools regularly.

HANGING TOOLS

● **Hand tools** Store hand tools off the ground to help keep them dry and to reduce the possibility of knocking them over or hitting them.

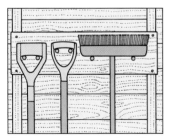

Constructing a tool rack
Make a tool rack by laying the tools to be stored flat on a piece of wood. The tools will be hung on galvanized nails, so mark their positions with a pencil. Remove the tools, and hammer in nails.

STORING CORRECTLY

● **Plastic wrap** Never wrap tools tightly in plastic since condensation may build up and encourage rotting and rust.
● **Hooks** Heavy tools can be suspended above the ground on sturdy hooks, such as those used for storing bicycles.
● **Soil** Never store tools directly on soil. Hang them or stand them on a board wrapped in plastic.
● **Shed** Before using a shed as a storage area for tools, make sure it is dry and in good condition.
● **Power tools** Keep electrically powered garden tools in a dry place. If the storage area is excessively damp, consider storing this equipment in the house.

TRADITIONAL TIP

Maintaining a lawn mower
To ensure that a lawn mower works efficiently at the beginning of a new gardening season, have the machine professionally serviced before putting it into storage, and be sure to place it on a level, wooden base when it is not in use.

GREENHOUSES

CONSTRUCTING AND FILLING A NEW GREENHOUSE can be an exciting experience. However, greenhouses also represent a considerable financial investment, making appropriate and thorough maintenance essential.

CLEANING GREENHOUSES

The type of maintenance needed to keep a greenhouse in pristine condition varies according to its construction. However, there are tasks that are common to all types that should be carried out annually in autumn in order to prolong their effectiveness.

CARING FOR PLANTS

● **Providing light** Clean both sides of the glass to remove debris. This is essential if plants are to benefit from natural light during dark winter months.
● **Protecting plants** If using a commercial cleaner, remove all plants from the area, or cover them with plastic.

WARNING!

Before cleaning a greenhouse with water, it is essential that the electricity supply is turned off and that all sockets are covered securely.

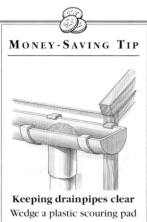

MONEY-SAVING TIP

Keeping drainpipes clear
Wedge a plastic scouring pad or a ball of galvanized wire netting into the opening of a drainpipe. This will act as a filter and prevent falling leaves and other debris from clogging up the pipe or entering a water barrel.

CLEANING A ROOF

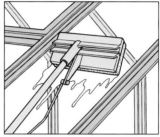

Reaching the roof
Use a long-handled floor mop to clean the upper sections of the roof on the inside and outside of a greenhouse. If the glass is very dirty, add dishwashing liquid or detergent to the water.

PROTECTING METAL

● **Fittings** Although aluminum frames should not rust, treat any other hardware of metal fittings to prevent corrosion.

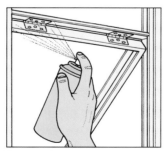

Preventing rust
To avoid stiffness and rust, apply a thin film of light oil or a layer of antirust paint regularly to metal hardware. Replace corroded hinges and screws with galvanized ones.

REMOVING PESTS

Scrubbing T-bars
Pests may lurk in the T-bars of aluminum greenhouses and remain there unless removed. Use a stream of water and a scrub brush to clean out these areas. If pests persist, rub with steel wool.

MAINTAINING INTERIORS

● **Contents** Sort through the contents of your greenhouse every year, and throw away anything that is not needed.
● **Plants** When cleaning a greenhouse interior, use the opportunity to remove dead flowerheads and leaves.
● **Surfaces** Clean flooring using garden disinfectant. Rinse with clean water. Paint or spray on diluted disinfectant to clean shelves and other surfaces.
● **Drafts** Check vents and doors for drafts, and replace insulation tape if necessary.
● **Insulation** To reduce heat loss during winter, install strips of bubble plastic along the bottom panels of a greenhouse, and put sheets of plastic on the floor.

REPLACING GLASS

Clean, undamaged glass is essential for a productive greenhouse. Cracked panes will make it impossible to maintain temperatures accurately and can be dangerous. Most metal frames use a system of clips to secure the glass panes; putty is necessary for wooden frames.

REPLACING GLASS
● **Positioning** Replace broken glass in wooden frames only if you feel confident handling and positioning glass. If in doubt, call a professional.

Installing replacement glass
Chisel away any old putty, and replace with a fresh layer. Press the edges, not the middle, of the pane to make contact with the putty. Hold in place with a second application of putty.

WORKING WITH GLASS
● **Damaged glass** Do not wait to replace a pane of glass that is broken. Once a pane is damaged, the whole pane may fall out, with dangerous consequences.
● **Selecting panes** Use special greenhouse glass to replace any panes that are broken or damaged.
● **Clips** To replace glass held in place with clips, unhook the clips and remove the pane, then slide in the new glass and fasten the clips.
● **Cleaning** Remove dirty marks from a new pane of glass with a cloth soaked in denatured alcohol.
● **Trees** If you cannot prune a tree that regularly damages a roof, replace the roof glass with a high-impact polymer.

USING PUTTY

● **Storing** Roll unused putty into balls and store in jars of water. Label the storage jars carefully, and keep out of the reach of children.
● **Positioning** Apply putty at an angle to ensure that rain and condensation do not collect on a wooden frame, which may lead to wet rot.

MAINTAINING FRAMES AND GLASS

Greenhouse frames are available in a variety of materials, which will determine the type of maintenance required. All glass needs regular cleaning, since debris and algae reduces the penetration of light. Dirt inside may also provide a hiding place for pests.

TREATING FRAMES
● **Aluminum** Do not remove the gray patina that forms on aluminum. It will protect a frame against damp weather.
● **Steel** Although steel greenhouse frames are strong, they are also prone to rust. Treat them regularly with a coat of antirust paint. Replace the paint promptly if the surface is scratched.
● **Wood** Hardwood frames need little maintenance. Treat softwood frames with wood preservative every two years (see p. 162). Use a plant-friendly solution, or remove plants until the solution is dry.

REMOVING DEPOSITS

Cleaning between panes
To remove all deposits from overlapping panes of glass, slide a plastic plant label or a piece of thin, flexible plastic in between the panes. Wash off the loose debris with a clean, damp cloth.

CLEANING GLASS
● **Timing** Avoid cleaning glass on hot days; loosened dirt may dry in the heat.
● **Cleaners** Use a commercial garden disinfectant or cleaner on persistently dirty areas or those harboring pests. Be sure to remove plants from the area beforehand.
● **Ventilation** After cleaning interior glass, ventilate the greenhouse thoroughly to reduce moisture in the air.
● **Leaves** If the roof is often covered with leaves, drape lightweight garden netting over the affected area. Empty the netting regularly.

SPRING TASKS

AREA OF THE GARDEN	EARLY SPRING
THE ORNAMENTAL GARDEN Once weather conditions improve and plants begin to grow, there is a great deal to do. There are many seeds that can be sown now, especially those that are sown directly into open ground. Some transplanting and dividing is also possible. The mild conditions of spring stimulate the germination and growth of weeds, as well as the development of many pests and diseases. Prompt action is therefore essential in order to prevent serious problems from developing later in the year. *Snowdrops*	● Turn the soil over, remove weeds, and fertilize the soil before sowing annuals. Those that can be sown now include *Adonis aestivalis, Brachycome, Centaurea cyanus, Clarkia elegans, Convolvulus tricolor,* and *Eschscholzia californica.* ● Plant out hardy bulbs that have grown inside over winter. Feed and water them well. ● Lift, divide, and replant crowded clumps of snowdrops as soon as the flowers have faded. ● Lift, divide, and replant established or oversized herbaceous plants, discarding any weak sections. ● Plant summer-flowering bulbs and perennials if the ground is not frozen or waterlogged. ● Prune hybrid bush roses, cutting out any frost-damaged, dead, or crossing stems.
THE VEGETABLE GARDEN Warm weather encourages the growth of many vegetables. Toward the end of spring, many tender vegetables can be planted outside, provided that the frosts are over. Pests and weeds may multiply rapidly, so keep a close watch on all crops. *Broccoli*	● Sow broad beans, cauliflower, brussels sprouts, carrots, onions, radishes, spinach, and parsnips. Make a second sowing of early peas. ● Dig well-rotted manure into celery trenches. ● Plant early potatoes and onion sets. ● Apply a balanced fertilizer to lettuce that will be harvested in early or late spring. ● Prepare runner-bean trenches by digging in compost or well-rotted manure.
THE FRUIT GARDEN Although the first garden-grown fruit does not ripen until toward the end of spring, there is still a lot of watering and feeding to be done to ensure that fruiting trees, bushes, and canes all perform well. *Strawberries*	● Prune back the stems of newly planted and two-year-old gooseberries by about one-half. ● Plant currant bushes and raspberry canes, and water in thoroughly. Cut the canes down to 12 in (30 cm) above the ground. ● Spray gooseberries and black currants for gooseberry mildew. ● Protect strawberry plants with cloches. ● Spray apples and pears prone to scab infection.
THE GREENHOUSE As the days become warm, windows and doors will need to be left open on sunny days. They should, however, still be closed up at night. The overall atmosphere should be reasonably dry. Thoroughly clean all of the glass, both inside and out, to let in the maximum amount of light.	● Begin sowing herbs. ● Take cuttings of bedding plants such as fuchsias, heliotropes, marguerites, and pelargoniums. ● Sow seeds of *Anemone coronaria, Antirrhinum majus, Aster novi-belgii, Dianthus chinensis, Lobelia erinus, Petunia, Salvia, Tropaeolum peregrinum,* and *Verbena.*
THE LAWN Having spent most of the winter virtually dormant, the lawn grass will suddenly start to grow. Any damage incurred during the winter must be tended to before summer arrives. Now is the time to begin regular lawn maintenance.	● Rake the lawn clear of twigs, leaves, and other debris that may be clogging the surface. ● To prevent scalping, cut the lawn with the lawnmower blades set reasonably high. ● Neaten lawn edges with edging shears. ● Brush off worm castings regularly.

MIDSPRING	LATE SPRING
● Continue to direct-sow annuals such as *Linaria, Mesembryanthemum,* annual *Rudbeckia,* sunflowers, *Tagetes,* and Virginian stocks. ● Prune shrubs grown for their decorative winter stems, such as willows and dogwoods. Prune *Forsythia* as soon as it has finished flowering. ● Plant out *Antirrhinum* and *Penstemon* raised from autumn cuttings or sowings. Make sure to harden them off gradually first. ● Take root cuttings of *Delphinium, Lupinus,* and herbaceous *Phlox.* ● Apply a high-phosphorus fertilizer around the base of summer-flowering shrubs, including roses. ● Layer shrubs and climbers such as *Carpenteria, Fothergilla, Kalmia, Lonicera,* and *Syringa.*	● Stake young, herbaceous perennials. ● Harden off bedding plants in preparation for planting them in open ground. ● Plant young perennials grown from seed into a nursery bed where they can grow until autumn. ● Begin to thin out seedlings of any annuals sown directly into the ground. ● Tie new, vigorous rambler-rose growth gently, but securely to supports. ● Sow seeds of *Achillea* spp., *Alcea rosea, Aquilegia vulgaris, Delphinium elatum, Erigeron speciosus,* and *Lychnis chalcedonica.* ● Plant up hanging baskets, barrels, and other containers. Leave them in a greenhouse or cold frame until all danger of frost has passed.
● Thin out overcrowded vegetable seedlings. ● Harden off young plants from winter sowings of cauliflower, leeks, onions, lettuce, peas, and broad beans before planting out. ● Prepare and plant new asparagus beds. ● Support peas with sticks or netting. ● Sow broccoli, leeks, kohlrabi, and cauliflower for planting out in early summer. ● Sow cabbage in fertile soil.	● Thin seedlings from root crops and onions. ● Direct-sow runner beans, squash, pumpkins, cucumbers, sweet corn, peas, endive, green beans, leaf lettuce, Chinese cabbage, and chicory. ● Transplant brussels sprouts and leeks; water in. ● Form a little mound of soil over young potato shoots to protect them from frost. ● Sow cucumbers in mounds enriched with plenty of well-rotted manure and compost.
● Feed summer-fruiting plants with potassium sulfate to promote good flowering and fruit. ● Control weeds around bush and cane fruit. ● Check for pests and diseases. Use sprays at dusk to avoid harming pollinating insects. ● Thin heavy-cropping nectarines and peaches when the fruit is ½ in(1–1.5 cm) in diameter. ● Feed blackberry and hybrid berry plants with ammonium sulfate or other high-nitrogen fertilizer.	● Mulch raspberries and other cane fruit. ● Carefully remove runners from strawberries. Place mats or straw beneath stems with developing fruit to keep them off the ground. ● Control slugs and snails in strawberry beds before they start to attack the fruit. ● Tie new raspberry canes to supports. ● Keep all fruit well watered, especially those on light soils, and those that are trained against a wall.
● Plant greenhouse tomato plants in large pots, or plant them in grow bags. ● Start to harden off bedding plants. ● Introduce biological controls to keep down pests such as greenhouse whiteflies and spider mites. ● Pot established begonias, chrysanthemums, *Cyclamen,* and gloxinias as necessary.	● Apply a high-phosphorus liquid fertilizer to any tomato plants with setting fruit. ● Protect greenhouse plants from heat with greenhouse shading or special shading paint. ● Water seedlings with a copper-based fungicide. ● Check for powdery mildew, gray mold, aphids, and other problems. Take immediate action.
● Apply a spring fertilizer to stimulate growth. ● Remove weeds such as dandelions. ● Thoroughly prepare the ground to be seeded or sodded. Fertilize it with a complete fertilizer. Sow grass seed unless the soil is still very wet. ● Protect new seed from birds, and water regularly.	● Control lawn weeds. Remove by hand, or use an appropriate weedkiller. ● Level off uneven areas of the lawn. ● Repair or replace worn-out or bare areas of turf. ● Use a half-moon edger to neaten any ragged squashed, or damaged lawn edges.

SUMMER TASKS

AREA OF THE GARDEN	EARLY SUMMER
THE ORNAMENTAL GARDEN Warm weather continues to encourage all plants to grow rapidly, although this growth may slow down considerably if it becomes very hot and dry. Regular watering and feeding are essential to ensure that the garden stays colorful and thrives throughout the summer. Many plants will need to be tied to supports, and prompt action must be taken with any outbreaks of pests and diseases. Lilac	● Continue to plant out annual bedding and to fill baskets and other containers. Hang up and display any baskets that have been kept in the greenhouse. ● Prune back *Arabis, Aubrieta,* and perennial candytuft as soon as they have finished flowering. ● Divide crowded clumps of primroses, and water irises as soon as flowering is over. ● Remove flowerheads from lilacs and late-flowering camellias as soon as the flowers fade. ● Remove suckers from roses. Be sure to cut them off close to the rootstock. ● Water all ornamental plants regularly to prevent developing buds from dropping off. ● Sow biennials and perennials, including *Aubrietia, Coreopsis,* delphiniums, and wallflowers.
THE VEGETABLE GARDEN There is a great deal to do in the vegetable garden in summer. In order for vegetables to grow as they should, they need a constant supply of water and careful feeding. Weeds compete for water and nutrients, so weed control, although time-consuming, is vital for a healthy crop. Asparagus	● Make successive sowings of lettuce, turnips, runner beans, green beans, endive, radishes, and kohlrabi. Sow Chinese cabbage. ● Pinch out the tips on broad beans to encourage good pod set and to deter attack from aphids. ● Stop picking asparagus so that the plants do not exhaust themselves. ● Plant outdoor tomatoes, and tie them gently, but firmly, to stakes to secure them.
THE FRUIT GARDEN Summer is when you can begin to enjoy the fruit from many of your trees, bushes, and canes. The plants themselves need relatively little maintenance, except for regular watering, some feeding, and possible spraying against pests and diseases. Peaches	● Spray raspberries against raspberry beetles. Apply the first spray as soon as the first fruit turns pink. ● Hang codling-moth traps on apple trees. ● Spray against apple scab, mildew, and aphids. ● Tie new canes of blackberries and hybrid berries to a system of support wires, allowing a maximum of eight canes per plant. ● Summer-prune gooseberries by cutting back sideshoots to five leaves.
THE GREENHOUSE Prevent high temperatures in the greenhouse from damaging plants. Open doors, vents, and windows, and damp down regularly to increase the humidity.	● Water and feed tomatoes, cucumbers, and peppers, never letting the soil dry out. ● Attach slings or nets to melons as they swell. ● Continue to remove sideshoots from tomatoes.
THE LAWN Lawn grass grows strongly throughout the summer, so regular mowing is one of the most frequent tasks. Wear and tear is often at its height, too; the lawn is heavily used for parties, sunbathing, barbecues, and playing. The amount of mowing and watering required will be greatly influenced by the weather, and this may vary considerably from year to year.	● Mow as often as necessary, taking care not to cut too short, especially in hot, dry weather. ● Control broadleaved weeds by handweeding or by using suitable commercial weedkillers. ● Water regularly with a sprinkler, but first check to see if there are any local watering restrictions. ● If necessary, apply a nitrogen-rich liquid fertilizer to the lawn to make it greener and to encourage the grass to grow rapidly.

MIDSUMMER	LATE SUMMER
● Feed roses and other flowering plants in open ground and in containers with a high-phosphorus fertilizer to encourage flowering. ● Deadhead faded flowers to promote the formation of new buds and encourage growth. ● Trim hedges regularly to avoid having to cut them back too much at any one time. ● Weed carefully between plants in borders and beneath trees, shrubs, and climbers. ● Layer border carnations and propagate pinks by taking 3-in (7.5-cm) long cuttings. ● Transplant Canterbury bells, sweet Williams, and wallflowers into a nursery bed. Water in well. ● Take semiripe cuttings of many shrubs, including *Deutzia* and *Weigela*.	● Plant *Amaryllis belladonna,* autumn crocus, *Colchicum, Fritillaria imperialis, Lilium candidum,* and *Sternbergia* bulbs. ● Continue to deadhead all flowering plants, unless you intend to save seed. ● Control earwigs and powdery mildew on dahlias and chrysanthemums. ● Prune rambler roses once flowering is over. ● Spray roses against fungal attack such as powdery mildew, rust, and blackspot. ● Water all plants regularly, giving priority to relatively new plants and those that are particularly intolerant of drought. ● Move layered border carnations to their permanent locations.
● Spray outdoor tomatoes and potatoes with a fungicide to protect them from blight. ● Mound soil around celery stems, and tie together. ● Harvest herbs for use in the winter, preferably before they begin to flower. ● Start to make successive sowings of spring cabbage. Sow turnips and rutabagas. ● Harvest runner and green beans as soon as they are ready. Freeze while they are still tender.	● Ripen onions by lifting them gently and leaving them in place for a couple of weeks. ● Sow onions (for an early crop next year), plus spinach, radishes, beets, and chard. ● Continue to water crops regularly, especially those that bolt or fail if allowed to dry out. ● Weed regularly between rows of crops. ● Use a commercial spray on all crops, particularly cabbages, to prevent attacks by caterpillars.
● Prune fan-trained cherries and plums to prevent excessive growth toward the wall or fence. ● Remove and dispose of any apples and pears showing signs of pest infestation. ● Water apple trees regularly and thoroughly to decrease the risk of bitter pit developing. Spray developing fruit with calcium nitrate. ● Erect netting around developing fruit to protect them from being attacked by birds.	● Control woolly aphids on apple trees. ● Prune summer-fruiting raspberries. As soon as they have finished fruiting, cut all the raspberry canes that have just fruited back to ground level, and tie new canes to supports. ● Remove old leaves and runners from strawberries once they have finished fruiting. ● Start to prune apples, and continue to prune cherries, plums, apricots, nectarines, and peaches.
● Continue to water tomato plants frequently to prevent the development of blossom-end rot. ● Remove excessive leaf growth from tomatoes. ● Add extra shading to the glass if necessary.	● Take cuttings of ivy-leaved and zonal pelargoniums, and pot them up. ● Take semiripe cuttings of *Berberis, Camellia, Ceanothus, Cotoneaster, Daphne,* and *Mahonia.*
● Protect areas that are frequently used by children, or move swings and other play equipment around to spread the wear and tear. ● Continue to water regularly, if possible. Water in the early evening to minimize waste. ● Control any ants that may be in the lawn. ● Drench any areas of lawn that have been urinated on by pets and wildlife. ● Leave grass clippings on the lawn in dry weather.	● Apply a lawn fertilizer with relatively high phosphate and potassium levels to encourage the development of strong roots. ● Trim back herbaceous plants that have grown excessively and flopped over the lawn edges. ● Continue to water regularly and thoroughly during hot, dry weather. Always water well after applying any kind of fertilizer. ● Continue to mow the lawn regularly.

Autumn Tasks

Area of the Garden	Early Autumn
The Ornamental Garden Summer borders have now begun to deteriorate. You will need to neaten the plants for the winter, weed, and in some cases divide and replant crowded clumps. Damp weather often encourages an outbreak of diseases, so you may need to control these, too. Remove fallen leaves, since they may harbor diseases and overwhelm small plants. Autumn is a good time to plan next year's planting. *Schizostylis*	● Plant daffodils, hyacinths, crocuses, scillas, iris, and most lilies for a spring display. ● Remove the remains of summer-flowering annuals, and prepare the soil thoroughly for winter-flowering bedding plants. ● In light, well-drained soils, direct-sow hardy annuals, including *Alyssum, Calendula,* candytuft, *Clarkia, Nigella,* and poppies. ● Lift and store gladiolus corms. ● Place nets over ponds to prevent the water from becoming polluted by falling leaves. ● Continue to prune rambler roses. ● Make sure that autumn-flowering herbaceous plants are properly staked. ● Rake autumn leaves regularly.
The Vegetable Garden Some vegetables will be used immediately, while others can be harvested carefully and stored. There is also a considerable amount of clean up to do in preparation for new crops. Remove all diseased debris and dispose of it well away from the vegetable garden. *Squash*	● Harvest carrots, potatoes, and beets, preferably when the soil is not wet. ● Plant spring cabbage. ● Lift parsley seedlings from around the parent plant, and plant them in containers or directly into a cold frame or cold greenhouse border. ● Harvest and store the bulk of the squash crop. ● Pick outdoor tomatoes, and ripen them in a warm spot indoors, away from the frost.
The Fruit Garden Most fruit trees yield the majority of their fruit during autumn. Late varieties of some bush and cane fruit are productive now, too. Many apples, and some pears, can be stored for use later in the year. *Grapes*	● Plant peaches and nectarines, preferably in a sheltered spot, and trained against a sunny wall. ● Begin planting blackberries and hybrid berries. ● Prune raspberry canes that fruited in the summer back to soil level. Carefully tie new canes to the support system. ● Rake up and dispose of fallen leaves from scab-infected apple and pear trees, and from any rust-infected plum trees.
The Greenhouse Before cold weather arrives, move tender plants into the greenhouse for protection over winter. Reduce ventilation and humidity levels.	● Take off all shading from greenhouse glass. ● Pot up bulbs for winter displays. ● Sow lettuce, radish, and carrot varieties for subsequent growing under cloches.
The Lawn The lawn can now begin to recover from the heavy use it may have sustained over the summer months, as well as from any damaging dry periods when adequate watering may not have been possible. As autumn approaches, grass growth slows down, allowing much essential maintenance work to be done. Work carried out now will benefit the lawn throughout the coming year.	● Rake fallen leaves off the grass as soon as possible, especially if the weather is wet. ● Reseed any worn patches in the lawn. ● Prepare areas ready to be sodded or seeded. ● Aerate the lawn to encourage good drainage and to stimulate root growth. Use a garden fork for small areas or a powered aerator for large areas. ● Apply an insecticide drench if Japanese beetle grubs are present in the lawn.

MIDAUTUMN	LATE AUTUMN
● Pick and dry attractive seedheads for use in dried-flower arrangements. ● Protect alpines, which are intolerant of wet conditions, with a pane of glass. ● Cut back chrysanthemums to about 6 in (15 cm) above ground level, lift, and store in boxes. ● To prolong the flowering period of *Schizostylis*, pot up garden-grown plants, and overwinter them in a greenhouse or cold frame. ● Plant winter and spring bedding plants such as *Bellis,* forget-me-nots, *Polyanthus,* pansies, and wallflowers. Plant lily-of-the-valley. ● Remove dead and dying herbaceous plants, leaving enough foliage behind to protect the crowns from severe winter weather.	● If necessary, transplant trees and shrubs while the soil is still warm and moist, but not too wet. ● Prune deciduous hedges, and carry out any necessary major cutting back. ● Protect half-hardy bulbs such as *Agapanthus*. ● Plant tulip bulbs, preferably in a sunny, sheltered border, or in containers. ● Plant spring-flowering plants for added color to fill any gaps between shrubs next spring. ● Continue to remove the last of the weeds, taking care not to spread seeds. ● To ensure good bud formation for plenty of spring flowers, provide all plants with enough water during dry spells. ● Remove fallen leaves from gutters.
● Harvest onions and cauliflower. ● Remove leaves showing signs of infection from lettuce and brassicas. ● Harvest chicory as the foliage dies back, and store in a cool shed in boxes of sand. ● For a winter crop of spinach, put cloches over late spinach sowings to protect them from frost. ● Cut back foliage of asparagus crowns planted in midspring. Mound soil over crowns.	● Sow broad beans in a sheltered spot to obtain a very early crop without the aid of a greenhouse. ● Harvest and store parsnip, horseradish, and Jerusalem artichoke crops. ● Pick brussels sprouts when the buttons firm up. ● Harvest leeks, trimming off roots and carefully disposing of any outer, rust-infested foliage. ● Dig over vacant areas thoroughly, and allow the soil to be broken down by winter frosts.
● Plant black currants, red and white currants, and raspberry canes from now until early spring, provided that the soil is not too cold or too wet. ● Take hardwood cuttings from grapevines, black currants, and gooseberries. Root them in sandy soil in a sheltered spot. ● Remove all weeds from between strawberry plants, water well, and apply a mulch. ● Continue to rake up and dispose of fallen leaves.	● Cut canes of blackberry and hybrid berries that fruited this year back to soil level, and tie newly formed canes to supports. ● Plant gooseberries, apples, and pears, provided that the soil is not too wet or too cold. ● Prune back newly planted apple trees immediately after planting. Reduce all sideshoots by about one-half, and cut back maiden trees to approximately 20 in (50 cm) above soil level.
● Pick the last of the tomatoes. Remove and dispose of all the plant remains. ● Bring in the last of the chrysanthemums for protection during the winter months.	● Water overwintering plants occasionally so that they do not dry out completely. ● Lift crowns of lily-of-the-valley, and pot them up for an early, indoor, scented display.
● Seed new lawns, or lay sod. ● Scarify the lawn using a spring-tined rake, or a power rake for very large areas. This removes any dead matter and debris from the surface. ● Continue to rake up autumn leaves regularly. Use them to make leaf mold. ● Use a commercial moss killer for moss-infested lawns. To prevent the spread of moss spores, wait until the moss is completely dead before raking it out.	● Plant *Narcissus* and any other suitable bulbs in drifts or clumps in lawns. ● Repair any humps and hollows created by excessive summer wear and tear. ● Continue to trim back herbaceous plants that have flopped over the lawn edges. ● Clean up the lawn mower, and do any necessary repairs before storing it for the winter. ● Repair broken and crushed lawn edges.

WINTER TASKS

AREA OF THE GARDEN	EARLY WINTER
THE ORNAMENTAL GARDEN Frosts, freezing conditions, and snow may make it difficult, if not inadvisable, to do much work outside during a good part of the winter season. It is, however, possible to create a winter garden that has plenty of visual interest as well as fragrance. Temporary color can be introduced in the form of winter-flowering bedding plants as well as a few winter-flowering bulbs. Combine these with a selection of shrubs grown for their winter bark, flowers, and berries (such as *Skimmia*), or for their evergreen foliage. *Skimmia*	● Protect crowns of herbaceous plants from frost damage with straw or dry leaves. ● Protect root balls of container-grown plants by wrapping the containers in burlap or newspaper. ● Continue to clear vacant beds and borders. ● Where necessary, firm soil that has been lifted around shrub roots by frost . ● In a windy garden, prune back some of the top-growth on roses to minimize windrock. ● If soil in flower beds is very wet, try to avoid walking on it, which could compact it. Stand on a board so that your weight is spread over a large area. ● Sow alpine and tree seeds that benefit from exposure to frost, and leave them outside. ● Begin winter-pruning trees and shrubs. ● Browse through seed catalogs, and decide what to buy. Place orders to seed companies early so that you are not disappointed.
THE VEGETABLE GARDEN A carefully planned vegetable garden will continue to yield some fresh crops throughout the winter. Protect crops with row covers and cloches for best results. Cauliflower	● Continue to harvest trench celery. Check for slug damage, and take appropriate action. ● Continue to harvest leek, turnip, rutabagas, kohlrabi, and parsnip crops. ● Bend the leaves of cauliflower over the curds to protect them from frost damage. ● Plant chicory roots in pots, and place them in a dark spot at about 45°F (7°C). Harvest young shoots as they appear.
THE FRUIT GARDEN Winter weather provides a relatively quiet period in the fruit garden, since fruit trees and bushes are now fully dormant. Check fruit in storage, and remove any showing signs of deterioration or disease. Stored apples	● Prune red and white currants from now until late winter. After pruning, apply a mulch of well-rotted manure or compost. ● Prune apples and pears. Check branches, stems, and trunks for signs of fungal canker. Prune out and treat affected areas as necessary. ● Make sure that any stakes and ties around fruit bushes and trees are held firmly in place. ● Apply dormant oil or similar to help control overwintering pests and diseases.
THE GREENHOUSE Use a greenhouse to make early sowings of many vegetables and flowers. Check the thermometer regularly, and adjust the heating as necessary.	● Sow the seeds of herbaceous perennials such as anemones, *Canna*, columbines, *Dianthus*, hollyhocks, and poppies. ● Prune grapevines grown under glass.
THE LAWN The lawn needs little attention during the winter. Unless any urgent action is required, it is best to avoid working on the lawn much until spring.	● Continue to rake up any fallen leaves that have blown onto the lawn. ● Use a brush with stiff bristles to scatter any worm castings that have appeared on the lawn.

MIDWINTER	LATE WINTER
● Slugs may cause damage during mild spells, so control them before they attack any plant crowns that are left in the ground. ● Prevent the sides of ponds from being cracked by pressure from freezing water. Float a ball, empty plastic bottle, or log on the surface. ● Brush heavy snow off branches to prevent the weight from snapping them. ● Protect winter-flowering hellebores from being splashed with mud by covering them with cloches. ● Carefully fork over the surface soil in flower beds containing spring-flowering bulbs to break up compaction and to deter the growth of algae, moss, and weeds. ● Dig the soil in preparation for planting dahlias when all danger of frost has passed. ● Make sure that garden birds have a regular supply of food and water during the cold weather. ● Plant trees and shrubs on dry, warm days.	● Sow a selection of herbaceous perennials to incorporate into your flower borders in the spring. ● Once winter-flowering heathers have finished flowering, trim them back lightly. Do not cut into woody growth – just trim off old flowering stems. ● Plant *Tigridia* bulbs outside in a sheltered, warm spot. Also plant *Crocosmia.* ● Check dahlias in storage, and remove any that are showing signs of rotting. ● Prune winter-flowering jasmine as soon as the last of the flowers have finished. ● Prune and train stems of ornamental climbers such as *Vitis coignetiae.* ● Start to prune *Cornus* (dogwoods), that have brightly colored winter stems. ● Plant gladioli, anemones, lilies, *Ranunculus,* and hedges in mild areas. ● Feed established flower beds and borders with well-rotted manure.
● Continue to harvest winter cabbage, brussels sprouts, parsnips, and leeks. ● Spray brussels sprouts and other winter brassicas for whitefly. ● Harvest Jerusalem artichokes. Make sure that you lift every piece of tuber. Store tubers in a paper bag in a cool, well-ventilated shed or garage. ● Plant early potatoes in pots in a greenhouse or a cold frame to produce a very early crop.	● Choose a sheltered spot with moist soil, to make the first sowing of carrots. ● Sow early peas in a sheltered spot. ● Sow onions and scallions. ● Continue to harvest winter brassicas, leeks, celery, and root crops. ● Continue to spray against brassica whitefly. ● In mild areas shallots may be planted. ● Thin lettuce sown in midsummer.
● Spray peaches, nectarines, and almonds with a copper-based fungicide to prevent attacks of peach-leaf curl. Cover fan-trained trees with an open-sided plastic shelter. ● Start forcing rhubarb. Cover the crowns with a deep layer of leaves or leaf mold, then cover with a pot. ● Apply a mulch of well-rotted manure or compost around the bases of gooseberries. ● Complete the last pruning of apples and pears.	● Apply a second spray of copper-based fungicide to trees susceptible to peach-leaf curl about 14 days after the first application. ● Sprinkle sulphate of potash around the root-feeding area of apples, pears, and plums to encourage good fruiting later in the year. ● Prune autumn-fruiting raspberries. Cut back to ground level the canes that fruited last autumn. ● Prune back canes of raspberries planted last year to about 12 in (30 cm) above ground level.
● Start to sow seeds of *Antirrhinum,* begonias, pelargoniums, salvias, verbenas, and at 65°F (18°C). ● Take cuttings from perpetual-flowering carnations; root in sandy soil mix at 50°F (10°C).	● Water trays of seedlings with a copper-based fungicide to prevent damping off. ● Ventilate as much as possible to prevent the buildup of diseases in the damp atmosphere.
● Have your lawnmower serviced and repaired if you have not already done so. ● Make sure that all lawn tools are properly cleaned, oiled, and stored for the winter.	● Try to keep off the grass if it is frozen, since damage will encourage the onset of diseases. ● Lift loose or sunken stepping-stones in the lawn. Level them, and re-lay.

INDEX

ACKNOWLEDGMENTS

AUTHOR'S ACKNOWLEDGMENTS
I would like to thank Linda Martin and Jayne Carter for their help and
patience. Thanks, too, to the rest of the Dorling Kindersley team; to Justina
Buswell for her wordprocessing help; Alasdair, Fiona, Simon, John, and
various other friends for their advice.

PUBLISHER'S ACKNOWLEDGMENTS
Dorling Kindersley would like to thank the following: Linda Martin for
planting up the containers, Debra Whitehead and Kristina Fitzsimmons
for additional help, Peter Griffiths for making the model
on p. 64, and Ray Jones for making props for photography.

Prop loan Adrian Hall Ltd., Putney Garden Centre, London;
The West Hampstead Garden Centre.

Editorial and design assistance Emma Lawson, Adèle Hayward, and
Colette Connolly for editorial assistance;
Chris Bernstein for the index;
Austin Barlow, Jackie Dollar, and Darren Hill for design assistance.

ARTWORKS
Illustrators All illustrations by Kuo Kang Chen and
John Woodcock, apart from additional illustrations on
pages 12–13, 14, 21, 22, 29, 32–33 by Karen Cochrane,
and pages 124, 126, 128, 130–131 by David Ashby.

PHOTOGRAPHY
Photographers Andy Crawford, Steve Gorton, Gary Ombler.
Additional photography Jane Stockman, Peter Anderson, Andreas Einsiedel,
Graham Kirk, Matthew Ward, Jerry Young.

Hand models Toby Heran, Katie Martin,
Marlon Reddin, and Helen Oyo.

Picture Researcher Sarah Moule.

PICTURE CREDITS
Key: a above, b below, c center, l left, r right, t top

Garden Picture Library J. Baker 133c; A. Bedding 19bc;
J. Bouchier 74tl; L. Burgess 71bl; T. Candler 71tc; B. Carter 13tr;
J. Glover 17tc; 70bc; S. Harte 32br, 133cr; M. Howes 91bl; Lamontagne 70bl;
J. Legate 116c; J. Miller 15tl; C. Perry 111bl; J. Wade 112br; S. Wooster 28cl.
John Glover 16bl, 37bc. **Harpur Garden Library** 32bc, 34bl, 35bl, 37bl;
design: Chris Grey-Wilson 24ca; design: Yong Man Kim 27br;
design: Mrs. Wethered 28bl; design: G. & F. Whiten 26bl. **Holt Studios
International Ltd.** N. Caitlin 104cla, 106clb, 107tl, 107cla, 107clb, 107cbl, 112c,
115c, 115cr. **Frank Lane Picture Agency** B. Borrell 105br, 106cla;
E. & A. Hosking 105clb; R. Wilmshurst 110br. **Andrew Lawson Photography**
76cb. **Natural History Photographic Agency** S. Dalton 110bc.
Photos Horticultural 104bcl, 105cl, 112cr, 116cl. **Harry Smith Photographic
Collection** 17tl, 17bl, 28tr, 36, 37bc, 71tr, 74tc, 76bl, 104bl, 122c, 122cr.

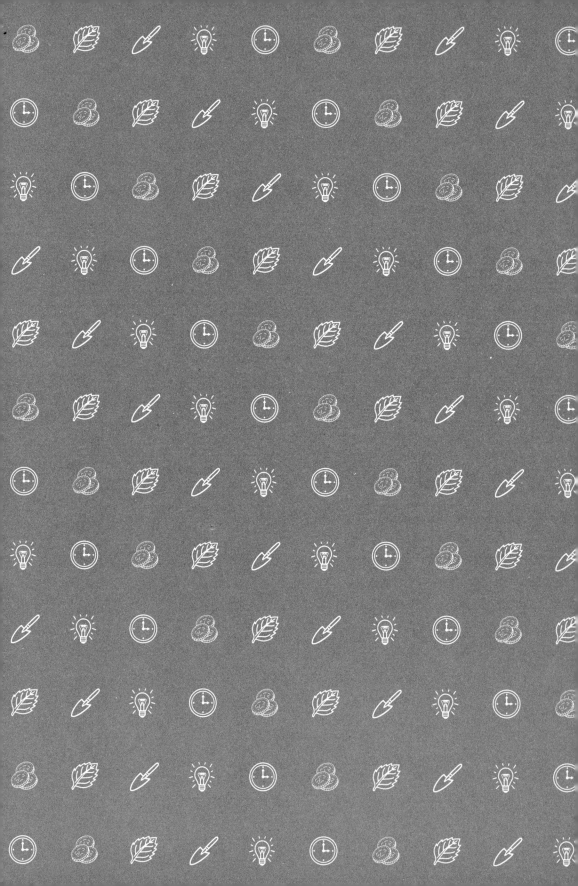